RECLAIMING JOHN STEINBECK

John Steinbeck is a towering figure in twentieth-century American literature; yet, he remains one of our least understood writers. This major reevaluation of Steinbeck by Gavin Jones uncovers a timely thinker who confronted the fate of humanity as a species facing climate change, environmental crisis, and a growing divide between the powerful and the marginalized. Driven by insatiable curiosity, Steinbeck's work crossed a variety of borders – between the United States and the Global South, between human and nonhuman life-forms, between science and the arts, and between literature and film – to explore the transformations in consciousness necessary for our survival on a precarious planet. Always seeking new forms to express his ecological and social vision of human interconnectedness and vulnerability, Steinbeck is a writer of urgent concern for the twenty-first century, even as he was haunted by the legacies of racism and injustice in the American West.

GAVIN JONES is the Frederick P. Rehmus Family Professor of the Humanities at Stanford University, where he has taught American literature since 1999. He is the author of *Strange Talk: The Politics of Dialect Literature in Gilded Age America* (University of California Press, 1999), *American Hungers: The Problem of Poverty in US Literature, 1840–1945* (Princeton University Press, 2008), and *Failure and the American Writer: A Literary History* (Cambridge University Press, 2014).

RECLAIMING JOHN STEINBECK

Writing for the Future of Humanity

GAVIN JONES

Stanford University

CAMBRIDGE
UNIVERSITY PRESS

CAMBRIDGE
UNIVERSITY PRESS

University Printing House, Cambridge CB2 8BS, United Kingdom

One Liberty Plaza, 20th Floor, New York, NY 10006, USA

477 Williamstown Road, Port Melbourne, VIC 3207, Australia

314–321, 3rd Floor, Plot 3, Splendor Forum, Jasola District Centre, New Delhi – 110025, India

79 Anson Road, #06–04/06, Singapore 079906

Cambridge University Press is part of the University of Cambridge.

It furthers the University's mission by disseminating knowledge in the pursuit of education, learning, and research at the highest international levels of excellence.

www.cambridge.org
Information on this title: www.cambridge.org/9781108844123
DOI: 10.1017/9781108933483

First published 2021

Printed in the United Kingdom by TJ Books Limited, Padstow Cornwall

A catalogue record for this publication is available from the British Library.

ISBN 978-1-108-84412-3 Hardback

For My Teachers, Especially John Comerford, Val Skinner, Nigel Smith, and Hans Aarsleff

Contents

Figures

Acknowledgments

I wrote this book in part to feel more rooted in the place where I live. I would thus like to thank the many students (and teaching assistants) in my Stanford course, English 146A, who listened patiently to my developing ideas, with a shout-out to Jenna Garden and Courtney Douglas. For opportunities to present my work, I thank the Stanford Alumni Association, the Stanford Historical Society, Debra Satz and Stanford's Office of the President, Stanford's Bill Lane Center for the American West (especially Bruce Cain and Priti Hehmeyer), Gregory Jackson, Mark Eaton, Susan Shillinglaw, William Gilly, Sylvan Goldberg, Michael Collins, Rachel Bolten, and Dietmar Meinel. Stanford University Libraries staff, especially Rebecca Wingfield and Tim Noakes, have been extremely patient and helpful, as has Peter Van Coutren at the Martha Heasley Cox Center for Steinbeck Studies, San Jose State University. I benefited from the expert research assistance of Ekalan Hou, Josh Mann, and Julie Plummer, and from the wise advice of Anna Mukamal and Ato Quayson. I thank William Souder, Robert DeMott, Mark McGurl, Paula Moya, Shelley Fisher Fishkin, Ken Gonzales-Day, Mary Ellen Hannibal, Nick Taylor, Alexander Nemerov, Barbara Heavilin, Sami G. Alvarez, Luchen Li, Kevin Hearle, Igor Maver, and Tom Kealey for their encouragement along the way. I am grateful for Ray Ryan's incisiveness as an editor at Cambridge University Press, and for the able assistance of Edgar Mendez. A revised version of my article "*To a God Unknown*: Drought, Climate, and Race in the West," which appeared in *Steinbeck Review*, Vol. 14, No. 1, 2017, pp. 1–22, is used with permission of Penn State University Press. Unpublished manuscript materials by Steinbeck are used courtesy of the Department of Special Collections, Stanford University Libraries, and the Martha Heasley Cox Center for Steinbeck Studies, San Jose State University. Thanks are owed to Fred Rehmus and the wonderful Rehmus family for their support, and to Stanford's H&S Dean's Office for ongoing research funding. Having served as my department's chair,

I appreciate the sureness of the two chairs under whom I wrote this book, Alex Woloch and Blakey Vermeule, and the staff of the Stanford English Department, not least Patrick Heyer and Maritza Colón. Finally, this book and so much more would be impossible without the love, support, and understanding of my family, Judy Richardson and Hazel and Eli Jones.

INTRODUCTION

Loving and Hating Steinbeck

The crowds had gathered at San Jose State University to celebrate the 50th anniversary of the publication of John Steinbeck's *The Grapes of Wrath* (1939). Leslie Fiedler, the fiery critic known for his controversial psychoanalytical readings of American literature, was to deliver the keynote address. How would Fiedler, the great American critic, account for the success of *The Grapes of Wrath* – the Great American Novel, some would claim, the novel largely responsible for Steinbeck winning the Nobel Prize for Literature? Fiedler's answer brought members of his audience to tears. Steinbeck's novel, he argued, was middlebrow schlock. It was ruined by didacticism, sentimentality, and melodrama, by hopelessly contradictory politics and equally sloppy writing. To admire Steinbeck, thought Fiedler, was to have a second-rate mind.[1]

By the time of the San Jose conference in March 1989, critical frostiness toward Steinbeck's writing was well established. If his works had generated divided, often extreme reactions through the 1930s, then by 1940 the East Coast critical establishment became settled in its view. "None of [Steinbeck's novels] that I have read seems to me precisely first-rate," wrote Edmund Wilson in an influential essay. Steinbeck fails at representing human beings, Wilson remarked, because he reduces them to the level of animals and produces them with stagey self-consciousness, leaving them like "actors giving very conscientious performances in a fairly well written play."[2] When Steinbeck received the Nobel Prize in 1962, Arthur Mizener in *The New York Times* dismissed the award as mere nostalgia for a moral vision of the 1930s, a nostalgia blinding readers to the "tenth-rate" philosophizing that overwhelms Steinbeck's books.[3]

The degree of animosity marking these overviews has continued in more recent criticism. Writing in *The New York Review of Books* in 2008, for example, Robert Gottlieb concluded that the Library of America's decision to reprint Steinbeck's entire canon was a mistake; his work was appropriate only for junior high school readers.[4] Certainly, Steinbeck has had his dedicated followers and fans over the years, including many critics who *only* work on Steinbeck.[5] And without doubt, Steinbeck has an enormous general readership (virtually all of his works are in print), an important place in the curriculum (if not typically at elite universities),[6] and an iconic presence in twentieth-century American culture. In 2016, Barack Obama included Steinbeck's *In Dubious Battle* (1936) as the only novel on a shortlist of "essential reads."[7] Two years later, PBS canvassed public opinion to rank *The Grapes of Wrath* in twelfth position on a list of 100 "Great American Reads," far higher than anything by other American Nobel laureates Ernest Hemingway and Toni Morrison (William Faulkner is not mentioned).[8] But still, a significant and troubling disconnect separates Steinbeck and many literary scholars. Even when scholars recuperate the left-leaning culture of the Great Depression and the "Popular Front," Steinbeck's work is considered too politically ambivalent or "successful" to completely fit.[9] Steinbeck has been omitted from leading-edge critical debates owing to assumptions that his "extra-literary urgency," in the words of Jonathan Yardley, lies in the past.[10]

Yet Wilson's resounding claim that Steinbeck is more concerned with animals than humans looks very different from recent perspectives that seek to decenter the human from a view of history, making us aware of our "species-ism" (even Wilson begrudgingly admitted that something of value may lie in Steinbeck's biological interest in the process of life itself).[11] Opportunities await to develop emerging recognitions of Steinbeck's importance for environmental and ecological study, his concern with how we are altering our planet, with climate migration, and with species codependency and extinction.[12] Recent attention to Steinbeck's groundbreaking representations of Asian American characters could be linked to his much broader, and often problematic, interest in race.[13] Steinbeck's lifelong fascination with Mexico, I argue, should place his work at the forefront of American approaches to hemispheric studies and the Global South. And as we will see throughout this book, Steinbeck is also a significant and complex thinker about topics such as mental development, disability, and group behavior, in addition to his more recognized attention to poverty, inequality, and social justice. It would be difficult to find another American writer more interested in a radical interdisciplinarity capable of fusing the "two cultures" of humanistic and scientific inquiry.

Before turning to recuperation, it is worth pausing for a moment longer on the reasons for the critical disdain toward Steinbeck that runs through Wilson's and Mizener's responses and that culminated in Fiedler's San Jose address. It needs to be taken seriously because it persists. Mizener confessed to being made "uncomfortable" by Steinbeck's work, its demonstration of limited talent being overpowered by the corny and the third-rate.[14] Wilson likewise seems confused by the mixture of seriousness and trashiness in Steinbeck's work: "there are passages in some ways so brilliant that we are troubled at being forced to recognize that there is something artistically bad about them."[15] Fiedler draws from Wilson's judgment that Steinbeck's novels "mark precisely the borderlines between what is definitely superior and work that is definitely bad" in his characterization of Steinbeck's oeuvre as *middlebrow* – by which he means not the middle position along a spectrum of taste but an inherent contradiction that emerges from being both highbrow and lowbrow at once.[16] Critics seem confused, that is, by Steinbeck's variety, both between and within individual works. We might explain Steinbeck's fall from critical favor by comparing him with William Faulkner, whose recognizable brand of high modernism makes him central to his literary period. Faulkner also worked through a variety of modes, ranging from modernist stream of consciousness to the humor of the Old Southwest. And like Steinbeck, Faulkner wrote screenplays and was fascinated by film. But Faulkner did not, like Steinbeck, coauthor a marine biology textbook, write an award-winning Broadway play, produce recruitment propaganda for the US Armed Services, plan theses for John Cage to set to percussion music, translate an Arthurian classic from Middle English, or research a history of a leader of the Mexican Revolution. Faulkner may have remade the novel, but he did not, like Steinbeck, try to dispense with it altogether. At a basic level, to encounter Steinbeck is to grapple with a bewildering series of formal transformations to the extent that, as Wilson recognized, "when his curtain goes up, he always puts on a different kind of show."[17] Steinbeck may not be an experimental writer in the way that Fiedler considers Faulkner an experimental writer. But from another perspective, we can reclaim Steinbeck as twentieth-century American literature's *most* experimental writer – and not least for his engagement with scientific experiments, which made him biological researcher and novelist both.

The variety that most concerned Wilson, Mizener, and Fiedler was internal to Steinbeck's works. These critics detected an uncertainty of aesthetic tone, an unevenness in which low-status forms, such as sentimentalism and melodrama, frustrate the compelling, even poetic prose of a social realist. Good writing jostles bad. In this regard, it is difficult not to agree with Fiedler that Steinbeck's writing is, quite frequently, "problematical."[18] But problems are interesting, just as the sentimental to seize on a label often applied to Steinbeck – is a complex literary mode that can serve conflicting ethical purposes. We might agree with his harshest critics that Steinbeck's work stutters in several ways. What, however, is the nature of those breakdowns and contradictions? What do they tell us about the power and the limits of literature's claims to social power, epitomized by Steinbeck's famous remark about *The Grapes of Wrath* that he was attempting to write history while it was happening?[19] He may have gotten that history wrong on several fronts. As critics and historians have been quick to note, the striking laborers in *In Dubious Battle* and the migrant workers in *The Grapes of Wrath* were by no means as white as Steinbeck would have us believe.[20] But criticism should not end there. Meaning proliferates from these problems, just as the true interest of Steinbeck's writing lies in its clash of modes and styles, in the formal dramas that emerge from his literary experiments. If Steinbeck's work is nostalgic, as Mizener suggests, and if it is often sentimental, as Fiedler and others claim, then what do we mean by these terms, and how can Steinbeck's work offer new ways to understand and evaluate them? Is it true, as Fiedler argues when he turns to the "infamous schmaltzy" scene in the hamburger stand in *The Grapes of Wrath*, that Steinbeck "eschews evasive irony in favor of shameless sentimentality, thereby not only flattening out all nuances and ambiguity but also sacrificing plausibility for the sake of easy pathos"?[21] At stake here is the question of how we read Steinbeck, and the aesthetic judgments that we bring to his work. In other words, how "flat" are Steinbeck's engagements with the sentimental and the nostalgic, to choose the two faults he is typically said to display? And how might new interpretations of Steinbeck's bewildering experimentalism – a frequent source of critical discomfort – emerge from such questions?

Curious Experiments

It is difficult to forget the scene in the hamburger stand, not least because it is staged so effectively in John Ford's 1940 film version of *The Grapes of Wrath*. The scene begins with a close observation of something we find again and again in Steinbeck's writing – an observation of work, in this case Al the counterman's preparation of a hamburger sandwich, described in extensive detail:

> He presses down a hissing hamburger with his spatula. He lays the split buns on the plate to toast and heat. He gathers up stray onions from the plate and

> heaps them on the meat and presses them in with the spatula. He puts half the bun on top of the meat, paints the other half with melted butter, with thin pickle relish. Holding the bun on the meat, he lays the spatula under the thin pad of meat, flips it over, lays the buttered half on top, and drops the hamburger on a small plate. Quarter of a dill pickle, two black olives beside the sandwich. Al skims the plate down the counter like a quoit. And he scrapes his griddle with the spatula and looks moodily at the stew kettle.[22]

Patrick McDonald and his two sons had opened their first hamburger stand on Route 66 in Monrovia, California, just two years before the publication of *The Grapes of Wrath*; with it, they announced the democratization of the hamburger and the automation of its production. Uncannily intuiting the emergent (one of Steinbeck's great talents, as we will see), the methodical, assembly-line prose rhythms capture Al's moody entrapment in a labor process beginning to require greater homogeneity and speed. Al is attempting to cling to the craft of work, its joy (in the end, he spins down the plate like a quoit in a lawn game), but his vacant, uncommunicative stare at his griddle suggests that he is *becoming* this automated worker. A hallmark of high modernism is its recursive inclusion of metafictional concepts of artistic process: think of Ernest Hemingway's use of the bullfight in *The Sun Also Rises* (1925) to theorize his ideal of authentic feeling communicated in the graceful line of style. Steinbeck positions his metafiction at a different, "lower" level: Al's work with the spatula is also Steinbeck's work with the pen. The scene as a whole is slowly and patiently built up, like Al's hamburger itself, with the description unfolding materially in real time. And like a hamburger, Steinbeck's sentimental scene is easily accessible – taste is democratized – and composite in structure: Steinbeck sandwiches his juicy human-interest story between an external, roving narrative omniscience. (The novel as a whole works in a similar way, with closely observed dramatic episodes contained by the distancing poetics of the more philosophical interchapters.) The scene is a perfectly manufactured unit for us to take out on our journey through the novel.

Like a hamburger, Steinbeck's writing can indeed seem big and in your face ("New Start Big Writing," he jotted at the top of the manuscript of *Grapes*): hence the discomfort it creates in critics, the accusations of bad taste. But to say that Steinbeck's writing is then flat and simplistic is really to miss all the "fixings" that accompany it. Fiedler compares Steinbeck's sentimentalism with that of Harriet Beecher Stowe in *Uncle Tom's Cabin* (1852), a comparison that Steinbeck would surely have recognized.[23] To label Steinbeck sentimental does not close the matter, however, but opens the fraught debate over the power of the sentimental itself. As Ann Douglas and Jane Tompkins debated in the 1980s, we can read the sentimental in competing ways. We can view it as a conservative mask for middle-class ideologies and a rationalization of laissez-faire economics, in which feelings of empathy emerge only when the capacity to act has been suspended, to paraphrase Douglas.[24] Or like Tompkins, we can read it as a realm of social power and of salvation through motherly love. Here the sentimental becomes an agent of social critique and a call for a radical transformation toward higher values, based on a democratic extension of humanity to others.[25] Either way, the sentimental is known for its overly scripted quality. But is this the case in Steinbeck's hamburger stand? Eric Sundquist reads the death of Little Eva in *Uncle Tom's Cabin* as an excessively staged scene that opens a space for our emotional participation and allows the transference of our sentiment from the white child to the enslaved person.[26] Steinbeck's hamburger stand stages a similar scene of transformation. The motherly emotions of Mae the waitress appear to have degenerated under capitalism. She reduces individuals to their ability to spend and consume. But this view changes when she confronts the deprived Okie children: "Is them penny candy, ma'am?"

> Mae moved down and looked in. "Which ones?"
> "There, them stripy ones."
> *The little boys raised their eyes to her face and they stopped breathing; their mouths were partly opened, their half-naked bodies were rigid.*
> "Oh – them. Well, no – them's two for a penny."[27]

Echoing *Uncle Tom's Cabin*, and with ultimate literary self-consciousness, Steinbeck founds this scene of emotional transformation (Mae *has* to act) on the virtual death of the children within it: they stop breathing; their bodies become rigid. If anything, the scene is an experimental play with the sentimental rather than literary schmaltz, an experiment that leaves readers with a number of potential interpretations. Following Tompkins, we can read the scene as one of sentimental power. We ascribe humanitarian motives to Mae, who begins to care about the migrant family's future in California, hence aligning her feelings with our own (we wouldn't be reading the story if we didn't care about what happens to the characters). But given the dramatic nature of the presentation, we could equally read Mae as performing for the truckers who observe the interaction and who leave a hefty tip that more than compensates Mae for her generosity, just as Al wins on the slot machine at the end of the scene, literally making money from others' bad luck. Nothing really changes following this scene; actions merely repeat themselves as new truckers arrive to order pie, and Mae returns to her disempowered position. Class relations remain intact as the suffering migrants move on. Indeed, the scene ends with the most unsentimental of lines: "The cars whizzed viciously by on 66."[28] In essence, Steinbeck disrupts sentimentalism by refusing readers any comfortable footing. *Viciously* suggests that other emotions – anger and outrage – are the true agents of social power. "Anger is a symbol of thought and evaluation," opined Steinbeck in the late 1950s: "I think anger is the healthiest thing in the world."[29] In Steinbeck's work, sentimental tenderness is often the flipside of sharp outrage.

If Steinbeck's engagement with sentimentalism is dynamic rather than flat in the problems it provokes, then can we say the same for his nostalgia – that redolence of the 1930s that Mizener credits as the reason for Steinbeck's Nobel Prize? To find this nostalgic sensibility, we might look no further than Steinbeck's sketch "Breakfast," first published in the *Pacific Weekly*, included in *The Long Valley* (1938), and then reincorporated into chapter twenty-two of *The Grapes of Wrath*, at the threshold of the Joads' entry into the idealized government camp, Weedpatch. The sketch describes the narrator's brief encounter, one frosty morning, with a family of migrant workers camping in a California valley – a young woman nursing a baby, her young husband, and his father – who invite the narrator to breakfast before heading to work. "This thing fills me with pleasure," the sketch opens: "I don't know why, I can see it in the smallest detail. I find myself recalling it again and again, each time bringing more detail out of a sunken memory, remembering brings the curious warm pleasure."[30] Steinbeck was not alone in remembering the 1930s as "a warm and friendly time," as he would recall in a later sketch, a time of happiness and mutual caring (a special "warm spot" is exactly how Mizener describes Steinbeckian nostalgia).[31] True to the nostalgia that was first diagnosed among homesick Swiss soldiers in the seventeenth century, "Breakfast" is full of intensely remembered minutiae involving the human senses – the sucking sound of the nursing baby, the smell of the cooking bacon, the taste of the coffee.[32] This vision of the virtuous folk provides a temporary sense of home for our wandering narrator; at its center lie a nurturing, Madonna-like mother and child. Corresponding to the happiness of the narrator, the pleasure of reading this text might return us to Steinbeck's purportedly middlebrow aesthetic, or to what Roland Barthes calls the "readerly text," one that gives pleasure without challenging us as readers.[33] The symbolist technique of the sketch lends an accumulating obviousness to the beatific vision. It is a moment of dawn, with light reborn from the

East. The father and son emerge from the tent (itself a religious image for our transitory time on earth), their heads wet as if from baptism, to form a trinity with the mother. The meal itself seems a holy ritual: the biscuits act as sacramental bread, and the younger man exclaims "Keerist!" (Christ) at their smell, to make the point more obvious still.[34] We learn that the father and son have had twelve days of work, as if this is the twelve-day festival of Christmas. And in case we missed it, the point is repeated with a holy exclamation about the meal, "God Almighty, it's good."[35] We leave the family finally bathed again in morning light.

None of this is difficult or contradictory, quite the reverse. But given this apparent "readerliness," let's consider the short final paragraph in more detail:

> That's all. I know, of course, some of the reasons why it was pleasant. But there was some element of great beauty there that makes the rush of warmth when I think of it.[36]

Why that word "But" in the middle of the paragraph? It suggests not continuity between the various aspects of the story, but instead a tension. The final paragraph splits the story into three potential readings that correspond to the three sentences. The first reading: there is really no deeper meaning at all; the moment is just something that happened, something that does not necessarily add up to anything more. The third reading: the sketch is indeed the moment of nostalgic beauty described in obvious (or "readerly") religious symbolism. But in the middle of the paragraph is another possibility: some deeper, perhaps even contradictory meaning lies in the sketch. In other words, there may be a difference between the obvious beauty, the warm pleasure of the scene, and the reasons why the narrator finds it pleasant, reasons not fully revealed to us (or not fully known to the narrator: he only realizes "some" of them). We might, then, interpret "Breakfast" more along the lines of what Barthes calls the "writerly" text, one that forces us into a critical engagement with it, challenging us as readers to reenact the actions of the writer as we attempt to understand the text's shifting codes, hence giving us an enjoyment higher than mere pleasure or pleasantness.[37]

When we know more about its original conception, the sketch becomes significant for what it fails to say. Steinbeck may have based his sketch on an experience he had when visiting migrant worker camps in the summer of 1934. He was talking to various labor organizers, looking for material for a creative nonfictional piece, a diary of a communist labor organizer – material that would eventually inform his strike novel, *In Dubious Battle*.[38]

With this in mind, we might read the sketch's obvious religious imagery as *displacing* this context, turning a moment of labor unrest into a celebration of American workers able to transcend the Great Depression through moral resilience. This perhaps is a "reason why it was pleasant": it resolves the class antagonisms of the 1930s, sweeping under the rug any tensions that would disrupt a nostalgic view. In the same year as Steinbeck published "Breakfast," Dorothea Lange took her famous photograph "Migrant Mother," a picture of anxiety that draws stark contrast to the well-fed and feeding mother at the heart of Steinbeck's sketch. The apparently husbandless woman with her apparently fatherless children in Lange's photograph are replaced, in Steinbeck's sketch, by two strong men and a woman confident in her performance of femininity. The tent in Lange's photograph (made clearer in a companion photograph to "Migrant Mother," Figure I.1) acts as a stage to showcase poverty as hopeless stasis. The tent in

Figure I.1 Dorothea Lange, "Migrant agricultural worker's family. Seven hungry children. Mother aged thirty-two. Father is native Californian. Nipomo, California," March 1936. Library of Congress, Prints & Photographs Division, FSA/OWI Collection, LC-DIG-ppmsca-03054.

Steinbeck's sketch, however, presents dancing reflections of the mother's precise and graceful movements, the tent acting as a screen in a Hollywood rendition of the worthy poor (the men's dungarees are new, adding to this staged effect).[39]

If Steinbeck was researching striking workers when he conceived of "Breakfast," then the sketch is thrown into further relief when compared with a related account, from the activist and journalist Ella Winter's autobiography, *And Not to Yield*:

> I went to "Strike Headquarters," a small room with bare floor and one bench. A quiet spoken boy in a turtle-neck blue sweater pecked at a typewriter, and some Mexican women, their hair in matted plaits, sat around suckling their babies. Bits of paper tacked on a soiled board had ill-spelled messages in English and Spanish, and a list of names was printed in uneven letters on a gray cardboard from a Uneeda soda cracker box. There were flies and a smell of sweat.[40]

This may be a similar scene of women nursing their babies, but we have a very different sense of smell and presentation of food (here merely a label rather than actual substance; the box is empty and dismantled), highlighting again the romanticized nature of Steinbeck's description. And we are presented with a different racial situation: the presence of Mexicans along with whites seems more typical of the labor situation in the California fields at the time. As already mentioned, critics have noted how Steinbeck controversially omits nonwhite laborers from *In Dubious Battle* and *The Grapes of Wrath*. Elsewhere he seemed interested in the Okie immigrants *because* they were white, supposedly possessing a power to renew California with their Anglo-Saxon vigor – a question we return to later in the book. We might thus read the submerged secret of "Breakfast," the reason why it was pleasant, as a moment of racial harmony. This would explain the narrator's interest in generational continuity – father and son look much alike – just as images of mothers nursing babies were prominent in the era's romanticization of the racialized folk, most notably in Nazi Germany. With the constant sound of sucking in the background, we might go one step further and read the reason why it was pleasant as an erotic attraction to this racialized vision, announced in the ecstatic moment when the narrator first comes upon the scene: "Grey smoke spurted up out of the stubby stovepipe, spurted up a long way before it spread out and dissipated."[41]

To target Steinbeckian nostalgia, then, does not close off interpretation but instead opens up a fraught politics beneath the warm and friendly vision. Steinbeck would often claim that his work contains different levels of meaning in this way. And the remarkable point here is not that Steinbeck is looking back on the Great Depression from 1962, after all. He is generating nostalgia on the spot; the depression is becoming nostalgic even as it is being written in 1936. The meaning of nostalgia, for Steinbeck, is not retrospective but is more like the "modern nostalgia" that Svetlana Boym defines as a sideways not a backward glance, "a mourning for the impossibility of mythical return, for the loss of an enchanted world."[42] Steinbeck's nostalgia is a self-consciously fictional creation, as if he is trying to rescue a spiritual absolute from its inevitable dissipation. Hence the scene is something he recalls "again and again, each time bringing more detail out of a sunken memory." This is not a documented real but a moment that grows in the process of forced, motivated recall (which version is this, we might ask?) and fictionalization. There is something of this quality baked into the description itself:

> We filled our plates, poured bacon gravy over our biscuits and sugared our coffee. The older man filled his mouth full and he chewed and chewed and swallowed. Then he said, "God Almighty, it's good," and he filled his mouth again.
>
> The young man said, "We been eating good for twelve days."
>
> We all ate quickly, frantically, and refilled our plates and ate quickly again until we were full and warm. The hot bitter coffee scalded our throats. We threw the last little bit with the grounds in it on the earth and refilled our cups.[43]

Filling and filling, chewing and chewing, refilling and eating again, drinking and refilling: the repetition in the act of remembering the scene is being played out in the actions themselves. A compulsive repetition, a self-conscious creation and recreation of the scene, emerges before our eyes in an attempt to lend it solidity and to rescue it from oblivion. "Breakfast" is the ultimate writerly text in the ways it exposes its own processes of construction, highlighting the conflicts between its various registers. The ultimate conflict lies in the idea of nostalgia itself: it is not a middlebrow, sentimental celebration of beauty and happiness, but rather a modern happiness that is inherently transitory, fugitive, and precarious.[44] In the suddenness with which the scene breaks up, as narrator and characters go their separate ways, we glimpse what Boym describes as "a nostalgia for what could have been."[45] Returning us to Al making his hamburger in *The Grapes of Wrath*, "Breakfast" is also a story about writing itself as the compulsive attempt to rescue a present from loss. Steinbeck is nostalgic, just as he is sentimental. But he is inconsistently, unevenly, and fascinatingly so, his apparent flatness giving way to sunken levels of meaning that expand rather than reduce interpretation.

Steinbeck Country

The first, book-length study of John Steinbeck, Harry Thornton Moore's *The Novels of John Steinbeck* (1939), begins with a map of "The Steinbeck Country" (Figure I.2). Printed in green and centered on Salinas, Steinbeck's childhood hometown, the map highlights various locations associated with Steinbeck's life and the settings of his novels and stories up to and including *The Grapes of Wrath*, then hot off the press. A few years later, Malcolm Cowley would famously include a map at the beginning of *The Portable Faulkner* (1946), his anthology of William Faulkner's stories and excerpts from his novels, organized into a chronicle of Faulkner's fictionalized Yoknapatawpha County, Mississippi. Edmund Wilson would note this parallel conduciveness to mapping in his early overview of Steinbeck: "His exploration in his novels of the Salinas Valley has been more thoroughgoing and tenacious than anything of the kind in our contemporary fiction," Wilson wrote, with the exception of "Faulkner's intensive cultivation of the state of Mississippi."[46] Both writers have a commitment to place that absorbs their separate books into a greater cycle of stories about the fundamental relationship between humans and the land.

If Faulkner's map tells a history of Native American dispossession and the legacy of slavery in the South, the map of Steinbeck Country sets different coordinates, even as its predominantly Spanish names imply a prior history of colonization. Faulkner's map is quartered by roads and bordered north and south by meandering rivers; it seems a self-contained "postage stamp," as Faulkner would term it, if always a synecdoche for a larger history.[47] Steinbeck Country, however, seems incomplete – an arrow points to Fresno and the San Joaquin Valley where the Oklahoma migrants "come" (not *came*) to work; the mountains run south to a Greater California beyond the Mexican border; the tip of the San Francisco Bay top-left implies the great city to the north; the ocean ranges west toward Asia. Both maps tell a tale of labor in the land: the plantation labor in the South is continuous with the exploitation of migrant workers recorded in the map of Steinbeck Country (we are told that *In Dubious Battle* uses "incidents in a strike of cotton pickers near Fresno"). And over both maps broods authorial presence. "Surveyed & mapped for this volume by WILLIAM FAULKNER," reads the map in the Cowley volume,[48] while

Figure I.2 Map of "The Steinbeck Country," from Harry Thornton Moore, *The Novels of John Steinbeck: A First Critical Study* (Chicago, IL: Normandie House, 1939), p. 4.

Steinbeck's presence is dotted throughout Moore's map not only in his current and previous homes but also in the sites where Steinbeck has himself performed work in this landscape – on a ranch near King City, on the new road stretching south of Big Sur. "The Steinbeck Country" is a map about work, about self-making, about education. Steinbeck's mother once taught school near Big Sur, we are told. And then to the very north we have Palo Alto, with the words "Steinbeck went to Stanford University here." Steinbeck is everywhere in this landscape, as if the map is an effort to pin him down amid a variety of interests in an area whose borders are unclosed.

Like the map of Steinbeck Country, Steinbeck's ideas are sprawling, open ended, and always extending out to a wider world in all directions, always toggling between different, sometimes incompatible, registers of meaning. If Faulkner's interest in race – focused in his map on the slave plantation – has helped maintain his position at the heart of twentieth-century American literature, then Steinbeck is equally preoccupied with this great American subject.[49] Yet Steinbeck's understanding of race is quite different from Faulkner's concern with slavery and with the haunting problems its legacy poses for Southern history. Steinbeck's idea of race is not centrally concerned with the binary of black and white, but with the western conquest and destruction of native and Mexican peoples, and with the continuation of a Mexican and "Spanish" presence in the West. It is concerned with successive waves of immigration – not just from Mexico but also from the Philippines, Japan, China, and subcontinental India – often in response to the seasonal needs of California's enormous agricultural sector. It is an idea of race that looks outward to distant borders, to the Pacific Rim and to Mexico in the South. It is strongly tied to the realms of science and medicine, particularly through the eugenics movement, which flourished in the West because of its strong investment in agriculture and nature, and because of the regeneration and hence racial perfectionism promised by the frontier.[50] For Steinbeck, race is also about "the human race" – or rather, humanity as a species – and is centered on what Wilson recognized as Steinbeck's constant "preoccupation with biology."[51] (At Stanford, Steinbeck petitioned to take a course in the medical school on the dissection of cadavers, because he "wanted to know more about people."[52]) It is tied to holistic, even transcendental ways of thinking about the individual as part of a greater consciousness.

Reclaiming John Steinbeck is a book about Steinbeck's struggle to become that big-picture thinker capable of interrogating the nature of humanity as a species, the relationship of humans to the planet and to other life-forms upon it, and the structures of social organization that divide groups of people even as they offer the possibilities of liberation (or at least survival). My somewhat ostentatious subtitle, *Writing for the Future of Humanity*, marks Steinbeck's ultimate understanding of human interconnectedness, fragility, and malleability that might allow for wholesale transformation.

My subtitle also captures the signal temporality that runs through so many of Steinbeck's works, as he seeks to describe situations of social, historical, and biological change at the points of their emergence. This book is also about the difficulties of that vision – the ways that Steinbeck's prophetic ambitions to think globally are both energized and thwarted by more local and intransigent questions of history and identity. And finally, this book is about how those fundamental tensions in Steinbeck's writing become dramatically visible in the experimental possibilities and problems of literary form.

The book contains nine essayistic chapters intended to suggest the diversity of Steinbeck's interests and to provoke new awareness of his complexity and difficulty as a writer and a thinker. The chapters trace Steinbeck's work more-or-less chronologically from its beginnings to the point in the mid-1940s when Steinbeck's close involvement with the history and environment of California ended with his departure for New York to spend the second half of his writing career on the East Coast. We can debate whether Steinbeck's later career represents creative dissipation, but we can say for sure that a definite and strong arc of ideas runs from his first novel *Cup of Gold* (1929) to *The Pearl* (1947) – a short novel that nevertheless serves as a fitting culmination in the ways it embodies Steinbeck's collaborative mind-set and biological framework of ideas, his play with form that works across the boundaries of genre and media, his cultural and national border crossings, and – dare I say it – his fragile sense of hope in the future.

The first three chapters of the book center on race to explore three important aspects of Steinbeck's early career: his engagement with the institutional teaching of writing, particularly involving the short story (the first manifestation of Steinbeck's ongoing frustration with the genre of the novel); his early concern with environmental thinking as it relates to the climate of the American West; and his interest in the history of race relations in the West, especially the interactions – both in love and hate – of whites with African Americans and with Asian Americans. By exploring stories from Steinbeck's early short story cycle, *The Pastures of Heaven* (1932), and his major collection of stories, *The Long Valley* (1938), together with his neglected second novel *To a God Unknown* (1933), these chapters establish a crucial aspect of my argument as a whole. The way to appreciate Steinbeck, in all his fascinating unevenness, is to open ourselves to levels of formal complexity in his work. What critics often view as problems in early Steinbeck – for example, his uneasy mix of mythical and realist modes, the easy drift from character to caricature, the uncertainty of focus – are productive ways to understand a central and politicized tension that runs through much of Steinbeck's work: a conflict between the normative rules (and expectations) of narrative and the hybrid, emergent, or subversive forces that refuse containment by them. We will also see how Steinbeck's expansive efforts to understand the largest forces shaping the environment and determining the nature of human interaction are haunted by narrower problems of cultural conflict, particularly as they involve a fragile and confused whiteness attempting, and failing, to maintain its difference and identity in a multicultural West.

The middle three chapters of the book explore another of Steinbeck's major obsessions, human psychology and behavior, especially as they relate to nonhuman life-forms, and to nonnormative states of mind. Turning again to stories from *The Long Valley* together with Steinbeck's story cycle *The Red Pony* (1933–36) and his novella about disability *Of Mice and Men* (1937), this section tackles the most resounding critique of Steinbeck – that he is a "late naturalist" who writes mostly about plants and animals – by placing his work in the context of "critical animal studies" and related attempts to decenter the privilege of the human in its relation to the planet. In some of his most experimental stories, Steinbeck establishes the fragility of "the human" by exploring the subjective life of nonhuman animals, and by recognizing states of passive, non-exploitative, and receptive existence based on the human-plant connection. If Steinbeck at times approaches a post-humanist ethical pluralism, then such states of radical alterity are also tainted by problems of race and class emerging from colonial possession and from the prominence of eugenic thinking in the West. In *Of Mice and Men* in particular, we see again how alleged "weaknesses" in Steinbeck's imagination – for example, hollow characterization, brutal melodrama, sweeping determinism, and easy sentimentalism – are not the end points of argument but the beginning of an understanding of Steinbeck's complex play with literary form that embodies both the expansion and the limitation of human development.

The final three chapters of the book expand the focus to consider a crucial characteristic of Steinbeck's writing that was noted during his lifetime but has failed to gather full critical recognition: his view of humanity as a species inhabiting a precarious planet. Treating the major phase of Steinbeck's career that includes *The Grapes of Wrath* (1939), the coauthored *Sea of Cortez* (1941), and the novel/film *The Pearl* (1947), this section explores how Steinbeck's writing strives to create a vision that is at once biological, ecological, and political as he turned toward Mexico and to patterns of environmental destruction and social inequality in the Global South. Setting him apart from Faulkner, Steinbeck became deeply involved with Mexico, collecting marine animals with the biologist Edward F. Ricketts, and making a movie with the Mexican director Emilio Fernández, among other film-based projects south of the border. *Sea of Cortez*, like so many of Steinbeck's works, is a radical experiment in a new kind of writing, a writing at the interdisciplinary border of art and science, to describe new, non-teleological states of species-consciousness necessary for human survival in the face of extinction. If this experiment involved Steinbeck again in the racial contradictions we have seen throughout his career, then we end with Steinbeck's attempt to resolve his notorious political ambivalence – so clearly on display in the vagueness of the social philosophy in *The Grapes of Wrath* – in *The Pearl*. The transnational dialogue between the novel and film of *The Pearl*, and the curious temporality of a novel imagining itself impacting a public through cinematic engagement, create an experimental if idealistic work, one that recognizes the global structure of inequality and injustice, and that imagines the conditions of uncertainty and projected consciousness necessary to free the individual from the determinism of history in a revolutionary (and decolonial) moment of social transformation. A brief epilogue on *Cannery Row* (1945) reads that eccentric, episodic novel as a microcosm of an experimental career.

As perhaps our most read but least studied writer – oddly canonical yet neglected – John Steinbeck remains a critical curiosity. Indeed, curiosity was one of Steinbeck's favorite words, which he used to describe the peculiar effects that his works seemed to have on their readers, impacts that often seemed difficult to comprehend, describe, or analyze. What Alfred Kazin disdainfully termed Steinbeck's "valley-bred . . . slow curiosity" likewise highlights a special power in Steinbeck's writing to draw attention to ideas difficult to hold in view.[53] This book is an attempt to find a critical language for those experimental effects during the major phase of Steinbeck's career. It requires recognition of the dizzying variety of genres and forms in which Steinbeck wrote, and it requires an openness to contradiction and messiness and to the faltering inherent in experimentation. It is time to take a long look at Steinbeck, facing the achievements and difficulties in his work rather than flipping neglect into defense, or letting him slip away altogether. Reclamation is not necessarily celebration. We need to consider more deeply Steinbeck's place in literary history, because claims that he is a late naturalist or a middlebrow writer are reductive and inadequate. As we will discover where Steinbeck is concerned, matters are complicated, sometimes problematic, and always interesting. We can ignore Steinbeck. But as Leslie Fiedler's angry reaction revealed on that day in San Jose, somehow we cannot forget him.

CHAPTER 1

Short Stories in School and Lab: "Tularecito" and "The Snake"

Harry Thornton Moore's 1939 map of Steinbeck Country (see the Introduction, Figure I.2) represents Steinbeck's body of work as a cycle of stories that pivots on the history of a common ground. In the big picture, Steinbeck's works are – like William Faulkner's – bound together by a series of interconnections, repeated characters, and recycled thematics and story lines. Steinbeck's Mexican American characters (some would say caricatures) in *Tortilla Flat* (1935) are mirrored by Mack and the boys in *Cannery Row* (1945). Steinbeck's concern with poverty and exploitation would develop across multiple works as would his formal interest in the Arthurian quest narrative, beginning with his "juvenile" novel *Cup of Gold* (1929) and ending with his unfinished translation *The Acts of King Arthur and His Noble Knights*, which he began in the mid-1950s. Some critics have suggested that a "Doc Ricketts" character, based on Steinbeck's friend, marine biologist Ed Ricketts, is always broodingly present in a number of guises in Steinbeck's work.[1] There are unities in Steinbeck's multiplicity, just as Steinbeck's central philosophical interests concern the holistic relationship of parts to whole, as we will see throughout this book. Such connections between disconnected parts would be nowhere clearer than in Steinbeck's first "serious" work of fiction, the short story cycle *The Pastures of Heaven* (1932).

The prefatory story of Steinbeck's cycle finds the roots of local history deep in the colonial past. It tells the tale of a Spanish corporal who accidently discovers *Las Pasturas del Cielo* "some time around 1776" while hunting for the escaped Native American enslaved people who were molding adobe bricks to build the Carmelo Mission of Alta California.[2] The story cycle may discover an alternate national history in a West Coast 1776, though Steinbeck again parallels Faulkner in finding these origins in slave labor, and in the rampant miscegenation it produced. "His descendants are almost white now," says the narrator concerning the colonizing corporal who was "building a new race for California" (the corporal eventually dies of venereal disease contracted from a Native American woman).[3] And just as Faulkner began to develop his stories about the poor whites of Frenchman's Bend – stories connected to yet separate from his interest in slavery – so too would Steinbeck place these stories about white rural settlers atop a history of colonial exploitation. Predicting Will Varner's store that becomes central to Faulkner's stories about Flem Snopes and friends in *The Hamlet* (1940) and its sequels, *The Pastures of Heaven* is centered on "a general store and post office," with the addition of another key location: "half a mile above, beside the stream, a hacked and much initialed school house."[4]

The central presence of the schoolhouse is reflected in Thornton's map, where Steinbeck's hometown of Salinas appears between Big Sur (where Steinbeck's mother taught school) to the south and Palo Alto (where Steinbeck attended Stanford University) to the north. Steinbeck left Stanford without completing his degree; his relationship to the institution was inevitably fraught. But to describe that relationship as "puzzling, mutually unappreciative, even debilitating" is to miss a degree of institutional self-consciousness in Steinbeck's work.[5] Steinbeck's early training as a writer links his formal experimentation (specifically in the form of the short story, that most under-theorized of genres) to his interest in the legacies of colonization in the culture and society of the American West. Steinbeck's story about the character Tularecito, chapter four of the twelve-chapter *Pastures of Heaven*, brings those links to light, helping us to understand the work performed by clashes in stylistic register that critics tend to dismiss as mere inconsistency marking Steinbeck's oeuvre.

Mark McGurl's study of the influence of creative writing programs on post–World War II American writing, *The Program Era* (2011), has helped to establish the many ways that institutions shape the form and content of literary production.[6] Steinbeck may have been formally educated before the official establishment of creative writing programs; however, during the 1920s, the teaching of creative practice was not quite *not* instituted either. In fact, Steinbeck took a number of courses that taught writing in a variety of genres (he took all that were available at Stanford, except a course in play writing, to which he was not admitted by the professor).[7] He was a member of the Stanford English Club, in which he won an award in his final year for best essay,[8] and he attended a number of literary salons, including one organized by English professor Margery Bailey, an important influence. The greatest impact on Steinbeck's development as a writer came from Edith Mirrielees, another English professor, with whom Steinbeck studied and with whom he continued to share his work after his time at Stanford, eventually providing a preface for a paperback edition of her book *Story Writing* (1947).

Steinbeck's education came at the height of the short story as a commercial form, driven by the rampant popularity of magazines and promoted by story-writing handbooks, hundreds of which were published in the early decades of the twentieth century. During this period, the short story came to bear implicit ideological pressures.[9] It was viewed as a peculiarly American form, capable of absorbing native material, and particularly attuned to the nation's marginalized groups; by the end of the nineteenth century, it had become an important entry point to the literary market for women and for writers of color. Echoing the observations of Alexis de Tocqueville a century before, the short story seemed an inherently democratic form, easily disseminated, adaptable, and graspable by the masses.[10] Such democratic assumptions translated into views that the short story was easy to write: the handbook tradition implied that the art could be mastered by virtually anyone, and manufactured at scale. Handbooks urged writers to internalize market forces, to become efficient, and to conform to the conventions of popular taste. One handbook even had a section dedicated to the "obliteration of personal traits."[11]

From Steinbeck's 1962 letter to Mirrielees, which became the preface to a later edition of *Story Writing*, it is clear that Mirrielees resisted much of the conformism within the handbook tradition of teaching the short story. "The only way to write a good short story," Steinbeck recalled her saying, "was to write a good short story."[12] Mirrielees was known to be critical of the short story writing tradition that placed authors in a "strait-jacket."[13] There were "no rules," she made clear to Steinbeck, giving him the sense that "no two stories dare be alike."[14] She was resistant as well to the handbook tradition's hostility to the traditional canon of literature.[15] *Story Writing* taught principles through a canon of literary precedent, its aims always as scholarly as they were commercial. Yet Mirrielees followed the more popular handbooks in dividing stories into their component parts. Not unlike the Russian Formalist critics who were beginning to analyze and define literary language as a rule-bound realm, Mirrielees encouraged the marking and blocking of literary text to understand its working functions, such as "time," "points of observation," and "characterization." From the analysis of bodies of text, rules emerged. Time should be working properly, thought Mirrielees; its links should be clear and progressive if you cut into a text at any cross section. Literary "effect" (a term straight from Edgar Allan Poe's early theorization of the short story in his 1842 review of Nathaniel Hawthorne's *Twice-Told Tales*),[16] for example, was "the sum of general causes plus the inciting cause." "A neurotic, sure the world despises him, is driven to suicide by a thing so small as a child's scowling at him in the street," wrote Mirrielees: "If the general causes for his condition have been adequately shown, then the special cause is all-sufficient, remains all-sufficient so long as it bears upon his own particular hurt."[17]

This relationship between part and whole would surely have appealed to Steinbeck's organic way of thinking. If Mirrielees encouraged textual dissection, and if Steinbeck wanted to cut open cadavers to know more about people,[18] then the handbook literature on the short story also described the form working bodily like a drug, potentially leaving the mind in a jerky state.[19] Mirrielees's choice of a damaged neurotic as her example would also have resonated with Steinbeck, whose early stories followed in the tradition of Sherwood Anderson's "grotesque" characters who exist at the margins of normalcy.[20] Early reviewers of *The Pastures of Heaven* picked up this point. "It is the first flight of a fine writing talent which, while kindlier than that of Faulkner, is yet related to it in its preoccupation with the abnormal," wrote one reviewer.[21] "Some of the stories are grim," wrote another, "for when the local supply of epileptics, congenital idiots and lunatics runs low, the author imports one from San Francisco."[22] Like the stories themselves, Steinbeck's characters are interconnected but also walled off in their own eccentricities. They are "decentralized," noted one observant reviewer; they "do not live as individuals," opined another.[23]

André Gide, the French writer of fraught psychological fiction, thought that Steinbeck wrote "nothing more perfect, more accomplished, than certain of his short stories."[24] But *The Pastures of Heaven*, Steinbeck's first major publication, partially resists the popular craze for the short story by placing its individual parts in an interconnected cycle of narratives. Again showing the influence of Anderson's *Winesburg, Ohio* (1919), the decentralized characters of *Pastures* populate a cycle in which the stories neither stand alone nor come together into novelistic wholeness. As the critic Long Le-Khac writes in his study of the story cycle prevalent in recent Asian American and Latinx literature, the form moves between connection and disconnection, unity and multiplicity, individuality and collectivity, often in political situations involving the relationship between marginalized groups and a dominant culture.[25] By choosing a marginalized and hybrid genre – the short story cycle – Steinbeck returns through literary form to the history of possession and prior occupancy that haunts the Western land. Steinbeck's pastures are gloomy, threatening, populated by deserted houses and dark trees, "the shadows they throw on the ground have suggestive shapes."[26]

One such suggestive shape is his character Tularecito, an early example of the type of "unfinished," innocent, nonnormative character who would fascinate Steinbeck throughout his career. Steinbeck's chapter about Tularecito is the story of a suppressed indigenous presence in a colonized land. It is also a story about the discovery of narrative itself from these native materials, a story about the emergence of myth from the soil and from the racial conflicts it contains. If "Tularecito" (to give the chapter a story title) is part of the hybrid genre of the story cycle, then it is equally hybrid in its awkward combination of realist and romantic elements. This resonant hybridity lies at the heart of Steinbeck's creative imagination. As Steinbeck phrased it to Mirrielees, "there is a magic in story writing" itself.[27]

Unfinishing School

Sandwiched between two chapters about the violent jealousies, repressed desires, and psychological illnesses of the valley's white settlers, "Tularecito" is a story about the discovery of a strange baby and the subsequent attempts to educate and normalize the child within the white settler community:

> The baby had short, chubby arms, and long, loose-jointed legs. Its large head sat without interval of neck between deformedly broad shoulders. The baby's flat face, together with its peculiar body, caused it automatically to be named Tularecito, Little Frog, although Franklin Gomez often called it Coyote, "for," he said, "there is in this boy's face that ancient wisdom one finds in the face of a coyote."[28]

If the minor character Franklin Gomez (whose Native American servant first discovers Tularecito) embodies in his name a merger of the Anglo and the Latin, then Tularecito himself seems an ill-jointed mixture of contemporary and ancient cultures, white and native beliefs, animal and human natures, cross-racial interest and stereotype. His Spanish name, moreover, sets the character in a long tradition of literary precedent. In his physical description and native inheritance, we might relate Tularecito to Caliban from William Shakespeare's *The Tempest* (1611). Like Caliban, Tularecito is made to work like an enslaved person. Perhaps he harbors the smoldering colonized hatred found within Shakespeare's indigenous character, announced by Tularecito's first words allegedly uttered to Gomez's

Indian servant Pancho: "Look! I have very sharp teeth."[29] We might place Tularecito in the tradition of another Western frog, as in Mark Twain's "The Celebrated Jumping Frog of Calaveras County" (1865), a tall tale about innocence and gullibility in a Western community. Or we might think of Tularecito alongside Poe's "Hop-Frog" (1849), a physically deformed character who is taken from his homeland to become an enslaved person and court jester, only to take revenge on his captors; foreshadowing Tularecito's first words, Hop-Frog is repeatedly described as grinding his teeth.[30] Or further compounding these literary references, Tularecito recalls a passage from D. H. Lawrence's *Studies in Classic American Literature* (1923), a pioneering study that, one imagines, Steinbeck may have encountered as a student at Stanford. Lawrence draws on the presence of Caliban to describe the contradictions of American democracy and the haunting legacies of slavery and racism: "When you are actually *in* America, America hurts, because it has a powerful disintegrative influence upon the white psyche. It is full of grinning, unappeased aboriginal demons, too, ghosts, and it persecutes the white men ... until the white men give up their absolute whiteness."[31]

Which is all to say that Tularecito is such a self-consciously literary character. Indeed, the reference to sharp teeth seems to be merely that: a literary reference (the teeth hardly feature again in the story) designed to place the character in dialogue, perhaps, with Lawrence's grinning aboriginal demons or with "Hop-Frog" by Poe, a writer who loomed large as a theorist of the short story in the handbook literature of Mirrielees and others.[32] Like Pancho's original story about the discovery of Tularecito, which had to be "stretched out of its tangle of incoherencies,"[33] Steinbeck's "Tularecito" is on a higher level an allegory of artistic emergence. *Pastures* as a whole declares strong paternity in Anderson's *Winesburg*, in which characters constantly seek to escape their loneliness by expressing themselves through feverish actions of the fingers and hands. Like an Anderson character, Tularecito is described as "queer," "unfinished," and "misshapen."[34] Stunted, he seeks self-completion and connection through the action of his long, powerful, dexterous fingers, which strive to communicate by carving and drawing lifelike forms. Steinbeck is writing self-consciously in the school of Anderson, but Steinbeck's grotesque is very much a racialized one. Tularecito behaves like a mixed-race fugitive from an Anderson village, his appearance and gifts lying deep in a mysterious indigenous past. At once a story of the return of an "aboriginal presence" – undoubtedly primitivistic and reductive on Steinbeck's part – and a contemplation of the creative impulse itself, the main theme of

"Tularecito" is the relationship between artistic talent and the educational establishment.

Steinbeck fell under the influence of two English professors at Stanford, Margery Bailey and Edith Mirrielees. Tularecito likewise encounters two teachers in his enforced progress through the school, Miss Martin and Miss Morgan, with the latter establishing a reading club for her students, very much like Stanford's English Club where Steinbeck met his earliest audiences. Miss Morgan, the teacher who replaces Miss Martin, is a strong pedagogical presence: she has read studies about Tularecito's special needs, and – like Mirrielees – she teaches her pupils through the precedents of classic literature. Indeed, we might think of Tularecito's truncated nature in light of one of Mirrielees's educational tactics that Steinbeck recalls: "As an exercise we were trying to reduce the meat of a story to one sentence, for only then could we know it well enough to enlarge it to three or six or ten thousand words."[35] We can think of Tularecito as this "meat of a story," a kind of raw narrative material himself. Replicating Steinbeck's work with characterization, Tularecito compulsively draws different creatures of the animal world on the chalkboard. His obsessive actions signify narrative in its simplest form, a listing of one thing after another – a counting or sequencing without plot, structure, or development. As a student, Steinbeck was known for a similar compulsion: he would endlessly read or mumble his own stories, as if he could not help it.[36] He described himself as always writing, even in his most intimate moments, and would later characterize his obsession as a "nervous tick."[37] Like Tularecito's gift of drawing, story seemed to Steinbeck a magic urge that would possess him, lifting him at times above his "confused, turgid, ugly and gross person."[38] At other times, it was something to be feared. "Do you wonder why I keep writing when I know of nothing to be gained by it?" he wrote a friend in 1924: "I will tell you – when this clawed creature is tearing in my chest, the scribbling of words appears to propitiate it momentarily."[39]

Tularecito both embodies and performs this powerful and subversive creativity. His compulsive drawing seems at first a protest at the confines of the school. When the other pupils begin to erase the figures he draws around the chalkboard, Tularecito flies into a violent rage. He cannot accept revision – one of Mirrielees's crucial categories of story writing – just as he rejects the "honorable rules" of the school and the formulas of alphabetic writing, spilling rivers of ink in protest at prescriptive discipline and institutional confinement.[40] If Miss Martin encourages Tularecito's native genius toward "astonishing detail and veracity,"[41] then her replacement, Tularecito's second teacher Miss Morgan, encourages her pupils in the principles of romance. Like the Russian Formalists then decoding the deep structures of literature, Miss Morgan likes fairy tales (Margery Bailey, Steinbeck's teacher, also wrote children's books based on myth). She reads her pupils stories about elves, pixies, changelings, and gnomes. Moreover, she implicitly believes in the existence of such mythical creatures: "part of America's cultural starvation," she often said, "was due to its boorish and superstitious denial of the existence of fairies." She even begins to participate in a fairy story herself when on a walk she tears her finger on a thorn and draws a mark of her presence on a chalk rock. As a student of humankind's need for myth and story, she is led to speculate on the existential function of language as an archetypal form of marking through which we impose on the world the evidence of our being. "Life is so unreal," she writes in a letter: "I think that we seriously doubt that we exist and go about trying to prove that we do."[42]

Himself part-human and, apparently, part-gnome, Tularecito comes to feel the pressure of Miss Morgan's theories about the ontological need for story. "Here was paper on which to write" is how she thinks about Tularecito: "She could carve a lovely story that would be far more real than a book story ever could."[43] Tularecito does not believe fairy stories to be merely imaginative; they are real things, chronicles of actual events. He goes forth into the world to find communion with the gnomes, digging holes in the ground as if to discover the fairy tale's deep structures. Indeed, the two sides of Tularecito – the empirical and the mystical – are not unlike the two sides of Steinbeck himself. Few major American writers, either before or since, have known more about science, particularly biology, and have used such knowledge to shape their writing. But Steinbeck also claimed to believe in leprechauns and had a strong interest in magic, particularly in the early years of his career.[44] As we will see in subsequent chapters, so balanced were these aspects of realism and the magical in Steinbeck's mind that we can consider him, without much of a stretch, a homegrown magical realist. The principles of magical realism as a movement in the visual arts were formulated in Europe simultaneously with Steinbeck's early development as a writer, in the 1920s. Miss Morgan's mystical beliefs emerge from her understanding of life's inherent unreality, and the same was true for the art critics and theorists for whom magical realism was merely a recognition of the miracle of existence itself.[45] Never a fully formed artistic movement in the United States, strains of magical realism can be found particularly in the regionalist art movement associated with Steinbeck's contemporaries Grant Wood and Thomas Hart Benton, whose landscapes and portraits are hybrid fusions of realist representation and shimmering mystery. For subsequent Latin American writers, this magical realism would serve political ends by disrupting Western conventions of rationalism and causality, and by confronting dominant political and cultural structures with indigenous myths and communal mind-sets. We can find an incipient if faltering recognition of this potential in Steinbeck's "Tularecito."

Writing in 1949, the Cuban novelist Alejo Carpentier viewed magical realism as the heritage of all America, an effect of the wealth of mythologies that emerge from "the virginity of the land, our upbringing, our ontology, the Faustian presence of the Indian and the black man, the revelation constituted by its recent discovery, its fecund racial mixing."[46] Tularecito seems quite literally to represent this emergence of indigenous presence from the land; his hybridity is a mixture of racial mind-sets. Tularecito's drawing of coyotes, snakes, and other animals is reminiscent of the cave painting of certain indigenous peoples in the American West who depicted their ancestors as animal hybrids emerging from an underground world,[47] just as Tularecito goes off to "dig for the little people who live in the earth." (Steinbeck may have become aware of Native American art from the Panama-Pacific International Exposition of 1915, which he visited as a child, and which featured multiple forms of indigenous representation.) Tularecito's protest at the school is to some degree a racial protest; yet, it inevitably comes to serve the needs of the white community. Working against complete cultural erasure, his marvelous gift has the power to create magically real feelings in observers. "He might even find the gnomes, might live with them and talk to them," thinks Miss Morgan: "With a few suggestive words she had been able to make his life unreal and very wonderful, and separated from the stupid lives about him."[48] Tularecito is the magical meat of story on which Miss Morgan's mind feeds.

Tularecito ultimately represents a process of appropriation rather than a balanced hybrid of real and magical, white and indigenous elements. After all, Tularecito's belief in and search for supernatural beings are largely induced by the scholarly ideas of Miss Morgan. Raw material meets shaping influence, and their interaction leads only to partial education. Tularecito is left with the desire to return to the earth, to find his "race" of hybrid human-animal gnome-people by digging repeatedly in the orchard of Bert Monroe, the central character of the larger story cycle (to the extent that this cycle can claim to have a central character).[49] Tularecito seems trapped again in a compulsive pattern of narrative, digging his hole, having it filled by Monroe, only to begin digging again. If Tularecito seems trapped in narrative repetition itself, then we can read his act of digging as a search for deep structure, for the patterns at the heart of the folktales and fairy stories he is told. To follow this metafictional aspect of the story further, we might return to Stanford in 1961 – the year before Steinbeck wrote his letter to Mirrielees – and to a lecture delivered there by the Irish writer Frank O'Connor: "The Lonely Voice." Theorizing the short story as a form opposed to the normalizing tendencies of the novel, with its assumed identification between reader and character, O'Connor posited that the short story turns not toward a hero but instead toward a "submerged population group."[50] The classic short story, as O'Connor describes it emerging from American and Russian traditions, features the "Little Man" and "outlawed figures wandering about the fringes of society" – figures of intense human loneliness defeated by "a society that has no sign posts, a society that offers no goals or answers."[51] In a direct prediction of O'Connor's theory, Tularecito is a figure of "loneliness," "an alien, a lonely outcast," digging for his "little people" – his submerged population group – literally in the earth, only to find a lack of signposts to their presence: "from the gnomes he had no message."[52] Digging, then, has a multivalent function in the story. It represents a search for indigenous literary material while implying qualities of the short story form we will see Steinbeck exploit again in "The Snake" and, later, in "The Vigilante": that is, the short story's adherence to human loneliness, and its capacity to work not horizontally, through narrative extension, but vertically, through its layers of implied depth.

The story ends, rather abruptly, with a violent confrontation between Tularecito, digging his hole, and Bert Monroe, the owner of the orchard. Like one of Lawrence's "grinning aboriginal demons" – the return of a dispossessed racial presence – Tularecito is dealt with in the strongest terms by a local judge. "After a short deliberation," the story ends, "he committed Tularecito to the asylum for the criminal insane at Napa."[53] As he features in the cycle, Monroe is the ultimate colonizing force, a failed businessman who seems to escape the curse of bad luck through his possession of the land and his subsequently successful career as a farmer. The forced institutionalization of Tularecito thus acts to remove another of the ghosts that haunt this Western land. If the story cycle is a hybrid form that can destabilize the relations of power and territory at the borders of different genres, as Le-Khac has argued, then its "deterritorialized potential" is curtailed at the end of "Tularecito."[54] The violence, in which Tularecito assaults Monroe before his arrest and incarceration, is part of a necessary formal violence, as the greater pressure of normalized continuity in the "institution" of the story cycle overcomes the insurgent energies represented by Tularecito and his chapter. The story cycle allows for unruly, fantastical episodes while also finally reining them in. Monroe is the realist who denies Tularecito's digging for supernatural forces, viewing it as trespass and dangerous vandalism. His view overpowers any magical impulse. This haunting, magical presence must be dealt with for the (mostly) realist story cycle to continue.

In his 1909 preface to his novel *The Ambassadors* (1903), Henry James described "the Story" as "just the spoiled child of art." However we attempt to discipline it, the story has its own organic force that will inevitably "play up."[55] As a "queer, unfinished child" himself, Tularecito represents this power of story, a primal (and compulsive) human desire for fantastic narrative associated with childhood storytelling.[56] His "queerness" as a character, rooted in mystery and myth, runs rampant through much of the narrative. We can read the story as inevitably one of magical realism's suppression; Tularecito's mystical potential dissipates in a realist light. As story cycle rather than novel, however, *The Pastures of Heaven* never fully weaves its various episodes into a smooth, developmental structure. The book ends with a chapter about a bus tour of the Carmel Valley, in which a group of tourists pauses to gaze over Las Pasturas del Cielo, contemplating its beauty and ideal promise. "If I could go down there and live down there for a little," thinks an old man on the bus tour, "why, I'd think over all the things that ever happened to me, and maybe I could make something out of them, something all in one piece that had a meaning, instead of all these trailing ends, these raw and dragging tails."[57] But as early reviewers of the book recognized, the collection remains decentralized. Steinbeck was attracted to hybrid forms, forms that behave messily by keeping different interpretations alive simultaneously. The brutal way that Tularecito is treated in the discourse of the story – the primitivist paradigms that leave him unfinished as a character – meets a metafictional energy that suggests a resistance to the normalizing rules of narrative. Tularecito's rage against the educational establishment may thus embody something of Steinbeck's own frustration with the prescriptive principles he received in the classroom from teachers such as Mirrielees. Mirrielees called for the practice of a unified "point of observation" in the short story. "Tularecito," however, is anything but cohesive in this regard. It is difficult to say where the story's sympathies lie; the violent ending leaves us especially confused. Where Mirrielees called for a subtlety of implication, "Tularecito" is if anything clunky in its references, particularly the way it literalizes and reduces the idea of indigeneity by having Tularecito physically attempt to return to the soil. In terms of characterization, Tularecito is denied coherent persona. He seems more like what Mirrielees called *caricature*: he has "grown disproportionate," having "one over-swollen feature concealing all the rest."[58] And as we have seen, the story may engage with the magically real, but this hybrid form (emerging from the racial mixture of the Americas, as Carpentier suggested) finally collapses when Tularecito is dismissed as mad and sent away to an institution for the mentally ill. Alterity and possibility become disability and discipline.

The final, incomplete quality of Tularecito – both character and story – involves the place of race in Steinbeck's work more generally. The story recognizes the unfinished business of the colonial legacy in the California landscape. Story itself is generated by an encounter with a native figure whose resistance to institutions becomes fuel for the white imagination and victim to its normalizing structures. We can explain away such problems as conditions of Steinbeck's notorious ambivalence: he both recognizes and subordinates an indigenous presence. But the limits of "Tularecito" are more significant than that. The grotesque mixture of realist and magical modes, their failure to cohere into a unified aesthetic, suggests the work of emergence in Steinbeck's writing, an incomplete process toward a fuller recognition that fails to escape the primitivist fantasies of racial otherness that lie at its inception.

More Curious Experiments

We will encounter Steinbeck's fraught engagement with race, and its relation to problems of literary form, in subsequent chapters. It is worth pausing for a moment longer on the institutional contexts informing Steinbeck's writing, particularly his short stories, in relation to that other topic of enflamed debate regarding Steinbeck's work: gender. To say the very least, Steinbeck is problematic in his representation of women to the extent that even those figures (such as Ma Joad in *The Grapes of Wrath*) who occupy central positions in his narratives can seem like midwives to their own oppression, to paraphrase Vivyan Adair, or merely vessels for male desires and relationships, as Nellie McKay writes, or else their femininity can seem abstracted to serve the ideology of the New Deal, as Michael Szalay has argued.[59] We might attack or defend Steinbeck on the gender question, but the more important point is to recognize the complex ways that gender operates as a problematic in his work. The story I have in mind is "The Snake" in *The Long Valley* (1938). Its institutional context is not the school, with its prescriptive rules, but a site of experimentation: the lab.

The other major educational influence on Steinbeck's life, beyond the classroom, was the scientific laboratory, specifically the Monterey lab of Steinbeck's close friend Ed Ricketts. Steinbeck and Ricketts would journey together to the Gulf of California to collect marine specimens and would write about it collaboratively in *Sea of Cortez* (1941), as we will see in Chapter 8. Ricketts's lab served as an educational supply company that sold preserved animal specimens to schools. It also functioned as a meeting point for a diverse range of intellectual, artistic, and other countercultural figures in the area.[60] Ricketts had studied at the University of Chicago with Walter Clyde Allee, a marine zoologist and pioneering ecologist.[61] Ricketts never completed his degree and was never fully accepted as a scientist by his academic peers, which created a tension with traditional disciplines that must have appealed to Steinbeck. In the eulogy Steinbeck wrote for Ricketts after his untimely death in 1948 (his car was hit by a train on a railroad crossing), Steinbeck described Ricketts's role in disrupting conventional wisdom. "Far from learning," Steinbeck wrote in "About Ed Ricketts," "adults simply become set in a maze of prejudices and dreams and sets of rules whose origins they do not know and would not dare inspect for fear the whole structure might topple over on them."[62] Opposing such conformity, Ricketts was a latter-day transcendental philosopher as well as scientist and poet; his thinking gave Steinbeck a way to unmask ideologies and "break through" the obstacles of our anthropocentric assumptions to glimpse humanity's "complete existence" and deep integration into the universe.[63] Ricketts offered Steinbeck an education in a kind of observation or attention, a seeing of things as they are in themselves, free from the teleologies and preconceived value judgments we impose upon them. Steinbeck's term for this kind of probing observation was *curiosity* ("I think I use that word far too much," he wrote at the end of the journal he kept while writing *The Grapes of Wrath*).[64] Together with Ricketts, Steinbeck would theorize this ideal of observation in *Sea of Cortez*, as we will see later, and he would write about it in another work that fictionalizes Ricketts, his short story "The Snake." "Tularecito" marks an early point in Steinbeck's experiments with the short story, one that inevitably but productively fails in its unfinished attempt to mix magical and realist modes. "The Snake" offers a more synthesized play with the narrative techniques of story writing. A truncated experiment in point of view, "The Snake" is a study of curiosity that, as Steinbeck noted in "About Ed Ricketts," also provoked some "curious reactions" in its readers.[65]

The story of a mysterious woman who visits Dr. Phillips's lab one night, "The Snake" centers on a process of observation that predicts

Steinbeck's and Ricketts's ideas in *Sea of Cortez*, just as it reflects on an aesthetics of vision developing at that time in the art world of the Monterey Bay. Dr. Phillips (one of several versions of the Doc Ricketts character that spans Steinbeck's work) has collected starfish from the tide pool and is engaging in a process of observing the starfish at different stages of reproduction, working to preserve them over time by mounting them on microscope slides for biological study. In *Sea of Cortez*, Steinbeck and Ricketts would describe photography as the ultimate medium to observe and capture, through close attention, the shells and other marine invertebrates they collected in the Gulf of California (even if they struggled with the technology of the camera on the voyage itself). Shells were also one of the subjects of Carmel-based photographer Edward Weston, who would use extremely long exposure times to capture, through a process of pure vision, the "sheer aesthetic form" of the shell, its essential being (Figure 1.1).[66] Weston described this process as seeing through the eyes not with them so that all human thoughts disappear by observing the object in itself. Weston's friends, however, did not see things in quite that way. "I cannot look at them long without feeling exceedingly perturbed," wrote Tina Modotti, "they disturbed me not only mentally but physically. There is something so pure and at the same time so perverse about them. They contain both the innocence of natural things and the morbidity of a sophisticated, distorted mind. They make me think of lilies and of embryos. They are mystical and erotic."[67] If Weston's shells tended to make observers think of his nudes, then similar resonances can be discovered in reactions to "The Snake," a story that Steinbeck claimed was based on something that "just happened" in Ricketts's lab – an event lacking deeper meaning – but that generated accusations that Steinbeck had a "perverted imagination."[68]

This tension emerges at the heart of the story too, when Dr. Phillips's desire to hold his pure scientific vision to his starfish (he has the "pre-occupied eyes of one who looks through a microscope a great deal") is disrupted by the alluring presence of the woman who mysteriously walks into the lab one night, demanding to see a rattlesnake consume a rat.[69] The story treats the relationship between attention and distraction. In this study of focalization, our omniscient narrator tends to see things from Dr. Phillips's point of view even as we are watching the doctor from the outside. The nameless woman's intense desire to see the rattlesnake eat the rat makes Dr. Phillips want to attract her attention to himself – "A desire to arouse her grew in him" – but increasingly he cannot take his eyes off her, as the woman's curiosity in the snake occupies more and

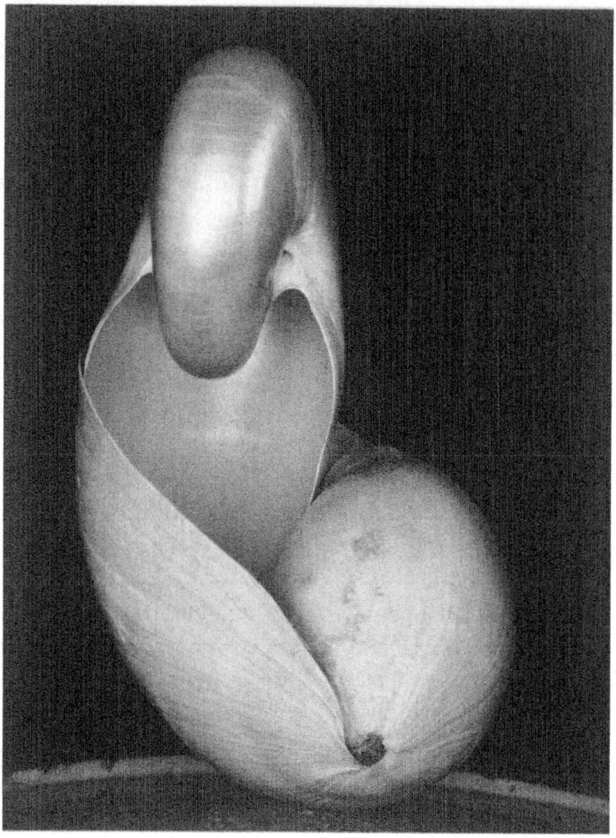

Figure 1.1 Edward Weston, "Shells," 1927. © 2020 Center for Creative Photography, Arizona Board of Regents/Artists Rights Society (ARS), New York. Photo © Tate, London 2017.

more of his (and the story's) attention. The woman thus becomes objectified, to the extent that even when her eyes were directed toward the doctor, "they did not seem to see him," thus making her very like the snake she is observing.[70] Dr. Phillips's experiment with the starfish fails because the woman herself has become a specimen through the arresting activity of his observation – a specimen that distracts by removing the agency of the enraptured observer. The experiment of the story lies in the way that, through Dr. Phillips's focus on the woman's act of watching, it brings attention *to* attention itself. The story becomes a study, in other words, of what objectifying observation looks like.

Returning to Mirrielees's theories of "points of observation" helps us understand more about Steinbeck's experiment with omniscience in "The Snake." "Omniscience," writes Mirrielees,

> allows for an observation of the mind as complete as that in the stream-of-consciousness story but allows for it from the outside. The author photographs minds; he does not enclose himself in them. And, as with all photographs, background appears as well as main figure. From his point of vantage, he finds and pictures relations, qualities, of which the individuals concerned know nothing.[71]

Mirrielees's turn to photography resonates with Steinbeck's story about techniques of vision, and indeed it seems directly relevant to the way that the story's omniscient focalization seems to objectify the woman by emptying her vision of subjectivity. "She continued to look at him," we read at the moment when the woman asks for a male snake, "but her eyes did not center on him, rather they covered him and seemed to see in a big circle all around him."[72] Rather than an empty look that does not see Dr. Phillips, the woman's vision is its own form of omniscience, rather like Mirrielees's idea of photography that reveals something beyond the knowledge of the main figure. Hence the story does not simply feature the dominant focus of Dr. Phillips; instead, it creates a double perspective in which Dr. Phillips's looking is itself being seen for what it is. Take these two moments from the climax of the story when the snake finally swallows the rat:

> The snake fitted its jaws over the rat's head and then with a slow peristaltic pulsing, began to engulf the rat. The jaws gripped and the whole throat crawled up, and the jaws gripped again. . . .
>
> He walked to her where she stood in front of the snake cage. The rat was swallowed, all except an inch of pink tail that stuck out of the snake's mouth like a sardonic tongue. The throat heaved again and the tail disappeared. The jaws snapped back into their sockets, and the big snake crawled heavily to the corner, made a big eight and dropped its head on the sand.[73]

The intensity of the woman's vision makes the doctor feel "sick," but the "perversity" (to use Steinbeck's word for his reader's reactions) of the story lies *within* the point of observation.[74] Through a double focus, Dr. Phillips's attention to the woman's attention becomes inherently sexual. These are not only descriptions of someone watching somebody else watch a snake eating a rat, in other words, but they are also descriptions of the oral sexual act that the male character implicitly desires.

The story as a whole contains a number of more obvious double entendres and sexual references. The snake seems to kiss the rat before eating it, just as the rat's legs kick spasmodically as if experiencing *la petite mort*, after which the woman "relaxed sleepily."[75] To underline matters further, the woman's voice is described as "throaty," and Dr. Phillips offers her a number of conventional "pick-up" lines ("I haven't anything to do for twenty minutes," he says at one point, and then later, "Would you like some coffee?").[76] And of course, the snake itself is the oldest phallic symbol in the book, as Dr. Phillips finally admits in a confused state: "'I've read so much about psychological sex symbols,' he thought. 'It doesn't seem to explain.'"[77] The story culminates in the doctor's ongoing, unrequited obsession with the woman, for whom he searches unsuccessfully in the streets. He becomes an agent (or victim) of unbounded, "bad" curiosity. But in a sense, all curiosity is bad in this story because vision comes unconsciously to embody arousal. As was the case with Weston's shells, the act of attention to attention cannot remain pure "is-thinking" that decenters the human in its contemplation of the essential quality of the object. Instead, curiosity is clouded by male desire to dominate, to conquer, to convert women into sexual animals, mere sex objects. Predicting the dynamic in Steinbeck's story, Weston's shells were haunted by his nudes.

In Chapter 3 we will see again Steinbeck's play with photographic perspective in the short story form. His career as a whole featured close collaborations with photographers such as Horace Bristol on an aborted photo documentary precursor to *The Grapes of Wrath* (1939), with John Swope on *Bombs Away: The Story of a Bomber Team* (1942), and with Robert Capa on *A Russian Journal* (1948). Steinbeck's imagination tended to move across both genre and media. Noting how photographers and short story writers talk about art in similar ways, the Argentine author Julio Cortázar (whose story based on a photograph was subsequently adapted into Michelangelo Antonioni's 1966 movie *Blow-Up*) described photographs and short stories as working in parallel: "cutting off a fragment of reality, giving it certain limits, but in such a way that this segment acts like an explosion which fully opens a more ample reality, like a dynamic vision which spiritually transcends the space reached by the camera." If cinema is an "open order" like the novel, developing through a synthesis of multifaceted elements moving toward a climax, then photography and short stories work inversely, through delimited image or event whereby readers move not horizontally, as in the novel, but vertically up and down in interpretive space.[78] "The Snake" works accordingly by creating a layered or hybrid vision in which the supposedly objective vision of the scientist merges with the literary imagination's power to pervert. The focused attention of the short story suggests how attention itself is never neutral. Thus, Steinbeck's work can present us with an unnerving variety of ethical positions concerning the politics of race and gender. In "Tularecito," the metafictional contemplation of the short story's institutional production depends on an appropriation of racial material that fails to recognize wholeness or depth in a supposedly native character. What is clearly a problem of race in "Tularecito" becomes a more subtle *problematics* of gender in "The Snake" because Steinbeck's story makes apparent the ideological structures buried in the process of seeing itself. The story provoked "curious reactions" in its readers, perhaps, because of this experimental play with curiosity in which the act of attention comes under the microscope to expose unconscious tensions and biases within the act of "straight" looking. The story helps us see the dynamics of dis-ease in the dominant imagination – a point that is partly true of race in Steinbeck's return to the subject in his 1933 novel, *To a God Unknown*.

CHAPTER 2

Drought, Climate, and Race in the West: To a God Unknown

Steinbeck's first published story, "Fingers of Cloud" (1924), follows the plight of Gertie, an eighteen-year-old white woman who is curiously intimate with clouds and with the rainstorms they produce.[1] Abandoned by her mother, Gertie leaves home but is caught in a storm, forcing her to flee to a Filipino migrant labor camp full of pockmarked laborers who surround their equally unattractive boss, Pedro. In an unlikely plot move,[2] Gertie becomes sexually attracted to Pedro, marries him, and lives as a queen among brown men until race consciousness enters the story. Gertie comes to realize – and despise – Pedro's blackness, exacerbated by his stereotypically "wet" back and his abusive and bizarre habits.[3] The story ends with Gertie's escape from the camp, as she takes her new knowledge of racial difference and heads into the hills to be near the clouds she loves and seems to be physically and emotionally activated by.

It may be difficult to agree with Jay Parini that the story is "a remarkable piece of work,"[4] but it does establish a number of themes and formal problems that would continue in the early period of Steinbeck's career, as we have seen already in *The Pastures of Heaven* (1932). "Fingers of Cloud" marks the beginning of a dominant if neglected theme running throughout Steinbeck's writing: the theme of race, in this case the consciousness of a white identity that is both attracted to and repulsed by the nonwhite characters laboring in the California fields. The story also treats another, crucial concern in the agricultural West: its climate.[5] And indeed, the story links these concerns (race and climate) in ways – as we shall see – that resonate with broader patterns of thinking during the period when Steinbeck was writing. Gertie is a kind of white goddess and a rain goddess; she is part heroine in a realistic story about migrant labor, part mystical presence in a tale that strays once more into the realm of myth.[6] An ambivalent move between realism and fantasy, an allegorical urge to treat complex questions of race in the West, a pressing interest in weather and climate: what "Fingers of Cloud" contains in germ would flower in

Steinbeck's second novel, *To a God Unknown* (1933). Neglected by critics, *To a God Unknown* deserves our attention not least for its pioneering fictional treatment of a timely subject in California: drought.

Magical Realism

Published in 1933 following a long and complicated gestation, *To a God Unknown* is the story of Joseph Wayne, a white Vermonter who migrates to the West in the early years of the twentieth century to escape the poverty of the East in the rich farmland south of the Salinas Valley. Joseph does not travel west alone. The spirit of his dead father follows him and comes to possess a large oak tree overtopping Joseph's new homestead. Joseph's three brothers follow too, and the Wayne empire grows when Joseph takes a wife, Elizabeth, a local schoolteacher. But all is not well on the Wayne ranch. The extreme difference in temperament among Joseph's brothers creates growing tensions, and Joseph himself becomes oddly obsessed with a grove of pine trees and a mysterious rock containing a hidden spring that lies close to his property – a rock that virtually becomes a character in its own right. The tree dies after Joseph's devout Christian brother girdles it in an attempt to destroy the idolatry it represents. Elizabeth too expires suddenly, appearing to be thrown from the mysterious rock. At this point, the weather changes as an emerging drought comes to dominate the story. Joseph and one of his brothers search for ways to escape the lack of rain but the only alternative seems to be subsistence living amid the redwoods on the foggy coast, or else an exodus to irrigated lands. Refusing to desert his ranch, Joseph is finally left alone to watch the gradual desiccation of the landscape. He retreats to his beloved grove where he tries to keep the mossy rock moist with water from the spring. But when the spring fails, Joseph cuts his wrists atop the altar-like rock in a self-sacrifice amid a growing storm that makes Joseph – prophetic to the last – believe his death has made the rains come again.

Early reviews of *To a God Unknown* were quick to note that it was a "strange and mightily obsessed book."[7] At the heart of reactions lay the novel's combination of realism, on the one hand, and symbolic, mystical material on the other. For appreciative critics, the book had "an uncanny, half-mad atmosphere which somehow binds the reader with its spell."[8] For others, such as the young V. S. Pritchett, Steinbeck failed "to understand that there is a difference between truth expressible in poetry and truth expressible in the novel."[9] The New York *Herald Tribune* perhaps put it best:

> This is a symbolical novel conceived in mysticism and dedicated to the soil. To this reviewer it is little more than a curious hodgepodge of vague moods and irrelevant meanings. It cannot be said to be successful even of its kind. It treads dangerous ground without a touch of that sureness and strength which characterize the very few good works of its order in modern times. The elements of realism and symbolism fail to cohere and it oversteps all the bounds of convincingness even on the mystic plane. *To a God Unknown* is a novel which attempts too much; and by any standards it achieves too little.[10]

Both for his admirers and detractors, Steinbeck was attempting a kind of writing that sought to fuse opposing literary modes. We saw the magical and the real collide in the problematic experiment of "Tularecito." Indeed, this tension between the late naturalist or documentary neorealist and the mystical believer in magical forces that connect humans to each other and to nature remains a dominant pattern throughout Steinbeck's career (we will see it again, for example, in the landscape descriptions of *The Grapes of Wrath* and in the character experiments of *Cannery Row*). *To a God Unknown* is the closest Steinbeck would come to fusing them together in an experimental form.

As we saw in the previous chapter, the term *magical realism* emerged in Europe in the mid-1920s to describe a magical sense of being that was finding form in the world of post-Expressionist art. In the words of Franz Roh, the German art critic who first used the term, magical realism "offers us the miracle of *existence in its imperturbable duration*: the unending miracle of eternally mobile and vibrating molecules. Out of that flux, that constant appearance and disappearance of material, permanent objects somehow appear: in short, the marvel by which a variable commotion crystalizes into a clear set of consonants."[11] Magical realism in art was also known as the New Objectivity because of its representation of objects in their ordinary settings. But these ordinary objects were penetrated by the artist's vision to reveal the mystical and often uncanny forces of life within, the sheer marvel of the world we experience every day. Through all its many definitions and manifestations – in post-Expressionist art, and in the Latin American writing of the 1960s and later, where it enters its major phase – magical realism returns centrally to a play with scale, a fusing together of worlds and spaces "irreconcilable in other modes of fiction" or art.[12] This delight in juxtaposing large and small, microcosm and macrocosm, yields what the critic Rawdon Wilson calls a hybrid quality of space, a "world interpenetration" in which the opposing qualities of the real and the marvelous can coexist.[13]

Expanding on concerns we saw in miniature in "Tularecito," *To a God Unknown* resonates with the broader, hemispheric understanding of the marvelous real that Alejo Carpentier discovered in the "racial mixing" of the Americas.[14] The major white characters in Steinbeck's frontier novel are accordingly framed by the "Mexican Indians" who lie on the story's edges, and by the native folklore and beliefs that seem to contain a truth-value greater than the displaced myths of white settlers.[15] The sedimentation of racial memories in the West remains a significant if minor element throughout the novel. More significant is the novel's uncanny layering of time periods – the way that Joseph is both a modern-day California transplant and an Old Testament patriarch or prophet, set apart from the other characters by the intense way that he embodies the inheritance of his father.[16] The possibility of communication between generations – and indeed the coexistence of different generations on a single plane of time – is realized in the presence of Joseph's father's spirit in the oak tree. "What lives here is more real than we are," says Joseph in a classic formulation of the magically real: "We are like ghosts of its reality."[17] The tree is granted this magical power in the novel – at one point, its gnarled limbs curve up protectively around Joseph's baby son – just as the death of the tree marks a tragic turn in the story's events.[18]

The magical real is felt most strongly in Steinbeck's questioning of conventional literary character (as one early review put it, the "chief characters are a man, a tree and an enormous stone").[19] Echoing magically real painting, there is a strong focus in Steinbeck's novel on objects, on the mysterious powers that vibrate within things, just as the giant rock that broods over the story seems to change its mood over time and to gain the agency necessary to kill Joseph's wife Elizabeth, who slips and falls from its mossy sides:

> It seemed to be shaped, cunningly and wisely, and yet there was no shape in the memory to match it. A short, heavy green moss covered the rock with soft pile. The edifice was something like an altar that had melted and run down over itself. In one side of the rock there was a small black cave fringed with five-fingered ferns, and from the cave a little stream flowed silently and crossed the glade and disappeared into the tangled brush that edged the clearing.[20]

We can think of such scenes alongside those of the American regionalist painter Thomas Hart Benton, whose curvilinear landscapes register a similar breakdown of distinction between human and nonhuman forms, and whose bouncy shapes resonate with an uncanny, even surreal energy. At times this power, which constantly pressures the surface representation in Steinbeck's novel, breaks through to reveal another order of magical reality beneath. When Elizabeth first arrives at the Wayne homestead, for example, her anticipated vision of the homecoming dissolves: the "room was swimming in a power beyond her control. She sat on the edge of a deep black pool and saw huge pale fishes moving mysteriously in its depth."[21] The novel demands that we accept a breakdown between the fantastic and the factual, to accept the reach of magic into the real. The landscapes of Steinbeck, like those of Benton, possess a hybrid quality of space. Steinbeck's characters contain the juxtaposition of different scales that makes magical realism so distinct. But to understand fully the nature of the uncanny forces intertwined with the social realism of *To a God Unknown*, we must return to Steinbeck's process of thinking during his long conception of the novel.

"Race Psychopathology"

Steinbeck wrote *To a God Unknown* for his friend Carlton "Dook" Sheffield, drafting the manuscript in a commercial ledger, and splicing into the growing story marginal notes intended for his erstwhile college roommate. "The story is a parable," he wrote to Sheffield: "The story of a race, growth and death. Each figure is a population, and the stones, the trees, the muscled mountains are the world – but not the world apart from man – the world *and* man – the one inseparable unit man plus his environment. Why they should have been misunderstood as being separate I do not know."[22] Clearly Steinbeck was attempting an ambitious novel. He described the story as being "too big": "I am so afraid of it sometimes – so fearful of its implications that I am tempted to burn it as an over-evil thing."[23] His subject, as he conceived it, was the relationship between human races and their environment, though his understanding of race was a complex one, as becomes clear in other letters to Sheffield written during the final stages of *To a God Unknown*.

In a letter to Sheffield dated June 21, 1933, Steinbeck describes the gradual process of observation and note-taking that accumulates into his understanding of how racialized human groups come into being in reaction to "topographical peculiarities" and other natural stimuli.[24] A couple of years later, under the influence of his marine biologist friend Ed Ricketts, Steinbeck would write "Argument of Phalanx," in which he further refines his understanding of group identity, whereby the unit-man subconsciously keys into a superorganism with its own pains, desires, hungers, and strivings that are different from, greater than, and hence influential on the nature of the individual (Steinbeck would return to this central idea in a number of ways, as we will see later in this book).[25] In his letters to Sheffield, this racialized, biological thinking is balanced with a mystical element, a belief in an unconscious force in which people

> seem to have worked under a stimulus as mysterious, as powerful and as general as that which caused the coral insects to build, and their product, while not built of their own bodies, is built of a fluid more fine, but none the less material. The human biologic unit has the ability to join with other units into a new unit so compact as to be thought of as a unit, a pathologic unit.[26]

The pathology of such units is key to understanding Steinbeck's ideas, which are far from a celebration of racial distinction even as they assert the power of racial consciousness to alter the biology of component units, to "control states of mind, alter appearance, physically and spiritually."[27] (Steinbeck would repeat this point in "Argument of Phalanx," stating that the group identity can change the birthrate, "stature, complexion, color, constitution" of its units.) These group units, or races, have "a soul, a drive, an intent, an end, a method, a reaction and a set of tropisms which in no way resembles the same things possessed by the men who make up the group." But it is the negative effect of such collaboration – "the desertion of localities, the sudden diseases which wiped races out, the sudden running amok of groups" – that commanded Steinbeck's attention, compelling him to begin investigation into what he calls the field of "race psychopathology."[28]

This interest in race psychopathology was more than just idle curiosity about the reasons for aberrant group behavior. It also presented Steinbeck with a problem of form: how to find "a fictional symbolism which will act as a vehicle" for his holistic ideas of group formation.[29] Just as individual units combine into greater races with the potential to disintegrate, so too did Steinbeck's many notes on the subject present fears of incoherence and possibilities of imaginative synthesis. Steinbeck would write in his journal again of the need to discover some new form to embody his discoveries: "I don't know how this thesis and theme are to be worked. I don't like to cast about for new forms, but the old forms seem inadequate. Such things as character, single stream, the mind of man – are out for this book is not about them. This book [must tap] the great ocean of the unconscious."[30] We can understand *To a God Unknown* – what I have been calling the magical realism of this novel – as one part of Steinbeck's attempt to find a new form, a new kind of symbolic expression, to embody such ideas of racial identity and dissolution.

In magical realist texts, according to recent scholarship, "societies, rather than personalities, tend to rise and fall."[31] This clearly jives with Steinbeck's characters who are imagined as whole populations rather than individual units. They have an allegorical function. As one character says to Joseph, in words that capture Steinbeck's own theories of man-beyond-the-individual, "You aren't aware of persons ... only people. You can't see units ... only the whole." To the characters in the novel, Joseph seems a godling, his figure growing large to overtop mountains, his being "a repository for a little piece of each man's soul." And to readers he occasionally grows huge *in* the narrative, literally making love to the earth at one memorable point, becoming a blue-eyed fertility god who thinks of endless increase not in his mind "but in his chest and in the corded muscles of his legs. It was the heritage of a race which for a million years had sucked at the breasts of the soil and cohabited with the earth."[32] Joseph's sensitivity to the deep time of his inheritance, and his Walt Whitman–like capacity to expand outward to contain multitudes – his ability, in other words, to serve a symbolic role in the novel – is a function of his racialized self. Admittedly, this is an ambiguous understanding of race. At times (and this is true throughout Steinbeck's career) "race" refers more generally to the human species, in a biological sense. But such holistic thinking contracts to a narrower understanding of race where Joseph is concerned, both in terms of the mythology that underpins his character (more on this later) and in terms of the pathology he embodies. Steinbeck's pathological sense of race, moreover, would depend on something that Steinbeck introduced into his story in its final draft: the element of drought that he wrote about to his agent Mavis McIntosh when planning his revisions:

> Do you remember the drought in Jolon that came every thirty-five years? We have been going through one identical with the one of 1880. Gradually during the last ten years the country has been dying of lack of moisture. The dryness has peculiar effects. Diseases increase, people are subject to colds, to fevers and to curious nervous disorders. Crimes of violence increase. The whole people are touchy and nervous. I am writing at such length to try to show you the thing that has just happened. This winter started as usual – no rain. Then in December the thing broke. There were two weeks of downpour. The rivers overflowed and took away houses and cattle and land. I've seen decorous people dancing in the mud. They have laughed with a kind of crazy joy when their land was washing away. The disease is gone and the first delirium has settled to a steady jubilance. There will be no ten people a week taken to asylums from this county as there were last year. Anyway, there is

> the background. The new novel will be closely knit and I can use much of the material from the Unknown God, but the result will be no rewritten version.[33]

The first drafts of *To a God Unknown*, titled "The Green Lady," already bore this interest in climate-related psychopathology. In a letter to a friend, Steinbeck described the story as offering "too many problems, not only psychological but anthropological. . . . I had to do too much research and consult too many psychiatrists and physicians and alienists. I hope the thing doesn't read like a case history in an insane asylum." (The original story is about a man who falls in love with a forest and, problematically, with his own daughter.) Describing his father's intense interest and final disgust in the story, Steinbeck continues:

> After my careful work in filling the book with hidden symptoms of paranoia and showing that the disease had such a hold to be incurable, my father expected Andy [the name of the character prior to its reconceptualization as Joseph] to recover and live happily ever after. I explained to him that with the ailment gone as far as it had, he must either turn suicide or homicidal maniac but that didn't make any difference. The American people demand miracles in their literature.[34]

Steinbeck understood the degree to which he was contravening popular taste in his developing narrative of the diseased American subject. But it would take his new interest in drought, with its emphasis on environmental influence, to unite aberrant psychology, racial identity, and formal experimentation. Drought enabled this conjunction by tapping into some powerful contemporary associations linking climate, race, and mythology.

Climate and Civilization

To a God Unknown is a work of magical realism to the extent that it holds together two time periods and two scales of existence. Steinbeck would not have had to look far to discover other parallels between California and deep history. Ellsworth Huntington, the Yale geographer who helped bring awareness to historical cycles or "pulses" in the earth's climate, made just such a comparison in his study of the giant sequoias of California. Huntington begins his essay "The Secret of the Big Trees" not in California but in the Holy Land:

> In the days of the Prophet Elijah sore famine afflicted the land of Palestine. No rain fell, the brooks ran dry, and dire distress prevailed.

> "Go through the land," said King Ahab to the Prophet Obadiah, "unto all the fountains of water and unto all the brooks; peradventure we may find grass and save the horses and mules alive, that we lose not all the beasts." When Obadiah went forth in search of forage he fell in with his chief, Elijah, and brought him to Ahab, who greeted him as the troubler of Israel. Then Elijah prayed for rain, according to the Bible story, and the famine was stayed.

The age of the giant sequoias of the Sierra Nevada – some as old as 3,000 years – allows direct access to these biblical times, linking "the ancient East and the modern West" in a collective story of drought, famine, and exodus. The successive growth rings of the sequoias enabled Huntington to read the history of climate in relatively deep time, leading to his theory of pulsatory changes in the location of the earth's population:

> It seems to have been interrupted by centuries of exceptional aridity on the one hand and of exceptional moisture on the other. When these pulsations of climate are compared with the course of history a remarkable agreement is noticed. Among a mass of minor details this apparent relationship may be concealed, but the broad movements of races, the rise and fall of civilization, seems to show a degree of agreement with climatic changes so great that it scarcely seems possible to avoid the conclusion that the two are intimately related.

Huntington produced a graph, stretching back more than 1,000 years BCE, demonstrating the persistent cycle of drought and wetness in California history, and demonstrating some correlation between that history and the history of Asia, with periods of extraordinary aridity occurring in the seventh or eighth century and again in the thirteenth century of the Common Era (CE).[35]

We know that Steinbeck read Huntington's major work, *Civilization and Climate* (1915); he refers favorably to Huntington's anthropological theories in a letter from 1933, in the final stages of writing *To a God Unknown*.[36] Huntington would have offered Steinbeck a compelling way to understand this relationship between man and environment, just as Huntington played an important role in introducing the environmental factor of climate into the consideration of human history and the distribution of what Huntington called "civilization." Huntington posited that a stimulating climate – one defined by the kind of moderate changes in weather found in regions with frequent patterns of cyclonic storms – increased mental activity and hence was an essential condition of "high civilization." Huntington's geographical interest in place combined with and qualified the supreme significance of race. Steinbeck's choice of a tree as a central character in *To a God Unknown* could well have been informed by the opening paragraph of *Civilization and Climate*:

> The races of the earth are like trees. Each according to its kind brings forth the fruit known as civilization. As russet apples and pippins may grow from the same trunk, and as peaches may be grafted on a plum tree, so the culture of allied races may be transferred from one to another. Yet no one expects pears on cherry branches, and it is useless to look for Slavic civilization among the Chinese. Each may borrow from its neighbors, but will put its own stamp upon what it obtains. The nature of a people's culture, like the flavor of a fruit, depends primarily upon racial inheritance which can be changed only by the slow processes of biological variation and selection.[37]

Huntington's bigger point may have been that trees need water to grow, but his environmental determinism was delicately balanced with his racial essentialism, just as his research into the climate-based distribution of civilization merely confirmed existing racial hierarchies. (Note how the passage moves from a recognition of racial variation to a more settled realization of racial inheritance.) Huntington was, in fact, a eugenicist who would go on to become president of the American Eugenics Society, an organization that encouraged race improvement through better breeding. He had a particular interest – as did most eugenicists at the time – in preserving the allegedly superior white race against the threat of contamination from inferior, nonwhite strains of "germ-plasm." Indeed, as the historian Alexandra Minna Stern has argued, early-twentieth-century interest in conserving the giant redwoods and sequoias of California was often underscored by a eugenic ideology. The stately trees were conceived as a great race, and conservationists as white knights striving to protect the trees' purity and superiority in an epic crusade unfolding across deep time.[38] Stern's broader point is to underscore just how widespread eugenic thinking was in California – defining its institutions and even its landscape – in the early decades of the twentieth century. Huntington's investigation of giant trees to detect patterns of climate change was thus a compounded racial inquiry, one in which the trees were both racial symbols and indices of climatic forces that determined hierarchies of civilization.

Similar ideas converge in *To a God Unknown*. If the tree that contains the spirit of Joseph's father is an embodiment of racial inheritance, then the moments when Joseph most resembles his people's fertility god are moments in which he is activated by the weather:

> The cavalry of clouds had passed and a huge black phalanx marched slowly in from the sea with a tramp of thunder. Joseph trembled with pleasure in the promised violence. . . . He stamped his feet into the soft earth. Then the exultance grew to be a sharp pain of desire that ran through his body in a hot river. He flung himself face downward on the grass and pressed his cheek against the wet stems. His fingers gripped the wet grass and tore it out, and gripped again. His thighs beat heavily on the earth.[39]

Huntington similarly observed that he had "seen Americans shout for joy because the clouds had come, and run out into the rain to let the cool drops refresh their faces."[40] Such moments of response to stormy weather, then, are implicitly racialized moments, just as they were in "Fingers of Cloud" (note the description of the clouds as a phalanx, Steinbeck's term for group identity). These moments connect Joseph not simply to the earth but to the memory of his race – a white race that, according to Huntington, came to fruition in the thunderous conditions that Joseph experiences. These moments become increasingly problematic, especially when drought begins to dominate the story.

The introduction of drought into the plot creates the essential difference between the published novel and Steinbeck's earlier drafts. It also marks Steinbeck's interest in what many would claim to be the West's defining quality: its aridity. Wallace Stegner famously claimed that "the primary unity of the West is a shortage of water." Climate, wrote Stegner, is the fundamental determinant of the Western landscape. Aridity impacts not just the geology, atmosphere, flora, and fauna of the West, not just its patterns of social development, but also the nature of thinking and of aesthetic perception: "You have to get over the color green; you have to quit associating beauty with gardens and lawns; you have to get used to an inhuman scale; you have to understand geological time."[41] Neither Stegner nor Steinbeck invented aridity as a theme of Western literature – Mary Austin's *The Land of Little Rain* (1903) was an important progenitor in that respect – but I would argue that *To a God Unknown* is remarkable in claiming climate as a crucial subject for fiction, and in striving for a form to express the impact of drought on the psychological well-being of its Anglo characters – and on the future of a white society – in the West. In this sense, we can think of Steinbeck's novel as a precursor to what recent critics have claimed as a new genre, "Climate Fiction" or "Cli-Fi," which has arisen in response to recognitions of detrimental human impact on the environment. A recent study of "Anthropocene fictions" – novels that recognize the current epoch of humanmade climate change – notes that "floods are the dominant literary strategy for locating climate change," creating plot movements based on an estrangement from place. Yet drought has received less attention: "the few novels that have tried to describe desertification have quickly veered away from a consideration of place, devolving to rather simplistic accounts of social conflict."[42] In its targeting of drought rather than flood, *To a God Unknown* stands apart, even as it seems to predict, in its magical realism, the rupture of conventional generic expectations that informs recent climate fiction: the hybrid combination of realist elements with fantasy (science fiction), for example, and the tendency to allow "nonhuman things to shape narrative."[43]

The connection between climate and a magically real aesthetic becomes apparent early in the novel, even before the possibility of drought is established. When Joseph enters the forest of Our Lady at the entrance to his valley, he feels half-drugged and overwhelmed by its luxuriance:

> There was a curious femaleness about the interlacing boughs and twigs, about the long green cavern cut by the river through the trees and the brilliant underbrush. The endless green halls and aisles and alcoves seemed to have meanings as obscure and promising as the symbols of an ancient religion. Joseph shivered and closed his eyes. "Perhaps I'm ill," he said. "When I open my eyes I may find that all this is delirium and fever." As he rode on and on the fear came upon him that this land might be the figure of a dream which would dissolve into a dry and dusty morning.[44]

Joseph's entry into the valley sees a clash between two symbolic, even ontological systems, the first a riparian world of fertility, of fundamental mythic archetypes of a natural divinity that are so overlain with symbolic meaning as to be virtually unreadable. Numerous critics have pointed to Steinbeck's interest in comparative mythology during this period, partly inspired by his acquaintance with the mythologist Joseph Campbell. The fertility imagery of the novel is clearly informed by works such as James Frazer's *The Golden Bough* (1890), which identifies the oak, as well as thunder and rain, as key aspects of an "Aryan" pantheon.[45] (At least in this regard, *To a God Unknown* is continuous with a high modernist tradition, found in works such as T. S. Eliot's *The Waste Land* [1922], which also drew from the ideas of Frazer and others.) Here we have a kind of American Gothic, a tapping into a racial memory or collective unconscious – Steinbeck was also influenced by Carl Jung's psychology of the unconscious, itself invested in an Aryan mythology – one that links the interlaced boughs of northern forests to the Gothic arch of the medieval cathedral. Yet this wandering in the psychological basement of race consciousness lies on the verge of its dissolution into dream, into a marvelous fantasy that threatens the deluge of symbolic meaning with drought. A riparian world of mythic archetypes is threatened by another system of meaning, and another "real." At times quite literally, the dream-world of characters is a realm of threatening dryness with a power to drive characters to suicide.[46] The gradual disappearance of landscape in the face of drought, the drying of the rivers, and the disappearance of flora and fauna are described as apparitions, revelations of another ghostly world whose bones begin to poke through a prior order,[47] creating a haunting, misty luminescence: "The land was unsubstantial under the misty, strained light; the dry trees seemed shapes of thicker mist. . . . The mountains seemed edged with phosphorous, and a pale cold light like a glow-worm's light seemed to shine through the skin of the land." (In this regard, Steinbeck's search for an aesthetics of drought predicts the documentary work of Farm Security Administration photographers such as Arthur Rothstein, who also combined realist and more mystical techniques to illustrate the emerging bones of a drying land; see Figure 2.1.[48]) Joseph may

Figure 2.1 Arthur Rothstein, "The bleached skull of a steer on the dry sun-baked earth of the South Dakota Badlands," May 1936. Library of Congress, Prints & Photographs Division, FSA/OWI Collection, LC-DIG-fsa-8b27761.

still dream of Ellsworth Huntington's ideal state of racial apotheosis enabled by the presence of frequent storms, "some cycle ... steady and quick and unchangeable as a fly-wheel," as he seeks to attain that larger-than-life stature of a rain god when he stands dripping with water amid the storm.[49] But the cycle he comes to realize is beyond the scale of his individual life. It is the cruel, long-term cycle of moist and dry weather that defines the Western climate. The dry years have, indeed, come again.

Magical realism is at heart a hybrid form in its fusion of different ways of being, both real and marvelous, different scales of time and of place. Its vehicle in *To a God Unknown* is the cyclical inevitability of drought in the longue durée. A new, dream-like order of reality emerges from beneath the world of moisture and fertility. Two lands seem to be present simultaneously. One could even say that the novel is magically real – it mixes together the quotidian world and the dreamworld; it strives to represent a real and a symbolic order of meaning; its characters are equivalents of actual persons yet allegorically larger than individuals – to the extent that this fusion is made possible by the remarkable reversals of climate and environment. The critics who considered the novel a success were those willing to live in this fictional world of juxtaposed eccentric and normal experience. "At the climax, dealing with drought, Joseph Wayne sacrifices his own blood to the rain god, and we are unconscious of absurdity," wrote one such reviewer at the time: "It is action for which Mr. Steinbeck's character-drawing of Joseph has prepared us; it is a poet-novelist's victory over common sense."[50] But I would like to return to what were, perhaps, the most common critical judgments of the novel's failure to hold these two worlds together, judgments that continue into later criticism, such as Warren French's description of the novel as an "overwrought allegory in which Steinbeck fails ... to fuse effectively realistic and symbolic elements."[51] The central problem, for critics, is the nature and the meaning of Joseph's death.[52]

The meaning of that death is connected to the meaning of drought for Steinbeck. Joseph dies taking his life on top of the rock in an effort to find some symbolic expression that will make the rains return, even as the rock remains beyond the pale of his racial memory: there was "no shape in the memory to match it."[53] Drought signifies more than just lack of water. It dictates the ability (or inability) to read symbolically, and it impacts characters both in terms of their represented bodies and minds and, indeed, in terms of their forms *as* fictional characters. In other words, it alters the nature of fictional characterization itself. Drought is defined by anxiety, by fear, and finally by a paranoia that the land itself is hostile to white civilization. This becomes clear in the ways that drought begins to creep in and finally comes to dominate the story:

> Slowly in his [Joseph's] mind there was arising the fear that the dry years had come. The dusty air and the high barometer did not reassure him. Head colds broke out among the people on the ranch. The children sniffled all day long. Elizabeth developed a hard cough, and even Thomas, who was never sick, wore a cold compress made of a black stocking on his throat at night. But Joseph grew leaner and harder. The muscles of his neck and jaws stood out under a thin covering of brown skin. His hands grew restless, went to playing with pieces of stick, or with a pocket-knife, or worked interminably at his beard, smoothing it down and turning the ends under.
>
> He looked about his land and it seemed to be dying. The pale hills and fields, the dust-grey sage, the naked stones frightened him. On the hills only the black pine grove did not change. It brooded darkly, as always, on the ridge top.[54]

Drought impacts the physiology and the psychology of the characters; sickness and a new nervousness break out from the dryness. And in a deeper, formal sense, character seems to be drying out as well. Joseph grows as lean and hard as the land, his muscles showing through the thin skin just as the bones of the earth come to poke through the dry land. His nervous, restless actions equate his own dry body with its surrounding objects. With the arrival of the drought, characters become increasingly confused about size relations and about their own relationship to the material world. For Elizabeth, "little things grew huge." In her growing nervousness, she comes to feel that somehow she had entered the rock, becoming it: "The little stream was flowing out of me."[55] The hierarchical relationship between humans and things becomes further confused a few pages later when Elizabeth suddenly slips on the rock and falls to her death. "It was too simple, too easy, too quick," says Joseph in words that read almost like Steinbeck's own comment on the suddenness of this death. "It was too quick," he says again:

> He knew that his mind could not grasp what had happened. He tried to make himself realize it. "All the stories, all the incidents that made the life were stopped in a second – opinions stopped, and the ability to feel, all stopped without any meaning." He wanted to make himself know what happened, for he could feel the beginning of the calm settling upon him. He wanted to cry out once in a personal pain before he was cut off and unable to feel sorrow or resentment. There were little stinging drops of cold on his head. He looked up and saw that it was raining gently. The drops fell on Elizabeth's cheeks and flashed in her hair. The calm was settling on Joseph. He said, "Good-bye, Elizabeth," and before the words were completely out

> he was cut off and aloof. He removed his coat and laid it over her head. "It was the one chance to communicate," he said. "Now it is gone."[56]

Elizabeth's sudden death embodies an increasing problem in this narrative: an imbalance, a problem of scale. Joseph cannot understand Elizabeth on a personal level. He can only understand her at an allegorical and symbolic level, just as she becomes associated here with the coming of the rain, which is in turn an apparent response to Joseph's own ritualized worship of water (when she slips, Joseph instinctively runs to the spring to fill his hands with water, failing to notice she is dead). If magical realism is a hybrid mode that depends on the merger of two scales of meaning, then here we can feel them pulling apart. The "higher" meaning of character – its symbolic level – becomes a problem of character. It is difficult to say for sure what the greater meaning of Elizabeth's death actually is, or what the "chance to communicate" may have been. The very process of attempting to understand character in this way becomes increasingly a function of Joseph's paranoia, itself brought on by a drought that threatens the entire intellectual framework by which he makes meaning and, indeed, makes a living.

Joseph becomes a study in what Steinbeck would call "race psychopathology" in his attempts to read himself at a higher, racialized scale, as the representative of an entire people. He cannot hold his attention at a local level; his thoughts spread out, "feeding in a hundred different places" in one of several moments in which "size changed, and time changed." Looking down at his slouched body and curved arms and hands resting in his lap, Joseph sees a "mountain range extended in a long curve and on its end were five little ranges, stretching out with narrow valleys between them." He comes to see his body as a land of fertile tillable earth and good fields, containing towns and houses full of little people: "High up on a tremendous peak, towering over the ranges and the valleys, the brain of the world was set, and the eyes that looked down on the earth's body." Two scales of space and time collide, as Joseph lets his body stand "a million years, unchanging and quiet," even though the brain knows it must move finally to destroy the work of tillage, the houses in the valleys, a whole world order. Joseph thinks that he witnesses human development – the growth and persistence of an entire people in a communal situation – and the final destruction of a race: "all the work of a million years was lost."[57] At these moments, the real and the magical fail to combine. Character cannot stretch coherently across these two time frames, or spatial coordinates. The individual character cannot at the same time be more than itself, cannot then also be a race of people. Or at least, the attempt to imagine the individual self as an entire population becomes a psychopathological projection, a delusion of the grandeur of race.

The final scenes of the novel involve Joseph desperately attempting to keep the mossy rock moist with water from its depleted spring, in moments that imply not merely a desire to survive within a vicious, dry land but also a desire to preserve a collective, racial memory based on water rituals and a verdant environment. The rest of Joseph's clan have migrated to wetter regions. The only escape from the drought – represented by an old man who lives near the coast and thrives, like the redwoods, on the moisture from the ocean fogs – seems a bizarre alternative. With his own rituals proving ineffective against the encroaching drought, Joseph finally cuts his wrists atop the rock:

> He watched the bright blood cascading over the moss, and he heard the shouting of the wind around the grove. The sky was growing grey. And time passed and Joseph grew grey too. He lay on his side with his wrist outstretched and looked down the long black mountain range of his body. Then his body grew huge and light. It rose into the sky, and out of it came the streaking rain. "I should have known," he whispered. "I am the rain." And yet he looked dully down the mountains of his body where the hills fell to an abyss. He felt the driving rain, and heard it whipping down, pattering on the ground. He saw the hills grow dark with moisture. Then a lancing pain shot through the heart of the world. "I am the land," he said, "and I am the rain. The grass will grow out of me in a little while."
>
> And the storm thickened, and covered the world with darkness, and with the rush of waters.[58]

His final vision of his own grandeur – himself as an entire land and the rain necessary to preserve its civilization – marks the novel's final failure to balance the real and the marvelous. The magnificent rising of Joseph's body is no longer a possibility within the logic of the narrative but rather a psychopathological projection, an individual fantasy or paranoid vision. The novel ends with another race of people – the Mexican Americans, the people of mixed Indian and Spanish blood whom Steinbeck would in *Tortilla Flat* (1935) call "paisanos" – performing their own ritual celebration of the coming rain, wearing the skins of animals, all under the tolerant gaze of a Catholic priest. Joseph's suicide can be read finally as a race suicide, to the extent that Joseph's symbolic outlook and collective unconscious are out of synch with this Western world of semi-aridity.

The final framing of *To a God Unknown* with these mixed-race and indigenous characters reminds us that magical realism, to the degree that it remains a coherent genre or movement, returns to postcolonial situations, to a world that Elleke Boehmer calls "fissured, distorted, and made incredible by cultural displacement."[59] Magical realism is born in the "gap between the belief systems of two very different groups of people."[60] It is defined by cultural heterogeneity, by the mixture and conflict between "first world" and "third world" belief systems that work to break down the distinction between what is real and what is magic. Steinbeck's novel shares some important traits with magical realism, particularly its cyclical rather than linear sense of time, and its questioning of the distinction between people and things. The novel recognizes too the power of indigenous beliefs. A ritualized adjustment to cycles of drought and moisture ensures the continuity of the indigenous characters beyond the bounds of the narrative. But again we encounter the limitations of Steinbeck's imagination, its inability to fully realize its nonwhite characters, and its treatment of interracial relationships as a source of conflict not redemption (as one early review pointed out, the chain of disaster that marks the second half of the novel begins when Joseph's brother Benjy "is killed in the arms of a jealous Mexican's wife").[61] Problems of form – the failure to sustain the hybrid vision of the magically real – perform the disastrous consequences of a logic within early climate science, one that linked racialized "civilization" to a thunderous wetness. Admittedly, *To a God Unknown* imagines little beyond the Anglo mind-set of Joseph and his clan. But the novel's vision of whiteness is anything but celebratory. The power of environment forces the colonizing presence from the Western landscape. The novel's decline from magically real possibility to the delusional projections of its suicidal protagonist represents a race psychopathology, a disease of whiteness that is out of place, unable to impose its mythological and agricultural vision in a land of little rain.

CHAPTER 3

Race and Revision: "The Vigilante" and "Johnny Bear"

On the evening of November 26, 1933, a crowd gathered outside the Santa Clara County Jail in San Jose, California. It wanted blood. Inside were two local men, Thomas Harold Thurmond, an unemployed house painter, and John Maurice Holmes, a Union Oil salesman, who were being held awaiting trial for the kidnapping and murder of another San Jose resident, the twenty-two-year-old Brooke Hart. Hart was the son of a famous San Jose family, and heir to a fortune founded in Hart's Department Store, an institution in downtown San Jose, and a symbol of the family's civic prominence in the successful and growing city. By all accounts, Hart was a likeable and popular young man. He was kidnapped on November 9, 1933, on leaving the store, after which the family received a number of ransom notes and calls. Thurmond and Holmes were arrested for the kidnapping in mid-November, after the police traced Thurmond's ransom call to the Harts, at which point Thurmond made a confused confession, naming Holmes as his accomplice (Holmes initially refuted the accusation and claimed innocence, supported by strong alibis). Media interest in the crime was intense, with transcripts of the confessions, full of gory details, appearing on the front pages of the local newspapers. Amid a national backlash against a slew of kidnappings in the 1930s, newspapers called for the severest punishment for the accused. When two duck hunters discovered Hart's disfigured corpse on November 26, public calls erupted for the lynching of the accused men, fueled by rumors of an insanity plea. Rounded up from the bars, urged on by local media, and with the tacit approval of California Governor James Rolph Jr., a mob stormed the jail, broke down the door with a length of pipe, assaulted the sheriff and deputy sheriff, and dragged Thurmond and Holmes – the former unconscious by this time from being knocked out, the latter resisting all the way – to adjacent St. James Park, where the two battered, partly naked men were hung from trees before a crowd that may have been as large as 15,000 onlookers, making it about the size of the larger "lynch carnivals" of the 1930s (see Figure 3.1).[1]

Steinbeck would turn these historical events into fiction in his story "The Vigilante," written in 1934 – when the events were still fairly fresh – first published in *Esquire* magazine (as "The Lonesome Vigilante") in 1936 and eventually included as the eighth story of *The Long Valley* (1938). Steinbeck undoubtedly knew the details of the Hart kidnapping and the Thurmond-Holmes lynching that took place in the hometown of Steinbeck's wife, Carol Henning. The story of the crime and lynching was all over the newspapers, both locally and nationally, not least because

Figure 3.1 San Jose, California: November 26, 1933. The body of John Holmes, alleged kidnapper and slayer of Brooke Hart, shown after a mob that dragged him from the county jail, completed its work. © Underwood Archives/age fotostock.

of the political circus that followed the lynching when Governor Rolph applauded the actions of the mob and was roundly condemned by President Franklin Roosevelt and former President Herbert Hoover. There are numerous parallels between Steinbeck's story and what we know of the events from various newspaper accounts. The locations are similar, the park (the scene of the lynching) being directly opposite the jail; the hang trees are elms in both factual and fictional accounts. The details of the extraction of the victims from the jail are very similar too: in both instances, the jail door is battered down by the mob, which at first mistakenly identifies the wrong prisoner, finally knocking the victim (Thurmond in the real events) unconscious in the cell before dragging him out. Steinbeck's use of the term "driving line" to describe the rushing mob suggests a direct borrowing from records of the actual event, in which sporting cries of "We want a touchdown" and "Hold that line!" marked the holiday-like atmosphere.[2] The breaking of streetlights, the stripping of the victim (Holmes in the real events), and the attempts to burn the victim's body are common to both fictional and historical versions, as is the subsequent obsession with obtaining souvenirs of the horrific proceedings.[3] In Steinbeck's version, however, there are not two victims of the lynching, only one. And he is not white, as were Thurmond and Holmes. The victim of the lynching, in Steinbeck's story, is one African American man.

But he wasn't always Black. At the beginning of the Long Valley ledger – the manuscript of this and a number of other stories – Steinbeck lists "The Vigilante" as the final story completed in summer 1934, giving it a culminating role in a series of stories that comprise the bulk of *The Long Valley*.[4] In this accounting, "The Vigilante" follows the stories "Flight" and "Johnny Bear," but in the manuscript ledger "Flight" is actually followed by an earlier, incomplete draft of "The Vigilante," or rather a quite different story based on similar events and ideas, an unpublished story called "Case History." "Flight" – the third story in *The Long Valley* – ends with the death of Pepé Torres, a young Mexican American who murders a man (presumably a white man, or at least, as Pepé recounts the events to his mother, someone who "said names to me I could not allow") in a bar fight. Nameless vigilante assassins subsequently pursue him into the mountains, where Pepé is gradually reduced to an animal in his desperate attempt to escape. When Pepé is finally shot by his pursuers (in the history of lynching in the West, those identified as Latin American or Mexican comprised the largest group of victims, followed closely by whites),[5] the language of a more conventional lynching shimmers behind the description: his "body jarred back. . . . Pepé swung forward and toppled."[6] Immediately following the end of "Flight" in the manuscript ledger, divided by an elaborate hashtag, comes Steinbeck's realization of his next lynching story:

> New work. One story which occurred to me last night is so delicate and difficult that I don't feel justified in taking regular work time to it. If I do it, it will be at night on my own time. This is not a time for experiments on company time. There is too much work to get out. This monday afternoon must be given to working out this weeks [*sic*] story and perhaps beginning it. New pen now. Gold colored one. It probably isn't gold. The back of it writes nice and fine though. Running all day today and is fine. Caught a whole can full of snails. The bottom of my stomach is dropping out with accumulated loneliness – not loneliness that might be mended with company either. I think Carol is the same way. There's a haunted quality in her eyes. I'm not good company to her. I can't help her loneliness and she can't help mine. Perhaps this is a good thing. It may presume some kind of integrity. Maybe it is exactly that kind of hunger that keeps us struggling on. I must get on to work. I'm wasting time now. Only work cures the gnawing. Maybe the work of last week wasn't good but the doing of it was good. I'll shave. That will make me feel better.
>
> – John Ramsey – hated the war and misses it. Came home to the quiet, the lack of design for the war was a huge design. Wanders lost on his farm looking for a phalanx to join and finds none. Is nervous and very lost. Finally finds the movement in a lynching. War shock not so much war as the ceasing of war drive. Hunger for the group. Change of drive. What does it matter. The mob is not a wasteful thing but an efficient thing.[7]

This personal aside is typical of Steinbeck's process of composition. As we have already seen, Steinbeck's writing was often a kind of dialogue, either with himself as in this case or with specific individuals to whom he would attempt to explain concepts and to overcome the loneliness of writing. Always so concerned with the tools of his trade and with his rate of production, Steinbeck turns to the task of work as an answer to his existential crisis. But work is not the right word for this new story, an experiment that is not only difficult but *delicate*: deeply intimate and personal. He shaves to prepare himself to tackle a question that can only be whispered to oneself in the dead of night. What does it feel like to participate in a lynching?

At least in obvious details, the protagonist of "Case History," John Ramsey, is quite different from Mike, the central character in "The Vigilante," although the name *Ramsey* does predict Mike's role as the front end of a human battering ram that knocks down the jailhouse door. Ramsey is explicitly a shell-shocked veteran of the Great War, which places the setting of the story back in the late 1910s or early 1920s. The story seems retrospective in terms of its place in literary history too. We might think of John Ramsey as an echo of Harold Krebs in Ernest Hemingway's "Soldier's Home" (1925), a classic story of trauma in which everything Krebs has experienced in the war is necessarily absent, displaced onto a need for order found in Krebs's fascination with the patterns on women's dresses or with the rules of a softball game.[8] Hemingway's story works by implication and omission, but Steinbeck's draft reads more like the writer himself is still working the details out. The plot is a clumsy effort to place Ramsey in a position to explain Steinbeck's theories of collective action to the reader. Ramsey's shell shock gradually develops; he goes to the hospital to treat his nervousness and then temporarily leaves his wife to live alone in a cabin on a nearby hill where he can read and think. Steinbeck seems eager to take Ramsey to a place where he can discuss matters at length, in an extension of the dialogic mode in which Steinbeck often contemplated the relationship between the individual and the group.[9] After Ramsey's friend Will McKay – the editor of the local newspaper – sees Ramsey participating in the lynching of an accused child murderer, all Ramsey wants to do is talk. What follows is a long dialogue, the bulk of the story, in which Ramsey tries to convince McKay of Steinbeck's holistic theory of the phalanx:

> Man is an unit in a greater creature which I call the phalanx. The phalanx has pains, desires, hungers and strivings as different from those of unit man as unit man is from unit cells. The nature of the phalanx is not the sum of the natures of the men who compose it, but a new individual, having emotions and ends of its own.[10]

Steinbeck abandoned this unfinished draft for good reason. The long-winded explanation of the power of groupthink may lead to Ramsey's self-awareness and partial cure, but to the reader it seems a long way from the details of the lynching that sparked such public interest. Not that "Case History" isn't based to some degree on the events in San Jose. We encounter several details shared with the newspaper accounts, some of which are carried over to "The Vigilante." The streetlights are smashed to throw the town into darkness; the jailhouse door is broken down with a battering ram; the victim is perhaps dead before being hanged; the crowd attempts to burn his feet with lighted newspapers.[11] In "Case History," the lynching victim's race is not specified. Presumably he is white in Steinbeck's mind at this point, although this early draft is not without its racial signifiers. Ramsey is typed as white: blond. The initial sense of urgency at Ramsey's nervous collapse emerges when he is "found dead drunk in a negro house of prostitution." We learn, too, from Ramsey's explanation to his journalist friend that the mob tore off the victim's genitals, in a "symbolic action which has full emphasis only in the phalanx mind." "The units wouldn't have thought of that but the phalanx nearly always thinks of it. It happens at nearly all lynchings," reports Ramsey, though such activity would more typically be reserved for African Americans accused of "crimes" against white women. (From what we know of the Holmes and Thurmond lynching, neither victim was castrated.) "Case History" leans further toward "The Vigilante" in the links it makes between lynching and sexuality, and in the importance of the spectacle of the lynching. The moment when the journalist McKay realizes that his friend is at the center of a lynch mob becomes a moment of photographic exposure: "At that moment a flashlight flare went out. The blue lighted picture remained before Will's eyes. Helping to swing the railroad tie against the door he had seen John Ramsey, blond hair flying, eyes wild."[12]

The second draft of "The Vigilante" is also in the Long Valley ledger. It is exactly three handwritten pages (the final words, "I feel," are made to fit by snaking vertically up the side of the page), about half the length of "Case History." The story is followed by one of Steinbeck's process notes in which he describes how another draft story, "The Cow," died of "something or other and was replaced by the little bit of a story called The Vigilante. That story even with the second draft only took two days."[13] The manuscript of "The Vigilante" in the Long Valley ledger is very like the final published version. It remains uncertain whether Steinbeck considers "Case History" to be the first draft of "The Vigilante," or whether another draft existed prior to the second version in the ledger, but the point is still good: the story flashes in his mind, occupying him wholly in an intense process of composition that is also an aftermath or revision of an initial attempt. Whereas "Case History" is set in Salinas, "The Vigilante" moves explicitly to San Jose. The manuscript version identifies specific streets (their names only slightly changed),[14] while the published version gets the time of the lynching almost exactly right.[15] Which is to say that "The Vigilante" moves closer to history (in terms of location, scene, the details of the lynching process), even as it steps further away by changing the race of the lynching victim in a switch that complicates an important detail. The victim in the story is the solitary and exceptional "nigger," as the other characters call him, though the story still contains a key detail in the original, historical events: the fear felt by the jail's other prisoners that their identity might be mistaken for that of Holmes or Thurmond, fellow whites (a fear surely redoubled because the mob was looking for two men, not one). We might say that the racial identity of the lynched character in Steinbeck's "The Vigilante" is produced *against* history, or at least in tension with the known and feasible details of the event.

One reason for this change of race, perhaps, was that Steinbeck wanted to disguise the location and divert attention from San Jose's "Night of Shame."[16] But then why lean so heavily on historical detail at all – indeed, why make the second version of the story adhere to the historical record much more closely than the first? Why not set the story in the American South (some critics mistakenly believed the story was set there) rather than having it part of the Steinbeck Country common to most stories in *The Long Valley*? After all, "Saint Katy the Virgin," another story in the collection, is set in medieval France. But instead we have a story focalized through a participant in a historical event who cannot quite remember it aright, a figure living in "a dream-like weariness, a grey comfortable weariness."[17] Mike's crisis of memory ties into broader problems that haunt the history of lynching in the United States, just as the change of race underscores lynching as a national not a Western outrage, one that targeted African Americans disproportionately and became a bloody cauldron of racist motivations that continued to receive national attention in the 1930s. The *way* that Mike tries to remember the lynching is significant regarding that history. Lynching was, in part, a crime of spectacle. Its horrendous violence was viewed by thousands at the time, including the photographers who memorialized events in lynching postcards that received wide distribution then and continue to draw crowds to exhibitions today.[18] When Mike looks back at the events of the San Jose lynching, the description evokes the specific medium in which such events were remembered:

> Mike filled his eyes with the scene. He felt that he was dull. He wasn't seeing enough of it. Here was a thing he would want to remember later so he could tell about it, but the dull tiredness seemed to cut the sharpness off the picture. His brain told him this was a terrible and important affair, but his eyes and his feelings didn't agree. It was just ordinary. Half an hour before, when he had been howling with the mob and fighting for a chance to help pull on the rope, then his chest had been so full that he had found he was crying. But now everything was dead, everything unreal; the dark mob was made up of stiff lay-figures. In the flamelight the faces were as expressionless

> as wood. Mike felt the stiffness, the unreality in himself too. He turned away at last and walked out of the park.[19]

Mike's moment of bewilderment and estrangement becomes an attempt to achieve photographic clarity: he wants a sharp picture as a memento of his experience. The split that he feels, between his thoughts and his eyes, somewhat corresponds to a typical lynching photograph in which the evidence of horrendous crime, usually in the upper half of the image, is juxtaposed with the disturbing "ordinariness" of the scene below, as in Lawrence Beitler's famous photograph of the lynching of Thomas Shipp and Abram Smith in Marion, Indiana, in which a crowd of white men and women mingle in flirtatious happiness and curiosity in the foreground (Figure 3.1 has a similar dynamic). Scholars of lynching imagery have described how photography was incorporated into the lynching itself, as the photograph came to mediate the experience both for viewers and, indeed, for some of the victims.[20] Images of lynching in general tend to make us aware of the taking of the photographs themselves as an act of memorialization even as they confront us with the uncanny presence of violent racism in American life. As Dora Apel observes, the spectacle of lynching embodied "the relationship of power to helplessness, citizen to outsider, privilege to oppression, jubilation to degradation, subjecthood to objecthood, community to outcast, pride to humiliation."[21] But in Steinbeck's version, feelings are more muted and confused, as if Mike himself is in disturbing ways also a victim of these events.

Steinbeck would undoubtedly have seen photographs of the San Jose lynching in the numerous newspaper accounts that reported it. The photographic record of the San Jose lynching is quite unusual in depicting the various stages of the event, from the breaking down of the jailhouse door to the hanged bodies of Thurmond and Holmes.[22] The photographs, in other words, form a narrative, and indeed specific images help us to understand key aspects of Steinbeck's story. (As suggested by the be-hatted crowd in Figure 3.1, another curious point about the San Jose lynching is that it occurred in a prosperous middle-class community, a point that Steinbeck emphasizes in his story.[23]) Steinbeck may even have seen souvenir postcards of the lynching, one of which spliced two photographs together to suggest that Thurmond and Holmes were hanged side by side, just as Steinbeck splices an African American character into the historical record. This postcard image would also have emphasized a quality that Steinbeck clearly drew from the lynching: its sign of the combined power of mob action. In another photograph (Figure 3.2), we see a group of

Figure 3.2 San Jose, California: November 26, 1933. The lynch mob using 30-foot-long pieces of pipe to break down the iron doors of the county jail. © Underwood Archives/age fotostock.

approximately a dozen men working together with the long pipe to break down the main jailhouse door. Concerted action – what Steinbeck called the phalanx – is produced from a disparate chaos of the crowd, the signs of its previous assembly strewn as garbage in the foreground.

Figure 3.2 is an image of implied process, of individuals becoming a collective group with a primordial power and motive direction beyond the official laws of the state – a power greater than the sum of its parts. The breakdown of social norms and values reflects the amoral, biological quality of the phalanx that Ramsey theorizes in "Case History." And as Mike's bewilderment implies, this mob action, because it is defined by a transitory moment of emergence, cannot quite be remembered or spoken into being.[24] We can understand the photograph's relation to history in a similar way. Figure 3.2 is documentary evidence of a social formation and mob action. But it is also severed from historical narrative, freezing this moment in time. The flash going off in the lower left of the image, lighting the scene of action, implies how photographers are another kind of phalanx, complicit with the action of the mob (the artist Ken Gonzales-Day, in his book about lynching in the West, observes among this garbage an unbroken flashbulb in what he describes as "one of the earliest uses of a flashbulb in the history of lynching").[25] But then the image is also inadequate or belated to what it sees precisely because of its awareness of the technology of seeing. An uncropped version of this photograph that appeared on the front page of the San Francisco *Chronicle* reveals in lower left the full figure of the photographer taking the photograph, making the image one of image making itself.

A study in focalization, the story's point of view is accordingly drawn to moments of self-conscious looking – the blue streetlight that illuminates the scene, the neon sign BEER that Mike follows into the bar, a patrolling policeman's flash that lights store windows – as if the narrator's own sight is stained by what was witnessed, or as if the story is cognizant of what Jacqueline Goldsby argues about lynching photography more generally: it makes vision itself "legible as a cultural operation."[26] But the story presents not a looking at but a looking back, an *afterimage* following a flash, in which photochemical activity continues in the retina. This phenomenon clearly interested Steinbeck for he would return to it at the climax of *The Pearl* (1947), when a fleeing Kino is able to sneak up on his trackers in part because a struck match "left a picture on Kino's eyes," one with an indexical quality that enables him to see how the men are positioned.[27] Mike is likewise trapped in a condition of melancholy belatedness in which he is recoiling from a flash, attempting to get back to that moment of becoming still burning in his eyes. We experience something similar in another moment when Mike looks back at the scene of the lynching:

> In the center of the mob someone had lighted a twisted newspaper and was holding it up. Mike could see how the flame curled about the feet of the grey naked body hanging from the elm tree. It seemed curious to him that negroes turn a bluish grey when they are dead. The burning newspaper lighted the heads of the up-looking men, silent men and fixed; they didn't move their eyes from the hanged man.[28]

This moment looks back in ways other than Mike's retrospective glance. It looks back implicitly to earlier lynchings that were illuminated by flares rather than by the car headlights or the photoflashes of the modern-day lynching. Metafictionally, it looks back to Steinbeck's source texts, the local newspapers in which he must have read the details and seen the photographs of the lynching. In its rather literal reference to details from these newspaper accounts – especially the attempts to burn Thurmond –

the moment suggests the parallels between the events of the San Jose lynching of white victims and the more violent lynchings of African Americans, as does the stripping away of clothes. Here the San Jose lynching is something of an exception to the general rule noted by scholars of lynching: that Black and white victims were treated very differently.[29] (The NAACP leadership was aware of the Thurmond and Holmes lynching. It responded to Governor Rolph's endorsement of the crime by organizing a Writers League Against Lynching, which petitioned Congress to pass an anti-lynching bill in the mid-1930s.[30]) But ironically, this moment suggesting parity between the races is the point at which Steinbeck changes the racial identity of the victim from white to Black, indicated here by the dubious racial "fact" concerning skin color change. The "bluish-grey" of the dead African American victim reflects the "blue street light" that first illuminates the scene, as if the racial change has been produced *by* the flash of electric light, just as the flash of composition in which Steinbeck changes the victim's racial identity makes this such a problematic short story. In her history of flash photography, Kate Flint writes that flash could ironically lighten the skin of its Black victims in a "bleaching glare" that carried, through the context of lynching, "additional, especially charged overtones of violence, exposure, and white racial hatred." The flash here, though, changes white to Black, hence literalizing a process that Flint observes more generally in flash photography's slicing of moments out of darkness: "the moment before the picture was taken and the moment afterwards are radically different in terms of lighting, shadow and visibility from the one that the flash lit up for us."[31] The flash here is a moment of compositional realization – that the victim, for the story to work, must be Black not white – which splits apart "Case History" and "The Vigilante."

If the story is one of looking back for Mike, then it is one of re-vision for Steinbeck. He rewrites the earlier version, adhering so closely to the historical record while departing vastly from it. Race, the difference between Black and white, is thus produced before our eyes. To Mike, the lynching is important as a spectacle: it is a "thing" that must be "[done] right," especially regarding the stripping and the hanging of the victim. Part of this logic of "doing it right," on Steinbeck's part at least, is altering the racial identity of the lynched victim to tap the filthy stream of racist motivation that made lynchings so sickeningly compelling to many white participants and observers. A central sign of this spectacle is the piece of torn blue denim that Mike helps rip from the pants of the victim. Souvenirs, bits of cloth from clothing, parts of the hang tree, even in some cases parts of the victim himself, were common in lynchings, and the San Jose lynching was no exception. (In Lawrence Beitler's photograph of the Marion lynching, two young women hold pieces of cloth, presumably souvenirs from the pants of the victim, perhaps charged with erotic power.[32]) After some haggling, Mike sells half of the cloth to the barman for a couple of dollars so that the barman can display it with a printed card. "The fellas that come in will like to look at it," he says.[33] A souvenir, Susan Stewart argues, maintains its power because it is a *partial* trace of a previous authentic experience, one that does not simply record the event but rather allows the possessor to describe experience through the "invention of narrative." Quoting G. W. F. Hegel, Stewart describes the original, authentic experience as "the bacchanalian revel, where not a member is sober," the escaped materiality of which is recaptured through the viewed object. Having a metonymic relation to the original scene even as it divides past from present, the souvenir "will not function without the supplementary narrative discourse that both attaches it to its origins and creates a myth with regard to those origins."[34] But in "The Vigilante," the patch of denim leads only to a partial narrative – Mike tells how he helps remove the victim's clothes – echoing how the characters in the story are unable to narrate their own experiences. "It don't make you feel nothing," says Mike, other than to feel "cut off and tired, but kind of satisfied, too." In fact, Mike does what should be impossible regarding a souvenir, according to Stewart's argument at least: he sells it.[35]

Mike's division and sale of this small patch of textured experience equates him with Steinbeck the short story writer making literary material from a truncation and hacking of a historical event. The relationship between "Case History" and "The Vigilante" is also embodied in that patch of denim: the former story explains the sexual motivations that often underpinned lynchings, while the latter story implies it through this artifact and the thin threads of Mike's conversation with his wife at the end. With characters unable to recall the nature of their experience, "The Vigilante" works through fragmentation and allusion; rather like Stewart's idea of the souvenir, it implies an attachment to historical origins while also creating a myth of those origins.[36] The story is itself the curiosity in its sustained description of bemused recoil, as if Mike is also recoiling from the flash: he cannot see in the same way again as he descends from an ecstatic metamorphosis to an isolated, human present, one of confusion and mourning for a lost fullness of group belonging. "The Vigilante" is a kind of souvenir in the way that it participates in a historical moment while revising it to resonate with the national horrors of a racialized – and racist – imaginary. This participation in the historical moment is perhaps why the story leaves us with more questions than answers, why it produces such a confused array of possible responses. Goldsby describes this confusion as characteristic of reactions to lynching in general, the way that it leads to various theories because people seem at a loss to account for its presence in American life. Thus lynching could be explained as a peculiarity of the South, as a fulfillment of Freudian sexual pathologies, as a process of "making" whiteness and masculinity, or as a condition of the anxieties of emerging industrial modernity.[37] Accordingly, the point of the story is its refusal to explain. By changing the race of the victim from white to Black, Steinbeck aligns his story with the art of protest in the decade of the Scottsboro Boys even as it removes subjectivity from the Black victim of the lynching (whose guilt is never questioned) and refuses to see Mike and the other townsfolk as the agents of terror.

It is an easy critical gesture to explain Steinbeck's work as confused on a number of political questions, as we will see when we turn to *The Grapes of Wrath* (1939). In "The Vigilante," the silences concerning the racism at the heart of the mob's actions create problems that are difficult to reconcile on the grounds of ambivalence (Mike and the bartender may debate whether all African Americans are "fiends," but the motives of the mob are unambiguous: they were out for the blood of a "nigger fiend."[38]) The switch of the lynched victim from white to Black distances "The Vigilante" from the historical record. But more significantly, it compromises the kind of theorization – the "species-sense," the interest in the biological nature of human group formation – that marks so much of Steinbeck's thought. The point here is that Steinbeck could have written a story about the power of the superorganism without changing the race of the victims of the San Jose lynching. In fact, the shared whiteness between mob and victim, the lack of racist motivation, would have made the point about group psychology stronger still. What makes "The Vigilante" "work" as a short story – its refusal to explain, the falling away of the explicit theorization that mars "Case History" – is the specter of racism in American life, a haunting reality that Steinbeck's imagination is, in this particular case, incapable of confronting.

The Photographic Voice

Steinbeck's problematic experiment in "The Vigilante" is thrown further into light by a story always closely paired with it in Steinbeck's mind: "Johnny Bear." ("Johnny Bear" follows "The Vigilante" in *The Long Valley*, while in the manuscript Long Valley ledger "The Vigilante" is the final story, following "Johnny Bear"; both are included in its initial list of stories.) "Johnny Bear" is narrated by an unnamed worker on a dredging crew cutting a drainage canal near the fictional town of Loma in Steinbeck Country. Deciding to stay at a boarding house in Loma rather than on the floating bunkhouse with the crew, our narrator encounters the dull village's celebrity, an autistic savant called Johnny Bear, who entertains the patrons at the village bar with his exact reproductions of overheard conversations. If "The Vigilante" works formally like an afterimage of photographic flash, then Johnny Bear's talent is also described in photographic terms. A "kind of recording and reproducing device," Johnny can "photograph" voices so realistically that the narrator can visualize the exact physical features of two of Johnny's subjects of representation: the Hawkins sisters, Amy and Emalin, who function as the community's moral conscience.[39] Or at least they do until Johnny begins to reproduce their conversations for the price of whiskey from his audience. This power of mimesis is one of the sources of Johnny's "monstrosity" that the other characters understand through a racial analogue. The narrator's friend Alex compares Johnny to Blind Tom Wiggins, an African American formerly enslaved person who became a celebrity after the Civil War for his uncanny ability to remember and reproduce pieces of music note-for-note on the piano. According to Willa Cather, who saw the pianist perform when she was young, Wiggins's "queer actions" produced "interestingly unpleasant" reactions owing to his apparently objective description of his own "idiocy" (he would refer to himself in the third person) and in the challenge his odd genius posed to the boundary between sanity and insanity.[40] Wiggins's performances held his audience spellbound, and Johnny Bear possesses a similar power in Steinbeck's story:

> His name described him better than I can. He looked like a great, stupid, smiling bear. His black matted head bobbed forward and his long arms hung out as though he should have been on all fours and was only standing upright as a trick. His legs were short and bowed, ending with strange, square feet. He was dressed in dark blue denim, but his feet were bare; they didn't seem to be crippled or deformed in any way, but they were square, just as wide as they were long.[41]

According to our narrator's view, Johnny exists on the edge of the human, at the boundary of the nonhuman animal, though his curious power lies not in his abnormality but in the uncannily alternative version of the normal that he represents.[42] He turns things inside out, questioning the superiority of a dull, everyday world that comes to depend on Johnny's "curious pantomime" for its entertainment. This need is reflected in the given description of Johnny, who draws the narrator's eye into a moment of stasis that simultaneously implies the narrator's anxiety over his own descriptive powers ("His name described him better than I can"). Rather than a passive presence to be described, Johnny has an active power that impacts the narrator on their first encounter. Johnny's performance impersonates the narrator's voice and identity when he repeats the overheard romantic conversation and sexual exploits of the narrator and Mae Romero, a female acquaintance with whom he strikes up a relationship as relief from the boredom of village life and from the equally unappealing world of the all-male dredging crew. Johnny's "photographic" voice is aligned with photography's uncanny power to decenter its subjects, to make us unfamiliar to ourselves – an analogy with photography that emerges from the association with the African American Wiggins, just as Johnny's power to verbally photograph our narrator exposes his interracial relationship with a "pretty half-Mexican girl."[43]

The tensions within the story involve distinctions between the powers of description and narration, as Johnny holds people in a trance through the completeness of his descriptive art. Hence our narrator, threatened by this power, seeks in turn to objectify Johnny through his own detailed descriptions – "I saw a big fly land on his head, and then I swear I saw the whole scalp shiver the way the skin of a horse shivers under flies" – but this only reveals the narrator's continuity with Johnny ("I shuddered too, all over") and the essential codependency in their relationship.[44] Johnny is able to animate people, to make the whole village shudder out of its dull, nondescript, repetitive, everyday reality through a power beyond mere mimesis. The villagers are not interested in realistic description for its own sake – they will not pay for uneventful details, say of a person's visit to the butchers – but instead they want suspense and sensation. Johnny is successful, then, in the degree to which he can master narrative as well. He serves as a principle of omniscience in his miraculous ability to move invisibly around the community to observe and record its most intimate conversations. With an ear for selection, he holds his audience most enraptured by the central story he tells of the Hawkins sisters. Not only are the Hawkins sisters the moral conscience of the community. They are also landowners, part of a system of ownership that has divided up the land between capitalists and workers (they rent to industrious Chinese sharecroppers), an exploitation with which our narrator is also involved in his work "reclaiming" swampy areas for arable use. As the story of the Hawkins sisters unfolds through Johnny's recounting of overheard conversations, we learn that Emalin accuses Amy of a "monstrous" sexual act that leads to a suicide attempt and then to Amy's death from hanging by her own hand. From Johnny's eavesdropping we learn that Amy was pregnant, that Emalin may have delayed in assisting her sister because of the pregnancy, and that the village doctor will omit from the death certificate what he finds. Not only does Johnny therefore expose the hypocrisy within the community's standard of moral propriety: he also brings to light the nature of Amy's sexual transgression, which leaks out through an act of ethnic impersonation: "He was down on his stomach the way he had been when he got me. Sing-song nasal words came out, Chinese I thought. And then it seemed to me that the same words were repeated in another voice, slower and not nasally."[45]

Johnny repeats this detail toward the end, out of sequence with the order of his narrative. His rehearsal of "the other voice, slow, hesitant, repeating the words without the nasal quality" makes Alex leap to his feet to silence Johnny by striking his mouth.[46] The attentive reader has probably realized by now what our narrator claims not to have realized till the very end, when Alex reveals it. That second voice was Miss Amy's. Presumably, she has been having a sexual affair with one of her Chinese tenants. Indeed, it seems to be a love affair, implied by the intimacy with which Amy has been learning Chinese in an act of cultural sharing. And if the reader has *not* realized this, then perhaps it is because the reader has all along shared the same stereotypical, even racist views of the Chinese held by many of the characters, thus not suspecting this affair as a possibility.

Which is all to say that "Johnny Bear," despite its interest in the photographically faithful, is a classic study in unreliable narration. Through much of the story, our narrator appears unable to break out of the sequence of Johnny's telling, even though he is recalling events and telling the story in the past tense and would (we can suppose) have known the final revelation all along. He seems bound in his telling by Johnny's spell, and he even begins to echo unconsciously the intonations of other characters.[47] The narrator's revelation at the end of the story can be read as a seizing of narrative power from Johnny Bear in an effort to emerge from the ontological disarray of being merely the object of description. Our narrator is "reclaiming" more than swampy land. He is reclaiming his narrative identity by replacing Johnny's suspenseful description of Miss Amy's relationship with his own melodramatic revelation.

When we realize this truth, our attention falls on the structure and timing of the story, and the unreliability it implies. Johnny Bear is suppressed in the world of the story to protect the sanctity of a white culture from an exposure of the interracial and cross-class affairs at its heart (ones, of course, that our narrator participates in too). Here the story is significant for what it shows rather than for what it tells. Our diegetic narrator or narrator-as-storyteller becomes – again like Johnny Bear – a mimetic narrator, more significant for what his behavior reveals. We thus come to understand the process by which whiteness is constructed against realizations of its interracial desires. Unlike "The Vigilante," which is silent about and thus complicit in the racist action it describes, "Johnny Bear" finally exposes what is not fully seen or told: the subplot involving the crew on the floating bunkhouse. The sound of the dredging can be heard in the background throughout the story, a sign of how the central events are haunted by the capitalist exploitation and division of the land. We learn in bits and pieces about life among the crew: about the "pasty" looking cook whom the narrator dislikes for his horrible whiteness and his apparent queerness; about the series of accidents that leaves one man with his legs partially severed and another with a case of blood poisoning.[48] The story of the dredging crew never develops into a coherent plot – and that's the point. There is no normative center to the story. The all-white, homosocial world of labor seems pestilential and contaminated, thus unable to develop into full narrative being.

In their treatment of race and class relations in the West, both "Johnny Bear" and "The Vigilante" imply a photographic vision, and both stories operate through a retroactivity. The bemused recoil of "The Vigilante" compares with the revelation at the end of "Johnny Bear," which forces readers to revisit the story's treatment of narrative showing and telling. The effect, in both stories, depends on their curtailed status *as* short stories, their refusals to explain completely. We saw in Chapter 1 of this book how Steinbeck's short stories (particularly "The Snake") resonate with photographic seeing, as they delimit reality and move not horizontally but vertically through layered acts of attention. This parallel between the short story and the photograph is at least as old as Edgar Allan Poe, who offered one of the first theories of each medium. Both are temporally delimited, capable of "unity" of effect, productive of a special kind of attention, and responsive to forces within democratic culture.[49] Subsequent writers have thickened the links between photographs and short stories. Eudora Welty – photographer and short story writer both (and indeed another white writer who tells a lynching story from the lyncher's problematically unjudged point of view[50]) – saw both forms as snapshots, offering a "peripheral awareness" of their subject.[51] We have already encountered Julio Cortázar's idea of the short story as a fragment of reality exploding into meaning like a photograph in ways very different from the synthesizing "open order" of the novel (and film).[52] Making us think of the treatment of vision in "The Vigilante," Nadine Gordimer writes: "Short-story writers see by the light of the flash; theirs is the art of the only thing one can be sure of – the present moment." Its photographic capturing of isolated moments of consciousness rather than the cumulative arc of a life makes the short story – unlike the novel – correspond to the loneliness and isolation of the individual in modernity and to the breakup of the conditions of middle-class life.[53] Such loneliness and isolation, as we saw, haunted Steinbeck when he turned to the story of "The Vigilante."

Recent work on the novel has stressed its world-building potential. As Yi-Ping Ong has argued from an existential perspective, novels tend to assume a totality and autonomy, a completeness of readerly experience that is related to the free, inward subject of liberalism and to the novel's ability to make knowable (and hence to sanction) the larger classes and institutions of which it is part.[54] Steinbeck's short stories "The Vigilante" and "Johnny Bear" possess an opposing energy: they work to unmake the coherence and authority of the classes and institutions they represent, an unmaking that returns not to their purported totality as artworks but to the incompleteness of what they represent. Hence the undeveloped experience in the bunkhouse in "Johnny Bear" and the forbidden interracial love within the institution of middle-class propriety that we glimpse through the photographic power of Johnny's mimetic voice expose the contradictions of the white culture they represent. "The Vigilante" in particular behaves like a photograph in its peripheral awareness of events, although its ethical relationship to history is much more problematic, again suggesting the range of positions that Steinbeck's work is capable of occupying. The story shares many of the qualities and contradictions that Susan Sontag, Roland Barthes, and others have detected in the photographic image. Like Barthes's idea of the "mad" photograph that works through a revulsive movement of time, "The Vigilante" confronts "the wakening of intractable reality."[55] Mike remembers and reports the physical details of his experience, many of which are true to the historical record, yet he still cannot see enough, he still cannot recall the feelings motivating his participation in the lynching. The brevity, suddenness, and incompleteness of "The Vigilante" embody loneliness and disconnection, a splitting apart of society into individual fragmented experiences.[56] The experiences it represents are not totalistic but curtailed, not developmental but revulsive, not world building but defamiliarizing and difficult. Like Sontag's idea of the photograph, Steinbeck's story is not a statement about the world so much as a piece of it.[57] It is a "raw record," a participation, even an intervention in history.[58] Behaving like a lynching photograph itself, the story gains a photographic authenticity, but it lacks ethical responsibility toward what it captures. Its tone of bewildered recoil recognizes but fails to judge the shocking presence of racist violence in American life.

CHAPTER 4

Becoming Animal: Theories of Mind in The Red Pony

"The stories in *The Long Valley* are almost entirely about plants and animals," wrote Edmund Wilson in his seminal essay on Steinbeck's early work. "Mr. Steinbeck does not have the effect, as Lawrence or Kipling does, of romantically raising the animals to the stature of human beings," he continued, "but rather of assimilating the human beings to animals."[1] Wilson was not wrong about Steinbeck's 1938 short story collection as titles such as "The Chrysanthemums," "The White Quail," and "The Snake" all suggest. "Flight," "Johnny Bear," and "The Murder" treat humans who are either reduced to or exist on the borders of an animalized state. And of course *The Red Pony* (1933, 1936), with its three (later four) internal sections, remains one of the most widely read stories of human and animal interactions in American literature. For Wilson, Steinbeck was a throwback to the naturalism of his fellow Californians, Frank Norris and Jack London. He was a late naturalist, not a modernist, who reduced human experience to the animal within. Of all claims about Steinbeck's work, Wilson's has stuck the fastest; his resounding critique would dominate negative opinions of Steinbeck's work for decades to come. And of all claims about Steinbeck's work, none deserves stronger reevaluation in light of the reversal in critical vision that has moved nonhuman animals from the margins to the center of our attention.

The Long Valley has always posed structural problems for critics. *The Pastures of Heaven* (1932) is a short story cycle with recurrent characters acting in a distinct location, but *The Long Valley* breaks beyond the bounds of its title, with a number of stories stretching outside traditional Steinbeck Country. The collection includes *The Red Pony*, a short story sequence in itself. *The Red Pony* was published serially in magazines and then as a separate volume, originally without the final section, "The Leader of the People," but subsequently – and with some controversy – including this story (the final story of *The Long Valley*) as its final section. We have already seen the contrasting treatments of race in the stories "The Vigilante" and "Johnny Bear," and in general *The Long Valley* offers a variety of experiences, perspectives, and techniques. To realize a key theme that holds the collection together, we might look no further than the story that seems most beyond its pale: "Saint Katy the Virgin."

"Saint Katy the Virgin" is an animal fable set in fourteenth-century France. It is a story about a bad pig called Katy whose series of devilish deeds culminates in her abuse of two Catholic monks, who succeed in converting Katy to Christianity, after which she ministers to the afflicted and is eventually canonized. The story tends to be viewed as an immature, even blasphemous aberration in the collection as a whole; one early reviewer wrote that it "is quite as though Ernest Hemingway had come forth with an Uncle Remus story."[2] But the story fits closely with the collection's animal thematics and indeed serves as an important transition to the following *Red Pony* series by recognizing a very different, premodern attitude toward the animal world. Animal trials, which implicitly recognized animals as legal agents, were not unheard of in the medieval world: they signaled what Luc Perry calls "a *prehumanistic* . . . relationship to the animal kingdom as well as to nature in general."[3] An amateur medievalist, Steinbeck must have had some conception of the special position of animals during the premodern period (E. P. Evans's foundational *The Criminal Prosecution and Capital Punishment of Animals* was published in 1906), hence gaining a sense of what Joanna Picciotto calls the "prehistory of the posthuman."[4]

The rise in recent years of critical animal studies (CAS) is the culmination of a succession of critical efforts to focus on excluded others, to interrogate normative conceptions of the subject, and to deconstruct hegemonic categories – the rational; the logocentric; and, indeed, "the human" itself. Driven by recognition of the disastrous impact humans have had on the planet, and by recognition of our widespread cruelty to animals, CAS has sought to establish a "posthumanist ethical pluralism" that exposes the limits and dangers of our "speciesism."[5] CAS has discovered in literary texts varied power to realize and give voice to the animal on its own terms, to collapse the boundaries between "human" and "animal" as categories, and to recognize what Susan McHugh calls "orders of agency beyond the human subject."[6] Perhaps the greatest power literature possesses in this regard, as any reader of London's *The Call of the Wild* (1903) or *White-Fang* (1906) would attest, is the power to inscribe animals with personalities, perspectives, and character traits that direct attention away from the centrality of human life and, indeed, that question the uniqueness and higher claims upon which that species-bound life is founded. Enter Katy the pig. And enter Gabilan, the red pony.

Composed both in the hospital and in the family's home in Salinas while Steinbeck was taking care of his mother following a massive stroke that paralyzed her left side, *The Red Pony* was originally published in three parts ("The Gift," "The Great Mountains," and "The Promise") in the *North American Review* between 1933 and 1936. We might follow Wilson and others in reading it as a return to the world of Steinbeck's fellow Californians, Norris and London, whose works were part of what Michael Lundblad calls the "discourse of the jungle" that emerged during the Progressive Era. This discourse reflected an intense and controversial interest in animality, but often in the service of constructing the category of the human, and establishing differences (typically along lines of race and gender) between humans.[7] Like London's *Call of the Wild,* and like its British precursor *Black Beauty* by Anna Sewell (an 1877 novel narrated from the horse's point of view, in the cause of animal welfare), *The Red Pony* is also often read – echoing so many works of "classic" American literature – as a children's story, not unlike the animal fables of which "Saint Katy the Virgin" is an example.[8] Viewed as at once a regressive glance back to the naturalists and as a children's book that has not fully developed as a work of literature, *The Red Pony* deserves attention precisely for the ways it challenges hierarchical status divides (particularly between humans and animals) and the problems inherent in that destabilization. As is so often the case in American literature, the figure of the child becomes a means to contemplate some of the most intractable social and political questions, here regarding the status of the human itself.

Steinbeck wrote to his friends during the composition of *The Red Pony* series, describing his need for discipline during a distracting time: "It was good training in self control and that's about all the good it is."[9] He wrote in another letter:

> There is a good deal in it, first about the training of horses and second about the treatment of distemper. This may not seem like a good basis for a story but that entirely depends upon the treatment. The whole thing is as simply told as though it came out of the boy's mind although there is no going into the boy's mind. It is an attempt to make the reader create the boy's mind for himself. An interesting experiment you see if nothing else.[10]

In describing his knowledge of horses, Steinbeck was turning to his own experiences as a child – Steinbeck's father bought Steinbeck a red pony called Jill, which he shared with his sister Mary – even as he was using this experience to more experimental ends.[11] As Steinbeck's biographer once put it, no other writer "would write more closely from personal experience than Steinbeck, and yet no other writer could have been, at the same time, less specifically autobiographical."[12] "Treatment" is the subject of the story, hence the careful descriptions of animal sickness and medicine. We often find this recording of knowhow or knack in Steinbeck's work: *The Grapes of Wrath* (1939), for example, can seem indistinguishable at times from a car repair manual. But Steinbeck uses the term *treatment* twice, the second time as a literary term ("but that entirely depends upon the treatment") for the way the material is adapted or described. In other words, the story is, as Steinbeck conceived it, a treatment *of* treatment. It is a self-conscious literary experiment in medical and psychological matters, one that attempts to bring the reader to a "theory of mind" about its young protagonist Jody Tiflin.

Traditionally understood, theory of mind is a hypothetical concept. We cannot directly access another's mind, the argument runs, so we must posit a theory of that mind to understand its unique beliefs, desires, intentions, and perspectives.[13] Theory of mind is a kind of "mind reading" that can help us to predict actions and behaviors.[14] It is commonly opposed to behaviorism, the idea that all behaviors are produced by responses to certain stimuli in the environment or are consequences of an individual's history or education. The mind, in the latter view, is the product of reinforcement, repetition, and punishment – processes of conditioning that posit the influence of the external on the internal.[15] But in "The Gift," the first part of *The Red Pony*, rather than a story seeming to come out of the boy's mind – rather than making "the reader create the boy's mind for himself," as Steinbeck suggested it should – the opposite seems to be the case:

> The high jangling note of the triangle put the boy Jody in motion. He was only a little boy, ten years old, with hair like dusty yellow grass and with shy polite gray eyes, and with a mouth that worked when he thought. The triangle picked him up out of sleep. It didn't occur to him to disobey the harsh note. He never had: no one he knew ever had.[16]

Not only is Jody described from the outside in: he almost lacks an inside altogether. The passage resists a theory of mind in the way Jody responds, like one of Pavlov's dogs, to external physical stimuli. A bundle of disciplined habits rather than rational processes, he seems incapable of thinking in the abstract sense. His thought cannot exist freely from the movement of his mouth, making him an example of the psychologist William James's famous claim for purely embodied emotion: "we feel sorry because we cry, angry because we strike, afraid because we tremble."[17] And in general, the story offers an ethology of the human in minute detail, for example, when the stable hand Billy Buck blows his nose at the beginning of "The Gift": "Billy cleared each nostril by holding its mate closed with his forefinger and blowing fiercely."[18] Humans are reduced to external observations of their behavioral characteristics.

Jody's habitual actions are not just the result of external stimuli. They are also formed by the practices of his disciplinarian father, whose ideas seem a product of his own upbringing. The Progressive education movement that developed at the beginning of the twentieth century may have worked to educate the whole child by engaging their interest, but it still included a strong element of training to make students act "economically and efficiently," in the words of John Dewey. The school became a place where proper habits should be formed.[19] Any errant impulses Jody has – whether to crush a muskmelon with his foot or to point his rifle at the house – quickly fold under his father's training, the merits of which the narrator seems to sanction: "It was good discipline" is the judgmental response to Carl Tiflin's tendency to give gifts with instructive reservations.[20] The red pony is one such gift, which is also a test of whether Jody has the discipline to treat and train the horse properly (Carl says he will instantly sell the horse if not). Even the plot of the story – the pony becomes sick after being left out in the rain – is a direct result of Jody's inability to overcome the discipline of the school to play hooky and rescue his pet.[21] If human characters are products of their environment in this way, however, then the situation is very different in the animal world.

Gabilan is the prime example. In his training, he is not "force broke" (disciplined through punishment) but encouraged according to what other characters believe to be his inner thoughts and emotions. A number of assumptions are shared by both human characters and narrator alike: that horses are afraid of their feet; that they are able to feign fear; that Gabilan possesses a range of emotions – anger, fear, anxiety, curiosity, pleasure – all revealed by the position of his ears and by other forms of facial expression.[22] Indeed, all of Carl Tiflin's disciplinary philosophy collapses before the pony. He does not want Gabilan to become a "trick pony," to be "like an actor – no dignity, no character of his own."[23] Character is exactly what the pony possesses, to the extent that, on becoming sick, Gabilan bears the full emotional weight of the story. Animals are understood from the inside out in a story that constructs humans from the outside in. To the extent that human interiority exists, its emotions are occasional, uncontrollable, and usually minor and negative even if they can be powerful in effect. So completely does the character of Gabilan – always full of emotion, always sensitive to human conversation – overwhelm Jody that the boy lives in fear of the shame of losing power over his pet. According to psychoanalytic theory, shame is so powerful an emotion because it signifies a self-reflexive feeling of *being* a failure, rather than simply performing a failed action.[24] The course of events in the story charts the failure of Billy Buck – a character who claims to be half horse himself – to read the signs of animal nature and to predict what is happening on the inside of the sickening pony. And in an ontological sense, the human is marked by failure of a deeper kind.

It is worth returning here to Steinbeck's experience writing the story, which he records in another letter to his friend George Albee:

> I am typing the second draft of the pony story. A few pages a day. This morning is a good example. One paragraph – help lift patient on bed pan. Back, a little ill, three paragraphs, help turn patient so sheets can be changed. Back – three lines, nausea, hold pans, help hang bedding, back – two paragraphs. . . . That is a morning. One page and a half typed. You can see that concentration thrives under difficulties since I have a fear and hatred of illness and incapacity which amounts to a mania.[25]

Steinbeck turns to compulsive descriptions (or "treatments") of the medical treatment of the pony as a form of discipline or training in face of the ultimate human failure. This compulsive, disciplined sense of writing is embodied in the character of Carl Tiflin, whose own disciplinary obsessions similarly stem from his hatred of sickness. Disciplined description reaches its peak toward the end of "The Gift," after Gabilan wanders away from the barn to die, and Jody confronts the buzzards who begin to feast on the pony's carcass:

> Jody plunged into the circle like a cat. The black brotherhood arose in a cloud, but the big one on the pony's head was too late. As it hopped along to take off, Jody caught its wing tip and pulled it down. It was nearly as big as he was. The free wing crashed into his face with the force of a club, but he hung on. The claws fastened on his leg and the wing elbows battered his head on either side. Jody groped blindly with his free hand. His fingers found the neck of the struggling bird. The red eyes looked into his face, calm and fearless and fierce; the naked head turned from side to side. Then the beak opened and vomited a stream of putrefied fluid. Jody brought up his knee and fell on the great bird. He held the neck to the ground with one hand while his other found a piece of sharp white quartz. The first blow broke the beak sideways and black blood spurted from the twisted, leathery

> mouth corners. He struck again and missed. The red fearless eyes still looked at him, impersonal and unafraid and detached. He struck again and again, until the buzzard lay dead, until its head was a red pulp. He was still beating the dead bird when Billy Buck pulled him off and held him tightly to calm his shaking.[26]

Such a violent moment is told in measured prose, as if in calm recoil from the bizarre scene. We also here move even further away from Jody himself, who empties of emotion. He is pure behavior, objectively described. If Jody is groping blindly, then we are given the buzzard's point of view. Indeed, any categorical distinction between human and animal seems to collapse. The buzzards are a "brotherhood"; anatomically they have "elbows" and "mouths," and a power of detached observation that brings Jody into view. The passage does not simply impute mind or intention within the animal. Instead, we as readers enter a shared world of perception. When we read "red eyes looked into his face, calm and fearless and fierce; the naked head turned from side to side," it is impossible to say whether the buzzard or Jody is the subject of the sentence. It is impossible because the buzzards look on to a world in which the human is becoming animal as well. Picking up a primitive tool, Jody becomes possessed by primeval forces, "like a cat." His character reverts to basic instinct in a moment that leaps back in genre too, as we enter the worldview of medieval romance. Jody performs an act of heroism to defeat a larger-than-life (at least from the child's perspective) beast that preys on his beloved, anthropomorphized pony. Karl Steel has detected in certain medieval works of literature "the discursive inability – or unwillingness – to abandon either the category threat of the animal or the foundation of the human subject on a humiliated animal object."[27] We glimpse similar ambivalence in "The Gift." The human subject, so prone to shame, attempts to regain self-esteem through the destruction of an animal. Yet the animal is also a threat *to* the human in this moment of equalization, of shared agency, and of mutual violence.

We can read this scene as an ultimate moment of cognitive deficit. Rather than having feelings that remain unrepresented, Jody seems to lack them altogether. We cannot theorize a mind in a self that appears to be merely a bundle of habits, a collection of impulsive behaviors reacting to environmental stimuli. The scene may be jarring to us as readers because shocking violence is described with compulsive calmness. The matter-of-fact quality of the style also suggests how, for Jody, this moment is continuous with the world in which he lives. In effect, he sees the buzzard and his father *on the same level*, as equal external threats to his self.

The father's seemingly inappropriate response to Jody at the end – "the buzzard didn't kill the pony. Don't you know that?" – does more than simply unseat Carl's authority over the situation. It signals the profound inability of the characters to read each other and to interpret the situation, owing to the cognitive void of the human, shown dramatically in Jody's absent subjectivity in his fight with the buzzard. Theorizing mind in animals but not in humans, "The Gift" ends with Billy Buck's question to Carl, a question that can only be answered in the negative: "man, can't you see how he'd feel about it?"[28] Carl seems to lack the textured subject position from which any such empathetic evaluation would be possible, just as Jody ironically lacks the ability to feel at all.

"The Gift" is followed in *The Red Pony* by "The Great Mountains" (a story to which we will return shortly), but its concerns are repeated most closely in the third story of the sequence, "The Promise," to the extent that the latter feels like a compulsive narrative return to the former when Jody is promised another gift of a colt born from the family's pregnant mare, Nellie. "The Promise" dwells again on Jody's own compulsions: the story locates symbolic meaning in the repeated behaviors of its characters, such as Jody's repeated return to the brush line of the property. We are in the same behaviorist world, a pragmatist universe in which uses and effects seem to determine truths, leaving Jody uncertain over "what action might later be construed as a crime" by his disciplinarian parents.[29] "The Promise" builds toward another violent conclusion, the impact of which depends on the degree to which the story establishes sympathetic identification with Nellie as a character. The story extends a theory of mind to animals in more extreme ways than "The Gift." Nellie is humanized in the character of the pregnant mother ("her lips were curled," we are told, "in a perpetual fatuous smile"), and she even gets her own flirty love story.[30] If animal emotion seems to be motivating the story, then the human is again marked by a feeling of failure centered on Billy Buck's fallibility and lost prestige, which carries over from his botched animal treatments in "The Gift." Billy recognizes the universe as a risky one of appearance and uncertainty in which his agency is limited, especially concerning his ability to successfully deliver the colt from Nellie. The "promise" of the title is Billy's vow to give Jody a good colt, a promise that emerges from an exchanged look between Billy and the mare ("a thing horses practically never do," we are told) to become Billy's redemption from shame.[31] Facing a badly breached birth, Billy opts to sacrifice Nellie to make good on his promise, which he does by bashing in her skull with a hammer and cutting her open with a knife. And then:

> Both of his arms plunged into the terrible ragged hole and dragged out a big, white, dripping bundle. His teeth tore a hole in the covering. A little black head appeared through the tear, and little slick, wet ears. A gurgling breath was drawn, and then another. Billy shucked off the sac and found his knife and cut the string. For a moment he held the little black colt in his arms and looked at it. And then he walked slowly over and laid it in the straw at Jody's feet.[32]

Billy performs his heroic redemption – he is a figure of skill, control, calculation, and precision – literally within the space of the animal. Billy's fragile self-esteem is reestablished, reborn from the violently destroyed animal, but ironically only to the extent that any distinction between human and animal is fundamentally questioned. Jody's final reaction, as he stares stupidly at the foal, is one of being animal himself. He "trotted" out of the barn with stiff and heavy legs, unable to rise above his body to feel emotion or to recall anything but the bloody face and the haunted eyes of Billy.[33] Humans dominate, but only to the degree that they are just one species in competition with, and unable to transcend, other species.

Reading "The Gift" and "The Promise" in tandem, we might point to Steinbeck's ambivalence concerning the human-animal connection. At times our narrator enters the unique perspective of the animal to see humans as a biological species with its own ethology. At other moments, animals become dominated beings upon which humans vent their rage, or upon which they overcome minor emotions of shame and boredom in a romance of glorious identity. Hence in "The Promise," the merger between species suggests both the animality of humans (Billy Buck, we learn, is disciplined by a father who saddles him like a horse) and the potential of imaginative liberation from such confines in the stories' few moments when we do glimpse human interiority (when Jody dreams of his colt, Black Demon, he "was not a boy any more, and Demon was not a horse. The two together were one glorious individual").[34] The category of the human exists in a rhythm of destruction and reconstruction, as it emerges to minor triumphs against a sense of its own precariousness. But there is another aspect to Steinbeck's interest in the animal, one that becomes clear in "The Great Mountains" – the second story in the sequence – and in the final story, "The Leader of the People." These stories also help us to locate Steinbeck's place in the world of critical animal studies.

The Mind of the Race

"The Great Mountains" begins with Jody relieving his boredom through acts of animal cruelty, thus placing the story in the world of interspecies violence that runs through the *Red Pony* series. But into this world Steinbeck introduces another theme, that of the West, the frontier embodied in the unexplored, mythical country of the great mountains to the west of Steinbeck Country. Mounted cowboy figures would have been a common sight along the California highways at the time, as in Figure 4.1 (a boy's face is just visible in the left of Dorothea Lange's photograph, admiring the mythical merger of man and animal). Opposing the eastern hills that suggest colonial conquest and settlement, the mountains to the west become a threatening space of terrible vastness. Indeed, they come to provide what is largely missing from Jody in the other stories: a mind, an inner process of thought, just as the West had played a similar role in the formation of a national imaginary. Out of these mountains walks Gitano, one of Steinbeck's *paisano* characters, a person of mixed Native and white blood: a Mexican American. Echoing Tularecito in *The Pastures of Heaven*, Gitano is a displaced, indigenous presence returning to the place of his birth, the Tiflin ranch, to die. The story works through a series of

Figure 4.1 Dorothea Lange, "Cowboy bringing cattle in from range. Common sight on California highways. Contra Costa County," November 1938. Library of Congress, Prints and Photographs Division, FSA/OWI Collection, LC-DIG-fsa -8b32834.

analogies, the first between the imperturbable mountains, which threaten Jody, and Gitano who seems like a geological presence himself: "The skin of his face had shrunk back against the skull until it defined bone, not flesh, and made the nose and chin seem sharp and fragile."[35] Like the mountains, Gitano has a mysterious, inaccessible quality: an unknown "thing" lies behind his eyes. In his repeated refrain, "I am Gitano, and I have come back," Gitano is much like Herman Melville's Bartleby the Scrivener.[36] A simple assertion of inscrutable presence implies an ethical responsibility that tests the philanthropy of the dominant culture, which crumbles in both Melville's and Steinbeck's versions. Gitano's repetitious minimalism of language frustrates Carl's perverse logocentrism, his ability to probe people with festering words and to generate analogies. Denying Gitano's right of prior possession, Carl compares him to an old horse that deserves to be euthanized in a cruel analogy that is undermined when Gitano flees on the horse into the "great unknown country" of mountains that seems the equivalent of Gitano's inscrutable difference.[37] In his recaptured manhood and heroic gesture, in his merger with the animal and mineral worlds with which he had been compared, Gitano becomes a racialized and romanticized presence that is disappearing both into and from the landscape – a presence as threatening as it is irrelevant.

What Gitano leaves behind, however, is a feeling that ties the *Red Pony* stories together. Jody feels a "sharp loneliness," a caressing "longing," a "nameless sorrow" that overwhelms him.[38] This feeling of melancholy for something Jody is unable to identify or comprehend threads through the series as a whole. The feeling is responsible for any imaginative fantasies he is allowed to possess. It also motivates Jody's relationship with animals, particularly horses, that enables his entry into a romanticized level of heroic experience through a relational sense of belonging to a group. An instinct more than an autonomously generated idea, Jody's feeling of historical continuity and significance that emerges from his possession of the red pony, and establishes superiority over his classmates,[39] is developed further in the final story of the Jody Tiflin series, "The Leader of the People." Some critics have considered this final story, added later to the *Red Pony* series, a confusing digression.[40] The extent to which it fits with the collection as a whole depends on its contemplation of a relationship never far from Steinbeck's mind: the relationship between the individual part and a greater whole.

The story begins typically with Jody attempting to overcome his loneliness and boredom with acts of animal cruelty, but his plan to conduct a mouse hunt is interrupted by the surprise arrival of Jody's maternal grandfather, one of the original white settlers who led his people on their journey West. In the foreground, the story treats the generational conflict between the grandfather and Jody's father, who cannot abide the repeated stories of the frontier journey and what they imply about the diminished experience of the younger, settled generation. In the background of these stories lies a broader theory of human experience – one dovetailed with a national mythology – and its connection to the power of literary experience. The grandfather is himself uninterested in his own, overly scripted stories of battles with the Indians. They are not what he wants to tell; he only knows how he wants people to feel when he tells them:

> It wasn't Indians that were important, nor adventures, nor even getting out here. It was a whole bunch of people made into one big crawling beast. And I was the head. It was westering and westering. Every man wanted something for himself, but the big beast that was all of them wanted only westering. I was the leader, but if I hadn't been there, someone else would have been the head. The thing had to have a head.[41]

To understand the grandfather's ideas – and indeed to understand the problematic complexity of Steinbeck's interest in animality – we must return to Steinbeck's biological interests that we saw developing in *To a God Unknown* (1933) and reaching a disturbing power in "The Vigilante." (Mike in "The Vigilante" also plays the "head" of the human battering ram that breaks down the jailhouse door.[42])The idea of people uniting into "one big crawling beast," greater than the sum of its individual units, emerges from Steinbeck's long education in marine biology, much of which was influenced by Steinbeck's close relationship with Ed Ricketts. Ricketts's study of intertidal life reflected his interest in how individual organisms behave differently when they are part of a group or colony, as a "superorganism" begins to determine the behavior of its constituent parts.[43] These ideas culminate in Steinbeck's unpublished 1935 essay, "Argument of Phalanx," which develops concepts that Steinbeck was already working out in his correspondence with Carlton Sheffield in the early 1930s, as we saw in Chapter 2, and then expanded in his unpublished story "Case History," as we saw in the previous chapter. "Man is a unit of the greater beast, the phalanx," wrote Steinbeck in "Argument of Phalanx": "The phalanx has pains, desires, hungers and strivings as different from those of the unit man's as man's are different from the unit-cells."[44] Returning us to the problems of "The Vigilante" – the way that a theory of species behavior is compromised by the unexplored motivation of racism – "The Leader of the People" suggests the nature and the limits of Steinbeck's power as a theorist of animality.

Here we might compare Steinbeck's interest in animals with that of Franz Kafka, a writer whose animal stories lie at the origin of a concept crucial to critical animal studies – the concept of "becoming-animal." Exploring Kafka's desire to escape from the "diabolical powers" of bureaucracy, especially in his short stories, Gilles Deleuze and Félix Guattari define "becoming-animal" as more than simply an attraction to or an impersonation of non-human identity. "To become animal," they write,

> is to participate in movement, to stake out the path of escape in all its positivity, to cross a threshold, to reach a continuum of intensities that are valuable only in themselves, to find a world of pure intensities where all forms come undone, as do all the significations, signifiers, and signifieds, to the benefit of an unformed matter of deterritorialized flux, of nonsignifying signs.[45]

For Deleuze and Guattari, "becoming-animal" describes the movement of the individual self into collective "assemblages" that are "deterritorialized" or nomadic. It describes a collapse of the boundary between human and animal that liberates subjectivity and deconstructs language itself.[46] To some extent, Deleuze and Guattari's poststructuralist ideas share remarkable and perhaps surprising similarities with Steinbeck's concept of the phalanx. Steinbeck, together with Deleuze and Guattari, explores the collapse of the individual into a group identity: "A becoming-animal always involves a pack, a band, a population, a peopling, in short, a multiplicity."[47] They are all strongly influenced by Charles Darwin's understanding of subjectivity stretching across generations and keying into forces no individual has experienced but that "endure in the generic imaginary of the community."[48] They are all centrally interested in the *process* of becoming rather than the thing become. "What is real is the becoming itself, the block of becoming, not the supposedly fixed terms through which that which becomes passes," write Deleuze and Guattari, while for Steinbeck what gives the group its power is motion and emergence – being *in the middle*.[49] And finally, for all three thinkers, becoming-animal (or the move to a phalanx identity) involves a holistic transformation in identity that takes place at a deep, molecular level.[50]

The grandfather's feeling of westering in "The Leader of the People" resonates with these ideas of phalanx-identity, of group-man, of becoming-animal. It is a feeling of movement, collectivity, and non-identity, a feeling of overwhelming hunger (the grandfather must prevent the people from eating their own pack animals) and of flux that lies beyond the realms of conventional signification. This explains the scripted and repetitious nature of the only stories the grandfather can tell, and his final dissatisfaction with the power of language to capture this experience of deconstructed identity and collective assemblage. In a pattern we will see elsewhere in Steinbeck, events are explained according to fundamental animal urges: "We carried life out here and set it down the way those ants carry eggs."[51] The self is driven by behavioral compulsion throughout *The Red Pony* but nowhere more so than in the grandfather's compulsive retelling of the same stories over and again, in an effort to recapture that phalanx feeling when individual becomes collective experience in a process of protean emergence. Through these stories – ones that "only little boys like to hear" – Jody comes closest to possessing an internalized mind, though it is one that suggests distinct limits to Steinbeck's theory of "deterritorialized" identity:

> A race of giants had lived then, fearless men, men of a staunchness unknown in this day. Jody thought of the wide plains and of the wagons moving across like centipedes. He thought of grandfather on a huge white horse, marshaling the people. Across his mind marched the great phantoms, and they marched off the earth and they were gone.[52]

If Jody possesses an imagination at this point in the series of stories, then it seems like a blank screen on which heroic figures are projected like stars in a Hollywood western. Deleuze and Guattari may admit that the politics of becoming-animal can be ambiguous and has its limits in Kafka's stories,[53] but their idea of becoming-animal tends to be understood as a force of radical liberation for the human subject, one associated with "minoritarian groups, or groups that are oppressed, prohibited, in revolt, or always on the fringe of recognized institutions."[54] The grandfather's idea of westering, however, is also connected to the idea of the West as a dominant mythological construct and a realm of racial conquest and destruction. Like Frederick Jackson Turner's theory of the West as a process rather than a place, a continual return to the inherent democracy and freedom of "primitive" conditions,[55] the grandfather's concept of westering is a rejuvenating power only for the white men involved in this racial violence. If the *Red Pony* stories are Steinbeck's attempt to make readers "create the boy's mind" for themselves – to the extent that the series can easily seem like children's literature – then the ultimate imaginative target of that mind is an ideology of racial dominance inherent in Western conquest.

As a sequence, *The Red Pony* interweaves stories that deconstruct the frontier between the human and the animal with stories about the colonial possession of the West. It thus puts in conversation a species understanding of the human as a universal if precarious construct defined by an inherent animality and a more localized understanding of the white "race" in a story of Western conquest. At their most radical, the stories shift attention from the centrality of human life by positing a theory of mind in nonhuman animals while reducing humans to compulsive behaviors and minor emotions. But as the series progresses toward the final section, it moves to an awareness of the need for stories and myths by humans dominated by biological urges. "The Leader of the People" describes a regressive need for a primal pattern of narrative as a disciplining ritual and a communal impulse in response to the bareness of our species life. The grandfather's compulsive stories about westering are ultimately stories that strive to recapture a lost state of becoming-animal, a collective process of emergence. What the grandfather cannot fully articulate is never explicitly brought to light but implied by the alternate patterning of the stories themselves, most obviously seen in the insertion of the Gitano story between "The Gift" and "The Promise." Returning to the problems on display in "The Vigilante," westering is inherently a racialized concept. Hence there is a troubling politics submerged within Steinbeck's apparent privileging of the biological and the universal. Steinbeck's power to become a transcendent thinker about the nature and fate of the species is haunted by intransigent problems of history and identity. By framing the conflict as one between generations, with different relations to historical experience, "The Leader of the People" partially disguises the conflicts between whites and indigenous peoples at the heart of the story of the West. The compulsive repetition of the same story works to disguise the racial slaughter, colonial violence, and capitalist greed that lurk within nostalgia, and within an ongoing melancholy that cannot be spoken fully into being. No new stories can emerge from this situation, just as Gitano seems deprived of voice and identity beyond a gesture of romanticized return to the land, or receding disappearance into the West. If "The Leader of the People" is about the loss of a frontier mentality, then it is also about the loss of an ability – the loss of Steinbeck's ability – to bring new stories to light, new experiences that might question the power of the dominant culture beyond a self-indulgent contemplation of its nostalgic "greatness." The loss is a loss of political self-awareness, one that contradicts Steinbeck's transcendent biological explanation. The narrative compulsion in "The Leader of the People" and to some extent in *The Red Pony* as a whole is the stutter of a voice unable to speak forth historical trauma, genocide, and dispossession.

CHAPTER 5

What Is It Like to Be a Plant? "The Chrysanthemums" and "The White Quail"

Writing as a war correspondent from London on July 15, 1943, John Steinbeck was drawn to the margins of military experience when he noticed the vegetable gardens springing up on the edges of American airfields and between the barracks of troops. Far from home, the American soldiers were yearning to raise familiar vegetables or to escape feelings of homesickness by working with the soil to achieve a sense of normality and peace. This discovery clearly resonated with Steinbeck, an avid gardener throughout his life and now himself far from home. Possessed by a frantic hunger "to put my fingers in the soil," gardening was a constant cure for Steinbeck's depressive moods.[1] When he encountered these American gardens in the context of war-torn England, however, Steinbeck's mind turned quickly from psychological to political concerns. He noted an English cruelty toward vegetables, found in the English kitchens where vegetables were boiled to a submissive pulp that destroyed their "essential character." English gardens were "a kind of symbol of revolt against foreign methods," a site of eugenic selection and control.[2] Opposing this, the American gardens Steinbeck discovered were places in which vegetables were treated with latitude and respect, even if this American closeness to the vegetable world could have overwhelming effects. "In the American gardens," Steinbeck observed toward the end of his essay, "certain English spies have reported they have seen American soldiers pulling and eating raw carrots and turnips and onions" straight from the ground.[3]

Steinbeck's account is lighthearted to a degree, though its undercurrents of violence and nationalism tap into a darker stream in Steinbeck's lifelong consciousness of plants. In a letter to a friend written during the composition of *To a God Unknown* (1933), for example, Steinbeck described himself as having "a great many of the basic impulses of an African witch doctor" regarding his relationship with a tree:

> Now the lower limbs should be cut off because they endanger the house. I must cut them soon and I have a very powerful reluctance to do it, such

> a reluctance as I would have toward cutting live flesh. Furthermore if the tree should die, I am pretty sure I should be ill. This feeling I have planted in myself and quite deliberately I guess, but it is none the less [strong] for all that.[4]

If Steinbeck describes his self as a space in which thoughts could be "planted," then these thoughts are capable of growing to vast proportions, entwining his very identity with a vegetable world charged with mythical and supernatural powers. And how could it not be so entwined, growing up in the agriculturally rich Salinas Valley where – as Steinbeck writes in his story "Johnny Bear" – "lettuce and cauliflowers grow to giants"?[5] The wealth of Salinas sprang from the soil, its vegetable products dominating the lives and livelihoods of its population, turning them into what Steinbeck called "Lettuce People," "Carrot People," and "Cauliflower People" who had unrooted the earlier "Cattle People" from power.[6] Vegetables meant money, and with this money came a darker side to Salinas: "It was a blackness that seemed to rise out of the swamps," wrote Steinbeck in recollections of his childhood home, "a kind of whispered brooding that never came into the open – a subsurface violence that bubbled silently like the decaying vegetation under the black water of the Tule Swamps."[7] When Steinbeck evoked the symbolic economy of vegetation in his fiction, it rested on this real but murky economy of capitalist greed and scientific exploitation of the land, which forced workers to grapple with its planted products (see Figure 5.1). The "grapes" in Steinbeck's famous title were a source of California's food power.[8] But they were also the locus of a deeper human resonance with the vegetable kingdom, one that also held the potential for renovation and reform.

Steinbeck would write about vegetable matters throughout his career. After all, Edmund Wilson's famous critique of Steinbeck's naturalism in *The Long Valley* (1938) – his tendency to deemphasize humanity – was that its stories were "almost entirely about *plants* and animals" (my emphasis).[9] Two stories in particular center on this vegetable obsession and feature Steinbeck's interest in both agriculture and horticulture: "The Chrysanthemums" and "The White Quail," both in *The Long Valley*. They are stories in which the vegetable world rests on a bubbling subsurface of political concerns related to Steinbeck's always fraught engagement with gender and sexuality (and to a lesser extent with race), hence returning us to themes that run through other short stories in the collection. If Steinbeck's experiments with animal consciousness in *The Red Pony* (1933, 1936) are compromised by the emergence of an uncritical racial ideology, then his stories about plants possess a more subversive potential to impact the minds of readers. "It is entirely different and is designed to

Figure 5.1 Dorothea Lange, "Filipinos cutting lettuce. Salinas, California," June 1935. Library of Congress, Prints and Photographs Division, FSA/OWI Collection, LC-DIG-fsa-8e07356.

strike without the reader's knowledge," Steinbeck wrote to a friend about "The Chrysanthemums": "I mean he reads it casually and after it is finished feels that something profound has happened to him although he does not know what nor how. It has had that effect on several people here."[10] The curious "difference" of "The Chrysanthemums" – and "The White Quail" too – emerges from a play with language and literary form to explore both the possibilities and the limits of transformations in human consciousness, ones that lie along the human-plant connection.

Vegetable Plots

"The Chrysanthemums" is one of Steinbeck's most anthologized works perhaps because of its strong engagement with the politics of gender, which divides along the lines of horticulture and agriculture in the fertile setting of the Salinas Valley. The story centers on Elisa Allen, an avid horticulturalist known for her chrysanthemums of giant proportions. Costumed in masculine attire and armed with snips and knife, Elisa uses gardening as an outlet for her pent-up frustrations and loneliness within her marriage to the farmer Henry Allen (the couple is childless, we learn, and Elisa – who may be based on Carol Henning, Steinbeck's first wife and herself an avid gardener and activist – is thirty-five years old).[11] Her energetic work with plants is "over-eager, over-powerful," a substitute for involvement in a life of commerce or a surrogate for marital satisfaction that filters into the selective breeding of outsized specimens.[12] Yet her furious work is interrupted by the arrival of an itinerant tinker, who feigns interest in the chrysanthemums to gain some business from Elisa, fixing pots. Their conversation quickly turns to Elisa's special connection to her plants, her power of "planting hands" that she attempts to explain to the tinker:

> Well, I can only tell you what it feels like. It's when you're picking off the buds you don't want. Everything goes right down into your fingertips. You watch your fingers work. They do it themselves. You can feel how it is. They pick and pick the buds. They never make a mistake. They're with the plant. Do you see? Your fingers and the plant. You can feel that, right up your arm. They know. They never make a mistake. You can feel it. When you're like that you can't do anything wrong. Do you see that? Can you understand that?[13]

Elisa is attempting to describe an ecstatic moment of "breaking through" (as Steinbeck's great friend Ed Ricketts would term it),[14] a connection to the natural world that seems barely expressible in human language. The condition is one of being pure body, with the mind merely a distant observer of instinctive physical action that is a release from ethics ("you can't do anything wrong") and a deep involvement in the inevitable order of the natural world (you "never make a mistake"). Elisa becomes like the plant, liberated from her animal existence.

The struggle to imagine oneself as another life-form was famously articulated by the philosopher Thomas Nagel in his 1974 essay, "What Is It Like to Be a Bat?"[15] There is an essential difference, Nagel argues, between knowing what the experience of being a bat resembles, to a human, and knowing what it is like for a *bat* to be a bat. The experience of consciousness, in other words, is immune to objectivity in a special way, or at least it is so between different species because each species is entrapped in its own subjective viewpoint. Nagel admits in a footnote, however, that it "may be easier than I suppose to transcend inter-species barriers with the aid of the imagination," continuing that the "distance between oneself and other persons and other species can fall anywhere on a continuum."[16] Yet what if these species lie beyond the animal world altogether, to the extent that they seem to lack what we would call – thinking anthropocentrically – "consciousness" itself? Is the imagination adequate to this kind of task, Elisa's questions imply. In other words, can we ever approach what it is like to be a plant?

Elisa's implicit question here may seem outlandish, yet it returns to a point made recently in the wake of critical animal studies: nonhuman animals have become the privileged other, the locus of ethical criticism that works to decenter our humanness, not because they do not fully count biopolitically – that they have been forgotten or abused by humans – but "primarily because they are 'like us' in an originary way."[17] According to Jeffrey Nealon, the form of life that *is* more radically other, and hence more capable of displacing human dominance if recognized centrally, is the life of plants. Plants have no political existence even if, as life, they share many qualities with humans and other animals (they breathe, they move, they communicate, they reproduce sexually, they share much of their DNA with humans). We have seen how Gilles Deleuze and Félix Guattari's idea of "becoming-animal" helps us understand Steinbeck's interest in human emergence beyond the individual subject. And again here, Deleuze and Guattari's notion of the *rhizome* – a horizontally growing, underground system of roots, as opposed to the hierarchical concept of the tree – is crucial both to plant studies and to Steinbeck's interest in "plant-mindedness," to borrow Judith Richardson's resonant term.[18] According to Nealon, such notions might provide a "more open, free, 'better' version of posthumanist subjectivity," one that is not "tethered to the organism."[19] In the words of Laura Marks, "Deleuze and Guattari invite humans to be weed-like and celebrate 'drunkenness as a triumphant irruption of the plant in us,' an interconnected receptivity."[20]

In some ways, these ideas are nothing new. As Richardson argues, a rich history of human-plant connections runs through American literature, particularly in the nineteenth century. In general, Victorians were obsessed with the language of flowers and would send each other "talking bouquets" full of coded messages. The tinker in "The Chrysanthemums" provokes similarly coded conversations about plant life. He is not unlike that master of leafiness, Walt Whitman. Indeed, the word "Fixed" on the side of the tinker's wagon, with the paint of its black letters running "down in little sharp points beneath each letter,"[21] is not unlike versions of Whitman's title page for *Leaves of Grass*, whose letters seem to be sprouting little roots that imply a language organically emerging from the soil.[22] Yet the language Elisa attempts to find to describe her own plant-mindedness transcends such easy organicism to capture something extra-human, even as it verges on the sexual: "Elisa's voice grew husky. She broke in on him, 'I've never lived as you do, but I know what you mean. When the night is dark – why, the stars are sharp-pointed, and there's quiet. Why, you rise up and up! Every pointed star gets driven into your body. It's like that. Hot and sharp and – lovely.'"[23] We might read this moment as an expression of spiritual ecstasy, as Elisa is pierced, like Saint Teresa, by the arrow of God. At a social level, she seems to desire the free, romantic, wandering life of the tinker, to be pierced with the poet's "pointed" words. Yet at another level, Elisa is attempting to express a condition of passive receptivity beyond the human altogether, an autonomous existence as pure growth. In the words of Elaine Miller: "The plant is radically opposed to the figure of the organism as autonomous and oppositional; its stance toward the world is characterized by the promise of life and growth, not the avoidance of death or loss."[24] Rhizome-like, Elisa even attempts to reach out laterally to the tinker, to touch the cloth of his greasy black trousers with her planter's (and plant-like) fingers. As Louis Owens phrases it, her suspended life awaits the "fertilizing imagination" of the tinker.[25]

Within the gendered power dynamics and the pent-up sexuality of Elisa's encounter with the tinker, a different story grows. Elisa gives the departing tinker some chrysanthemum shoots that he claims he would like to take to another customer, but when he departs another transformation occurs:

> Elisa stood in front of her wire fence watching the slow progress of the caravan. Her shoulders were straight, her head thrown back, her eyes half-closed, so that the scene came vaguely into them. Her lips moved silently, forming the words "Good-bye – good-bye." Then she whispered, "That's a bright direction. There's a glowing there." The sound of her whisper startled her. She shook herself free and looked about to see whether anyone had been listening. Only the dogs had heard. They lifted their heads toward her from their sleeping in the dust, and then stretched out their chins and settled asleep again. Elisa turned and ran hurriedly into the house.[26]

We have already been introduced in the first paragraph to the "pale cold sunshine" that lights the "sharp and positive yellow leaves" across the valley.[27] Here, Elisa seems again to enter a plant-like passivity, a being of pure physical body, her head a flower directed toward the energy of the sun. She speaks a mystical language of plants seeking the glowing brightness of their life-force. She may not actually be photosynthesizing (even if some scientists believe that the human retina does indeed collect the energy of photons),[28] though here she approaches a pure plant-mindedness, only to spring back to her animal self amid the dogs that surround her.

Steinbeck would elsewhere explore these close connections between humans and plants. In "The Harness" – another story in *The Long Valley* – we meet a character who has been quite literally trained like a plant. Peter Randall's upright position of respect in the community stems from the webbed body harness his wife forces him to wear. He collapses after his wife's death into a rhizome-like planthood, his sagging body reflected in his successful crop of sweet peas that spreads vine-like across his land.[29] "The Chrysanthemums" takes this analogy to another level through a sustained and specific attention to the biology of the human plant, and its aesthetic resonance. Scrubbing with pumice her legs, thighs, loins, chest, and arms, then posing nude in her bedroom mirror toward the end of the story, Elisa has skin that glows like Edward Weston's "Pepper No. 30" (Figure 5.2). Indeed, the pureness we find in Elisa's contemplation of her naked existence seems to owe something to the vision of "pure" photography shared by Weston and his group of California photographers, whose work also juxtaposed plant life and human sexuality. Weston wrote of his desire to see a pepper purely for itself, with "no psychological attributes, no human emotions . . . beyond the world we know in the conscious mind," even as such images could not help but arouse human, sexual emotions in their viewers.[30] Elisa's vision in the mirror is similarly a merger of human sexuality and human planthood. Following this moment of Elisa's pure bodily contemplation, Steinbeck returns once more to his central focus:

> Then she went to the porch and sat primly and stiffly down. She looked toward the river road where the willow-line was still yellow with frosted leaves so that under the high grey fog they seemed a thin band of sunshine. This was the only color in the grey afternoon. She sat unmoving for a long time. Her eyes blinked rarely.[31]

The moment ends when Elisa's husband Henry enters the room and tells Elisa she looks "nice," hence provoking the kind of gender conflict, or Freudian pathologies, for which the story is known.[32] But within the parameters of this familiar marital tension, the story opens another space – the space of plant-mindedness. Again passive like a vegetable, Elisa's vision turns toward the sun, which locks her into a photosynthesizing stare as she

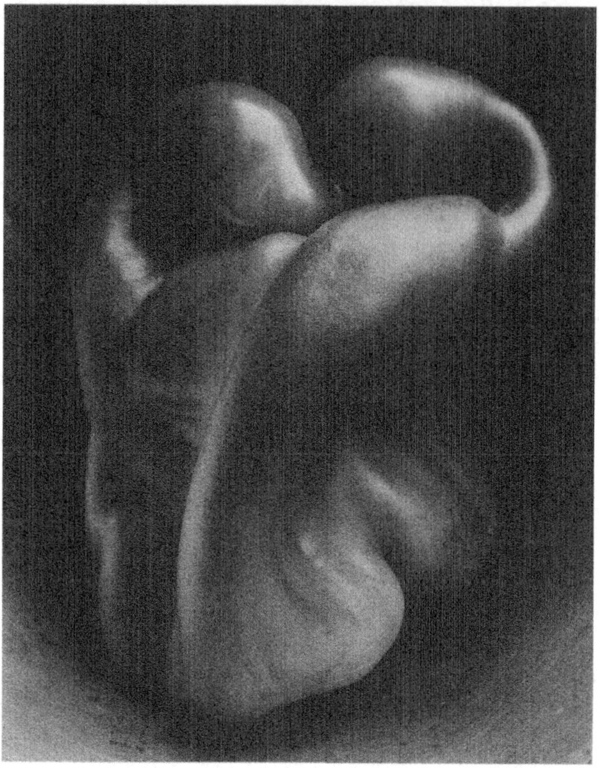

Figure 5.2 Edward Weston, "Pepper No. 30," 1930. © 2020 Center for Creative Photography, Arizona Board of Regents/Artists Rights Society (ARS), New York. Photo © Art Resource, New York.

soaks in its energy. Elisa's humanness has disappeared into another existential state. Her eyes are not seeing. They are absorbing.

It may be a stretch to suggest that Steinbeck imagined the "different" power of his story to "strike without the reader's knowledge" as itself a kind of photosynthesis, in which we absorb the text's meaning unconsciously to reach a profound transformation ourselves, fertilized by its radiant power.[33] At the very least, a different kind of reading is required of us to appreciate the transhuman undercurrents of the work. The story ends with the couple's journey to town to have dinner, during which they hold a conversation about boxing – a conversation that seems to embody all of the repressed frustration and gendered aggression of the story, at the end of which Elisa sits secretly crying, "like an old woman."[34] It is tempting to view the story's ending as a Hemingwayesque moment in which a seemingly distracted conversation has depths of meaning beneath its surface. Yet perhaps the conversation is just exactly that: a distraction from the more profound thematic, the deeper plot. On their journey into town, Elisa sees a dark speck on the road ahead and realizes that a crime has been committed. The tinker has simply dumped the chrysanthemums on the road, keeping the pot but killing the life within. This is a murder story, though no human is the victim. If we read deeply and well, then our sympathies have been relocated to another area of possibility and concern. In its attempt to articulate a condition of pure passive being in an ideal, non-exploitative relationship to nature, and in its story of the death of that transcendent condition of growth and of receptivity to the forces of nature, "The Chrysanthemums" has centered on a vegetable plot all along.

The Marriage Plot

"The Chrysanthemums" may take us to and even beyond the edge of human consciousness, yet it is haunted by another strain of ideas that were also connected to California's agricultural economy, ideas that we have already seen thread through Steinbeck's work. Elisa approaches a state of plant-mindedness, yet her engagement with nature is also a means of "over-powerful" control as she separates the weak from the strong to selectively breed "giant whites."[35] During the first half of the twentieth century, California had one of the most active eugenics programs in the world, its logic of "better breeding" motivated in part by the strength of an agricultural sector driven by its scientific and industrial desire to maximize output and to innovate new varieties. As Alexandra Minna Stern demonstrates in her history of the rise of eugenics in the West, the logic of better breeding shaped modern California, not only in terms of its inhabitants and institutions but also in apparently progressive areas of environmentalism and conservation. If Elisa is breeding "giant whites," then the Save the Redwoods League likewise found in the vast scale of California's plant life a metaphor for the preservation of (white) racial purity.[36] The purity of Eliza's plants, ironically, may be resting on hybridity, just as Elisa's beloved chrysanthemums were themselves being genetically manipulated by California's own "plant wizard," Luther Burbank, to become the hybrid Shasta Daisy. On his experimental farm in Santa Rosa, Burbank's selective breeding within and between plant species produced new varieties – the spineless cactus, the plumcot, the white blackberry – and indeed led to the era's most explicit exploration of the merger between human and plant identity, his 1907 book *The Training of the Human Plant*. Like plants, humans absorb their environment, they need sunshine, and their "fixed" traits can be trained and altered through crossbreeding, Burbank argued.[37] His belief that the American West could produce the finest race the world had ever known, from the vast mingling of peoples brought to California through immigration, was the flipside of more negative – and widespread – attempts to preserve racial "health" and hierarchy through forced sterilization of the "unfit" together with various anti-miscegenation laws and practices. Whether positive or negative, such eugenic beliefs returned to the same assumption. In the words of Paul Popenoe, editor of the American Breeders' Association journal: "The idea is to show that plants and animals obey the same laws of heredity, and that these laws are the ones which govern Homo Sapiens, as well."[38]

Popenoe studied at Stanford University – a hotbed of eugenic thinking – under David Starr Jordan, its first president, and went on to found the California chapter of the American Eugenics Society. As Stern demonstrates, Popenoe's road to human-centered eugenics involved a sustained engagement with plant breeding, which emerged from the family's date-growing business in the Coachella Valley (he imported and transplanted Middle Eastern varieties of date palms to California and published a book in 1913, *Date Growing in the Old World and the New*). Popenoe maintained his interest in plants as he turned to race "betterment."[39] His advocacy of sterilization for the allegedly unfit, however, was supplemented by another strain of "positive" eugenics still alive today. Popenoe founded the American Institute of Family Relations in 1930 as his attention turned to marriage counseling. "I began to realize that if we were to promote a sound population," he wrote, "we would not only have to get the right kind of people married, but we would have to keep them married."[40]

Following "The Chrysanthemums" in *The Long Valley*, Steinbeck's story "The White Quail" explores human-plant connections again in the context of the kind of fraught marital situation that occupies Steinbeck in the preceding story. Like Elisa and Henry Allen in "The Chrysanthemums," Mary and Harry Teller in "The White Quail" are a young-ish, childless married couple whose relationship is lived through the medium of the vegetable world. The opening of "The Chrysanthemums" introduces us to the agricultural landscape of the Salinas Valley, with the vision of "pale cold sunshine" and flaming "positive yellow leaves" foretelling the human plant-like desire to soak in the sunlight. "The White Quail" likewise introduces us to a landscape, the carefully tended garden of the Tellers, loaded with big colorful flowers, a landscape that again contains ideas: "At the edge of the lawn, a line of fuchsias grew like little symbolic trees. In front of the fuchsias lay a shallow garden pool, the coping flush with the lawn for a very good reason."[41] The very good reason is that of Mary Teller, whose obsession with her garden symbolizes for her a greater fight, to impose civilized order on the surrounding wilderness.

Mary's love of her garden carries the mystical sense that Steinbeck discovered in the world of horticulture – what Mary calls the "really-garden-time" in which the garden glows as if inhabited by "millions of not quite invisible fairies."[42] Following those modernist writers for whom vegetation myths had special force, the story inscribes plants with symbolic value. Fuchsias in particular stand like ceremonial objects holding back the wilderness that lies at the edge of the garden. Mary treats plants as if they were people, possessing agency and knowledge; indeed, she imbues the garden as a whole with a consciousness that aligns with her own: "She didn't think so much, 'Would this man like such a garden?' but, 'Would the garden like such a man?' For the garden was herself, and after all she had to marry some one she liked."[43] Not only is the garden an externalization of her mind; it also possesses its own point of view, allowing Mary to feel that she has vacated her body when she enters its sacred realm. Venturing outdoors one night to retrieve a pair of shears, she is able to look inside the house virtually from the garden's viewpoint: "She could almost see herself sitting there. Her round arms and long fingers were resting on the chair. Her delicate, sensitive face was in profile, looking reflectively into the firelight."[44] Echoing "The Chrysanthemums," plant-mindedness is a process of vision, though here it is also more profoundly a division, a splitting of the self in two ("There were two me's") that reveals some deeper tensions both in Mary and in the story itself.[45]

If Mary's self splits when she sees from the garden's perspective, then the story also places the garden's cultivated plants in a dialectical relationship with the animal life that inhabits them, especially the mystical white quail that comes to drink at Mary's pool:

> "Why," Mary cried to herself, "she's like me!" A powerful ecstasy quivered in her body. "She's like the essence of me, an essence boiled down to utter purity. She must be the queen of the quail. She makes every lovely thing that ever happened to me one thing."[46]

Playing with the idea of Narcissus's pool, in which the split self of reflection turns Narcissus into a flower, Steinbeck poses Mary between these two states of existence.[47] Her interest in entering different nonhuman states of existence (animal and vegetable) has a single aim, to exist in essential purity, in an ecstasy that is a condition of perpetual emergence, which

Mary expresses in a series of childhood memories: "The packages that came; untying the thing was an ecstasy. The thing in the package was never quite – ."[48] Even the first moment of loss when she hears of her father's death is an ecstasy of growth, though one that suggests a problematic division within Mary's relation to the nonhuman. The promise of perpetual life and pure passivity found in the vegetable world is haunted by the promise of death, and the struggle for existence found in the animal world (Mary is described as a "quiet gentian" in the story, a plant with a sterilizing power to kill bacteria). Mary's idealization of herself in the quail places that self in an evolutionary competition with other predatory creatures in her garden, particularly the cat that threatens to kill the quail. The plot of the story centers on Harry's quest to kill the cat, and we will turn to that in a moment. But first we need to recognize some other forces growing beneath the surface of the story.

Harry's reaction to his wife's obsession with her garden leads to an exchange that follows Mary's perfectionist claim that she would always maintain this order exactly by replacing any plants that die:

> "Curious little bug," he said.
>
> "Well, you see I've thought about it so long that it's part of me. If anything should be changed it would be like part of me being torn out."
>
> He put his hand out to touch her, and then withdrew it. "I love you so much," he said, and then paused. "But I'm afraid of you, too."
>
> She smiled quietly. "You? Afraid of me? What's there about me you can be afraid of?"
>
> "Well, you're kind of untouchable. There's an inscrutability about you. Probably you don't even know it yourself. You're kind of like your own garden – fixed, and just so. I'm afraid to move around. I might disturb some of your plants."[49]

Mary is a figure of intellect. When first in love with Harry, for example, she turns to writing in her copybook; the garden as a whole is a product of her "collected" and certain mind.[50] Yet one result of this externalization of Mary's mental life is an "untouchable" quality that manifests itself in a withdrawal of her sexual life from her husband. Mary locks her bedroom door – "The lock was an answer to a question, a clean, quick, decisive answer" – forcing Harry to try the door silently and to retreat from the bedroom in shame.[51] Popenoe's marriage counseling movement had a word for "untouchable" women like Mary: she is "frigid."

The language of "The White Quail" is suffused with the assumptions of eugenics. "Fixed" (Harry's term for Mary) is of course a synonym for sterilization (just as it recalls the tinker's acts of repair in "The Chrysanthemums"), and indeed Mary describes her fear of change as "like part of me being torn out." But "fixing" is also what Popenoe wanted to do with the failed marriages he saw all around him, the childless marriages and the "mental and nervous wrecks" who could not fulfill the procreative promises of the marriage tie.[52] "Sexual maladjustment" was allegedly at the root of this failure, and the blame was placed mostly on women like Mary, who in some cases needed surgical treatment – Popenoe believed – to make them more "ardent."[53] These collapsed marriages stoked fears of "race suicide," the overcoming of white birthrates by people of "inferior," "darker" strains of blood.[54] But for Popenoe and his collaborators, the problem was also internal, and education itself was partly to blame: "Many a college girl of the finest innate qualities, who sincerely desires to enter matrimony, is unable to find a husband of her own class, simply because she has been rendered so cold and unattractive, so overstuffed intellectually and starved emotionally, that a typical man does not desire to spend the rest of his life in her company."[55] Mary's intellect – her *mind* coming out in her garden – her "curse of imagination" that makes her see animals destroying her garden also renders her marriage childless, the story implies, and leads to an estrangement from her husband.[56] However, it also implies more ironic possibilities to cure the eugenic problems on which the failure of the marriage seems to lie.

The eugenic link between gardening and marriage is first established during the nighttime hunts that Mary and Harry enjoy when they destroy the slugs and snails that prey on their plants. The ideal of vegetation is involved in a competition for existence. This hunting develops into Harry's quest to destroy the cat that threatens Mary's quail – a quest that takes an ironic twist. Refusing to set poison for the cat and intending merely to scare it away with his air gun, Harry turns his fire on the white quail instead, saying to himself that he only meant to frighten it but shooting it dead in its tracks. Driven from the loneliness of the domestic sphere into the wilderness beyond the garden in search of a white animal to destroy, Harry's quest for the white quail might call to mind another literary quest for a somewhat larger white animal – not quail but *whale*, the parallel underscored by the homophonic pun.[57] That the quail symbolizes "utter purity" for Mary thus redoubles in significance in light of Herman Melville's novel. Here is D. H. Lawrence's interpretation of *Moby-Dick* (1851) in *Studies in Classic American Literature* (1923):

> What then is Moby Dick? He is the deepest blood-being of the white race; he is our deepest blood-nature.
>
> And he is hunted, hunted, hunted by the maniacal fanaticism of our white mental consciousness. We want to hunt him down. To subject him to our will. And in this maniacal conscious hunt of ourselves we get dark

> races and pale to help us, red, yellow, and black, east and west, Quaker and fire-worshipper, we get them all to help us in this ghastly maniacal hunt which is our doom and our suicide.
>
> The last phallic being of the white man. Hunted into the death of upper consciousness and the ideal will. Our blood-self subjected to our will. Our blood-consciousness sapped by a parasitic mental or ideal consciousness.[58]

Harry – locked out of the bedroom – is attempting to reestablish his own phallic masculinity, though the hunt is a lonely one in Steinbeck's version. The position of the quail in Mary's imagination perfectly stages this clash between blood (whiteness) and a desire for the ideal (purity). The racial valences of the whiteness of the quail become clearer still when we realize its role as the state bird of California (chosen as such in 1931, a few years before Steinbeck's story), the place where the eugenics movement, and its offshoot of marriage counseling, took such firm root. Always aware of the special scope and power of the short story, Steinbeck targets not the state of global capitalism and its racial hierarchies (the reading of *Moby-Dick* by Lawrence, and by C. L. R. James after him[59]) but something narrower even if pivotal to eugenic thinking: the idea, as we have seen Popenoe describe it, "to show that plants and animals obey the same laws of heredity, and that these laws are the ones which govern Homo Sapiens, as well." We can understand the white quail in Steinbeck's story, then, not simply as a symbol of the eugenics movement but as something deeper: the problem of symbolic identification itself. Harry wants to destroy "the thing she loved so much," the thing in which Mary locates her core of identity: "That white quail was *me*, the secret me that no one can ever get at, the me that's way inside," just as her garden "was herself."[60] The problem here is one of analogy. To link the human self so intensely to plants and animals is to use the kind of analogy that presupposes we can judge and encourage human betterment along the same principles of selective breeding that Gregor Mendel discovered in his sweet peas. The crucial irony of the story is that the attempt to think beyond our species – to enter a state of plant- or animal-mindedness – merely provokes the problematic racialized assumptions that divide the "weak" from the "strong."

To some extent, "The White Quail" turns this logic of eugenics on its head. Mary Teller's plant- and animal-based obsession with purity, located in her compulsive planning and thinking, turns her into the "frigid" woman targeted by the marriage counseling movement, thus exacerbating the very "race suicide" that eugenics sought to prevent. Of course, the woman character is still to blame in this critique, just as the man gets the quest narrative, his own "melodrama of beset manhood," to use Nina Baym's relevant phrase.[61] But on a deeper level, the symbolic patterning of "The White Quail" – and the way that it uses the truncated form of the short story to realign a larger mythology of race within the literary imagination, located in Melville's *Moby-Dick* and elsewhere – returns us to the maniacal sickness within the idea of whiteness.[62] The fate of the white quail, like that of the white whale, signals the doom of a white day.

Coda: The "Grapes" of Wrath

Both "The Chrysanthemums" and "The White Quail" reveal how Steinbeck's minute focus on vegetable life raises larger philosophical and political questions about the nature, fate, and limits of our humanness, and about the networking of plant life into realms of scientific (eugenic) control and industrial production in the context of what Allison Carruth calls America's burgeoning "food power" at mid-century.[63] We have already seen Steinbeck's interest in human-plant connections in *To a God Unknown* and we will see it again, of course, in *The Grapes of Wrath* (1939): "Can you live without the willow tree? Well, no, you can't. The willow tree is you."[64] It is worth pausing for a moment on the opening chapter of *Grapes* because it helps us to understand the nature and the limits of Steinbeck's attempt to see things from the plant's point of view, an attempt that has generated some of the severest critiques of the novel – for example, Michael Denning's claim that it reduces the political and economic causes of the Great Depression to the terms of natural history.[65] Steinbeck writes:

> To the red country and part of the gray country of Oklahoma, the last rains came gently, and they did not cut the scarred earth. The plows crossed and recrossed the rivulet marks. The last rains lifted the corn quickly and scattered weed colonies and grass along the sides of the roads so that the gray country and the dark red country began to disappear under a green cover. In the last part of May the sky grew pale and the clouds that had hung in high puffs for so long in the spring were dissipated. The sun flared down on the growing corn day after day until a line of brown spread along the edge of each green bayonet. The clouds appeared, and went away, and in a while they did not try any more. The weeds grew darker green to protect themselves, and they did not spread any more. The surface of the earth crusted, a thin hard crust, and as the sky became pale, so the earth became pale, pink in the red country and white in the gray country.[66]

Critics have tended to view such descriptions as acts of personification (or anthropomorphism) in which weather patterns, plants, and earth are inscribed with agency and intention.[67] At such moments the human seems deeply recessed, invisible except for that single reference to the plow working with disastrous consequences against the natural direction of the land. If the reference to the plow makes us think of Pare Lorentz's documentary *The Plow That Broke the Plains* (1936) – the first film the US government produced for commercial distribution – then we see how the "bayonet" of corn links plant life to an increasingly globalized and unstable industrial world order responsible for over-farming the land to the point of collapse (Lorentz's documentary juxtaposed through montage the military machines of the Great War and the mechanized farming of the land). But the slightness of Steinbeck's reference is really the point: we are not – at this point in the novel at least – in the realm of theory about the state of the globe. Echoing the attention to minor forms of life in Steinbeck's short stories, the eye is drawn instead to the small and the marginalized: the *partial*, the *gentle*, the *pale*, the *thin*, the *sides* of the road, the *edges* of the leaves of corn. The language of the small and the marginal returns in the second paragraph:

> In the water-cut gullies the earth dusted down in dry little streams. Gophers and ant lions started small avalanches. And as the sharp sun struck day after day, the leaves of the young corn became less stiff and erect; they bent in a curve at first, and then, as the central ribs of strength grew weak, each leaf tilted downward. Then it was June, and the sun shone more fiercely. The brown lines on the corn leaves widened and moved in on the central ribs. The weeds frayed and edged back toward their roots. The air was thin and the sky more pale; and every day the earth paled.[68]

Again, this is an environment of the pale and the thin in which edges are the center of attention. We are down at the level of ant lions and gophers, from where we see the plant in a primary position of subjective distress. As we glimpsed in Chapter 2, Roy Stryker and the photographic branch of the Resettlement Administration likewise sought to illustrate the impact of drought through photographs such as Arthur Rothstein's images of "Corn suffering from drought" from August 1935 (Figure 5.3), with their ground-level upward view toward wilting corn against a backdrop of high clouds. Stryker viewed his documentary photography as the momentary revelation of a "fleeting face" that could expand to reveal a larger truth and narrative about humanity's relationship with the land.[69] The "faces" presented to us at the beginning of *Grapes* and in Stryker's photograph are those of plant life rather than humanity. The striking parallels between Stryker's images of suffering corn and Dorothea Lange's later image, "Wife of a migratory laborer with three children" from June 1938 (Figure 5.4) suggest that the gesture of the human was *following* that of the plant, rather than vice versa. (Lange and Paul Taylor would likewise talk of "human erosion," the human

Figure 5.3 Arthur Rothstein, "Corn suffering from drought, Arkansas," August 1935. Library of Congress, Prints & Photographs Division, FSA/OWI Collection, LC-DIG-fsa-8b26767.

Figure 5.4 Dorothea Lange, "Wife of a migratory laborer with three children. Near Childress, Texas. Nettie Featherston," June 1938. Library of Congress, Prints & Photographs Division, FSA/OWI Collection, LC-DIG-fsa-8b32434.

again echoing the fate of the land.[70]) Such images predict Steinbeck's intense focus on the plant's melodramatic gesture of crisis and decline, a felt suffering of the corn itself. Drought is seen primarily through its impact on the vegetable world, before the human enters the picture.

In Steinbeck, as in Rothstein, we detect a biocentric awareness that seems squarely in a tradition of ecological writing about drought pioneered in Mary Austin's book about the Southwest *The Land of Little Rain* (1903), which we encountered in Chapter 2. Like Steinbeck after her, Austin was concerned primarily with edges, borders, in-between spaces, wastes, and small events as she sought to liberate her readers from the entrapment of "man-height" (Austin's point is that one must get down very low or up very high to recognize the presence of water in the land of little rain).[71] Again predicting Steinbeck, Austin sought to decenter human agency through an absorption in the land itself, although Austin's ecofeminist perspective becomes, in Steinbeck's version, a lack of implicitly masculine virility (the young corn becomes "less stiff and erect"). We have seen in Steinbeck's short stories how the relationship between humans and plants is intertwined with questions of human sexuality and reproduction. But if, in important ways, the human-plant connection displaces or supersedes such political concerns in the stories, then in *Grapes* – perhaps because of the narrative demands of the novel versus those of the short story – the opposite seems true. To a degree, human characters in *Grapes* are plant-like: they grow from the land; they have a primal need to be rooted in the soil. Hence in the first chapter we are presented with humans emerging from the barren ground: "a walking man lifted a thin layer as high as his waist."[72] There is no abnegation of the human here, as we might find in Austin's vision of the land of little rain.

The photographs of the Resettlement Administration may have pointed to the intellectual and cultural poverty on the Great Plains, the lack of educational and recreational opportunity and its dire impact on children.[73] But here, at the end of Steinbeck's first chapter, we encounter the reemergence of play, of normalcy in childhood behavior and relations. Children begin drawing figures in the dust, manipulating the dirt beneath them, as the faces of the men emerge from bemused perplexity to become "hard and angry and resistant." The grasping of little tools of sticks and rocks by the children, sitting on the verge of a domestic space divided into male and female labor, is reflected at the very end of the chapter, as the play of the children is taken up by the men: "The men sat in the doorways of their houses; their hands were busy with sticks and little rocks. The men sat still – thinking – figuring."[74] As the sun emerges from the dust, so too does the activity of expression and human imposition on the land. "Figuring" is statistical (just as documentaries like *The Plow That Broke the Plains* turned to statistics to justify government-planned resettlement of populations); it is a process of folk wisdom ("figger" is the phrase for this throughout the novel); and it is also inherently metaphorical, a promise of the figuration of language itself to move people into action.[75] We see the power of men specifically to emerge from ecological catastrophe, to dust themselves off and reimpose themselves as historical agents by writing with sticks in the ground.

At the beginning of *Grapes*, we become aware of drought through the life of plants, and plants remain the objects of occasional attention throughout. In chapter twenty-five, for example, we return to the world of scientific, eugenic manipulation of vegetation that occupies Steinbeck in "The Chrysanthemums" and "The White Quail." The plants of California agriculture are victims of men who operate like surgeons to increase fertility and eradicate disease. But the experimentation that Steinbeck attempts within the limited space of his short stories – the possibilities they describe of a plant-like consciousness – becomes a more familiar act of personification in Steinbeck's great novel. Accordingly, critics have pointed to the sexualized landscape in *Grapes*, seen in the "rape" of the environment through plowing and over-farming,[76] and in the theme of restoring male generative power through the female "body" of the land.[77] If plants are the victims of a crime in "The Chrysanthemums," then the victims shift in *Grapes* from the outsized, rotting fruit to the children dying of pellagra "because a profit cannot be taken from an orange." "Figgering" is again paramount, both in the sense that economic failure is the primary cause of the catastrophe and in the sense that the vegetable becomes primarily a figure for something else. The desire to eat vegetables in *Grapes* is not an existential question, as it was for Steinbeck in the military gardens where we began, but a physiological problem of need, an actual physical hunger. Hence plants become the tools of social power rather than the medium of altered consciousness. They are internalized as a metaphor for emergent human action: "In the souls of the people the grapes of wrath are filling and growing heavy, growing heavy for the vintage."[78] As we will see when we turn to *Grapes* in Chapter 7, however, the precise direction of that movement and what it means for the nature of humans are anything but certain.

CHAPTER 6

On Not Being a Modernist: Disability and Performance in Of Mice and Men

Steinbeck's short novel *Of Mice and Men* (1937) has always attracted public attention. A staple of California middle-school education today, the book has had an unusually close relationship to state institutions. Until recently, the state of Texas defined "that level and degree of mental retardation at which a consensus of Texas citizens would agree that a person should be exempted from the death penalty" according to the so-called Lennie standard.[1] Formulated in 2004 by Judge Cathy Cochran – a Californian who grew up loving the work of Steinbeck – the Lennie standard is a series of mental capacities (or rather, deficits) based on the character of Lennie Small in *Of Mice and Men*, the mentally disabled figure who accidently kills a woman and is euthanized by Lennie's friend George, presumably to save him from harsher punishment by others.[2] Lennie should be exempt from the death penalty, Cochran argued, because of his "lack of reasoning ability and adaptive skills."[3] Cochran's opinion has been criticized for basing its standards for exemption on "someone with moderate to severe intellectual disabilities,"[4] and for turning to a fictional character rather than to medical science in making real decisions about life and death. Yet Cochran's opinion also highlights a crucial question concerning disability itself: to what extent should disability be considered a physical reality, located in the person, or a social construct dependent on the discourses through which it is understood and defined against purportedly normative states? Because of its social influence (in Texas and in the classroom), *Of Mice and Men* lies like few other texts at the intersection of the discursive and the social in its representation of disability. It motivates decisions even as it complicates them (for example, it is unclear from Steinbeck's novel whether Lennie would meet his own standard).[5] The peculiar form of *Of Mice and Men* embodies a series of intriguing problems regarding what I term the "reach" of the literary into the social. Its experimental techniques ask us to think about the relationship between the novel and what Steinbeck called "physical contact with other people."[6] These techniques also help us reconsider the fraught question of Steinbeck's aesthetic value, how we judge and understand the quality of his work, which has always suffered from beliefs that there is – as Edmund Wilson once said – something "artistically bad" about it.[7]

Centered on Lennie, the mentally disabled figure, *Of Mice and Men* also resonates with modernism's fascination with developmentally challenged characters such as Benjy in William Faulkner's *The Sound and the Fury* (1929) or the parade of apparently disabled figures that threads through the work of Samuel Beckett. The formal difficulty of works such as *The Sound and the Fury*, critics have argued, can be understood as an effort to produce the intellectual distinction of their readers both through and against constructions of the un-intelligent.[8] Or in the case of Beckett, the very mark of the modernism of plays such as *Waiting for Godot* (1953) and *Endgame* (1957) returns to what Ato Quayson calls an "aesthetic nervousness" regarding the disability of their characters.[9] The "hermeneutical impasse" of these works – the resistance to mimesis, the fracturing in the representational surface, or what other critics call Beckett's existential phenomenology and deconstructive humanism – emerge from an incapacity to bring the pain of disability into the literary realm.[10] Such modernist difficulty could not be further from the feel of *Of Mice and Men*, a book that Steinbeck described as a "little study in humility," a book initially intended for children:

> I want to recreate a child's world, not of fairies and giants but of colors more clear than they are to adults, of tastes more sharp and of the queer heartbreaking feelings that overwhelm children in a moment. I want to put down the way "afternoon felt" and of the feeling about a bird that sang in a tree in the evening. . . . You have to be very honest and very humble to write for children. And you have to remember that children aren't gay.[11]

At the core of *Of Mice and Men* lies this juvenile conception of an aesthetic that seems the inverse of modernist difficulty, negativity, or self-reflexivity. Indeed, it seems decidedly "low," even *kitsch* in its desire for immediate, unimpeded, and un-ironic access to a world of pure feeling, unadulterated beauty, and libidinal energy.[12] Lennie as mentally disabled figure thus exists not in an ironic relationship to the novel's discourse – as in the case of Faulkner's Benjy – but rather as a figure for the book's initial intended audience (like Steinbeck's view of the child, Lennie is also overwhelmed by the desire to feel). If only he could read, Lennie would be the book's ideal reader. The form of *Of Mice and Men*, unlike that of high modernist texts, is not then part of a reaction against disability. The novel's plot finally deals with, rather than nervously avoids, Lennie's own "defectiveness": it faces the problem and shoots it in the head. This resolute ending suggests the generic borders of Steinbeck's book, its purported naturalism and its reformist intentions (in a passing reference to *Of Mice and Men,* Quayson aligns it with works in which "disability is used as a pointed critique of social hypocrisy and indeed of social institutions as such").[13] But there is also a quality in the novel that "defies analysis," as one critic puts it.[14] In uncanny ways, the ontology of the book (what *is* it, precisely?), its curiously curtailed state – its aesthetic "badness," if you will – responds to weakness, failure, and disability in ways that offer an experimental alternative to high modernist techniques. As I hope to convince the reader, the book is formally fascinating in its failures.

Initial responses to the novel recognized its simplicity. "It is a plot upon which the characterizations and story are laid as effectively as flesh upon bone," wrote one reviewer, recognizing a sparseness that defines the mood and the style of the work.[15] For Dorothea Brande Collins, writing in the *American Review* in April 1937, this elemental quality creates a peculiar effect for the "simple type of reader" who feels, "when he discovers that he has foreseen correctly any movement of a story, a kind of participation in the creative act of the author." Predicting Judge Cochran's confusion over fiction and reality, the novel seemed to be seducing its readers, co-opting them into its point of view. Collins associated this obvious pattern of foreshadowing in *Of Mice and Men* with the book's aesthetic faltering: "Steinbeck's work puts the average pulp writer to shame."[16] Such judgments of aesthetic limitation surface too in suggestions that the novel looks back to naturalism, that it has not fully grown up in terms of literary history. The language of "weakness" that runs through *Of Mice and Men* certainly connects to the logic of social Darwinism that inflects literary naturalism, and particularly to the eugenics movement that surrounded Steinbeck as a student at Stanford University. Stanford was the center of intelligence testing under the guidance of Professor Lewis Terman, who was particularly interested in the education of children by testing them and thereby ranking them in terms of intelligence.[17] To a significant degree, the assumptions of eugenics seem built into the structure of *Of Mice and Men.*

What Steinbeck called the book's limitation or "littleness" lies in its almost obsessive return to a narrow series of ethical questions about how to treat the socially marginalized. The key character here, in typically Steinbeckian fashion, is a dog: the old, gray, blind, moth-eaten "dragfooted sheepdog" that belongs to Candy, himself a disabled old man who is reduced to "swampin'" (mopping up) because he has lost a hand.[18] The degree of attention the novel pays to Candy's dog is the structural equivalent of the "greater clarity" that Steinbeck associated with writing for children. Like Candy's mopping, the book clears a space for the debate over whether it would be merciful to put the suffering dog out of its misery. Indeed, Steinbeck quite literally opens a space, an "offstage" space (more about this later) where the shooting is performed following a long moment of delay in which the characters' nervous shuffling scripts our ethical assent to the inevitability of the intervention. Again, we have that feeling of participation, as if – through this pause – we are being brought into the discursive construction of who has the right to live. We are being swayed by a deterministic escalation of events that lays the groundwork for the final scene and the necessity of Lennie's death.

Or are we? Judge Cochran certainly did not think so. The novel's sentimental treatment of Lennie's desire for friendship and happiness limits its naturalistic brutality, which perhaps explains why it led to confused reactions from its early readers. It will "appeal to sentimental cynics, cynical sentimentalists," wrote one reader; it is a "triumph of the sentimental macabre," wrote another.[19] Such confused reactions to the novel's tone suggest that the "weakness" in *Of Mice and Men* lies as much in its form as in its themes, a form that complicates the various ideas and theories the book strives to express. Steinbeck was not averse to strong theory: prior to *Of Mice and Men*, he published his brutal strike novel *In Dubious Battle* (1936), which offers his most sustained theory of the phalanx, his holistic theory of group behavior that explains the urge toward collective action and the basis of worker protest in the novel. But the theory offered in *Of Mice and Men* is – to follow recent scholarship in modernist studies – decidedly *weak*: its humility, or modesty, is an apparent refusal to round out its interventions or to amplify their implications.[20]

Formal Limitations

For an example of weak theory, take the book's relationship to the labor question. As "bindle stiffs,"[21] Lennie and George would have been recognizable social types (Figure 6.1), members of the itinerant labor force that emerged to harvest crops along the grain belt at the turn of the century, and that spread to Western states to work in irregular, low-paid, and harsh conditions in California's "factories in the fields."[22] And in the somewhat slapstick nature of their interaction, particularly in the first chapter of the novel (when the two characters first appear, Lennie nearly runs over George when the latter stops short), Lennie and George owe something

Figure 6.1 Dorothea·Lange, "Napa Valley, California. More than twenty-five years a bindle-stiff. Walks from the mines to the lumber camps to the farms," December 1938. Library of Congress, Prints & Photographs Division, FSA/OWI Collection, LC-DIG-fsa-8b32870.

to Charlie Chaplin's tramp – a figure who appears in movies such as *Modern Times* (1936), where he is literally caught up in the machine production of Henry Ford's America, desperately trying to preserve his humanity amid the forces of alienation.[23] To some extent, Lennie and George are studies in alienation: Lennie's uncontrollable desire to fondle soft things seems part of a basic need to get in touch with his own hands, just as the working characters are reduced to mere "hands" on the ranch (the fact that Candy is missing one of his hands places him at the bottom of the scale of laborers).[24] When Steinbeck first introduces Lennie, we are told that his "arms did not swing at his sides, but hung loosely,"[25] but then Steinbeck removes the following lines (the only strikeout from the first typesetting of the first edition, published by Covici-Friede; the entire page had to be reset): "and only moved because the heavy hands were pendula."[26] Steinbeck did not want Lennie to be a *mere* machine, unable to determine his life and destiny and to direct his own actions. But from the opposite perspective, neither did Steinbeck want his characters to be too aware of their own victimization, or too class conscious (the workers on the ranch, unlike the characters in *In Dubious Battle*, are a long way from labor organization). George is full of anger at the harsh treatment they receive. "Guys like us," he recognizes, "that work on ranches, are the loneliest guys in the world" because of their situation of constant displacement and social precarity.[27] Yet George's consciousness of their class situation becomes scripted and directed in formulaic ways precisely because of his relationship with the mentally disabled Lennie. George's class consciousness becomes trapped in a feedback loop, caused by Lennie's inability to fully remember their shared vision, which necessitates George's retelling of their codependency ("*I got you to look after me, and you got me to look after you*") and dream of living "*off the fatta the lan'*."[28] In other words, the disability narrative – the recursive need to care for Lennie, to respond to his need for a future vision of stability – disables the narrative of awakening class consciousness or a theory of their situation, which remains only weakly formulated. In a similar way, characters such as the one-handed Candy and the hunchbacked Crooks seem too weak to emerge into social action. In an interview with the *New York Times*, Steinbeck claimed that Lennie was based on a real person, someone who killed a ranch foreman.[29] If the story originates in this moment of labor violence, then it becomes displaced, from the foreman to the wife of the ranch owner's son, in *Of Mice and Men*. As critics at the time realized, the novel falls short of being a tale about the class struggle because of what Edmund Wilson called its "non-political point of view."[30] The obvious sentimentalism of Steinbeck's novel – centered on Lennie as a figure of pure feeling – resonates with Ann Douglas's understanding of sentimentalism as a conservative mode: feelings emerge in place of recognition of the structures of social power.[31] In these ways, *Of Mice and Men* never quite becomes a book about class or poverty.

If the themes in *Of Mice and Men* are unable to develop fully, then the same can be said of its characters. Enter Curley's Wife, a character without even a full name who nevertheless is the major force in the novel because of the tension and competition her presence creates among the men, and because she seems to motivate her own murder through her flirtation with Lennie when they are finally alone together. She seems to be a principle of dumbed-down femininity rather than a fictional person that the other characters or indeed we as readers might actually care about. What she represents makes other characters react so strongly and quickly to her and, indeed, makes them continue talking to her after she is dead, as if she matters merely for being sexualized flesh to be fondled and then brutally silenced.[32] The first major critical study of Steinbeck's work noted *Of Mice and Men*'s melodramatic qualities, its violence without tragedy, its lack of pathos.[33] Indeed, it seems to be a melodrama in a specifically American sense, what the feminist critic Nina Baym called a "melodrama of beset manhood," that classic dynamic in so many mainstream American texts in which women are the domesticators or entrappers and men are the complex, fraught victims, struggling to find their freedom.[34] (However, it would be difficult to argue, in line with Baym's thesis, that the male characters in Steinbeck's novel become "complex" through this struggle.) The novel hence fits into the mythological archetype that Leslie Fiedler – ironically Steinbeck's loudest critical antagonist – identifies in classic texts like Herman Melville's *Moby-Dick* (1851) and Mark Twain's *Adventures of Huckleberry Finn* (1885): a situation in which an interracial, homosocial male bond is formed in reaction to the threat of feminized domesticity.[35] Fiedler's harsh criticism of Steinbeck, as we may recall from the Introduction to this book, is that his major works like *The Grapes of Wrath* do not treat the Black-white racial relationship that Fiedler sees driving the mythic infrastructure of American "masterworks." *Of Mice and Men* is very much an exception to this rule since it features what one critic calls Steinbeck's only fully fleshed Black character: the "negro stable buck," Crooks.[36]

According to the African American writer Charles R. Johnson, the novel presents, through Crooks, "a strong and influential indictment of racial segregation, for which Steinbeck is still praised today, and rightly so."[37] It is fairer to say that the novel represents a weak indictment, or at least a highly delimited one. Crooks focalizes many of the central themes of the book: like Candy he is physically disabled (he has a crooked back), and like the other male characters he is a figure of loneliness – indeed, a redoubled loneliness since he is isolated from his own racial community as well as segregated from the white world. Crooks is also the novel's figure of intelligence (Johnson calls him a "victim-savant") and of literacy.[38] He lives in his books and hence is a kind of double for the author; he is versed in the laws of California (he possesses a copy of the California Civil Code of 1905, which would have granted him equal rights of accommodation before the law); and he is forceful in articulating his rights to privacy.[39] A master of irony and sarcasm, Crooks is also aware of his victimization and is the strongest critic of the ideology of success and the delusions of future stability that drive the other characters. As a figure of intelligence, Crooks highlights the generically white characters as figures of low intelligence even as his racial identity becomes an ultimate limitation when Curley's Wife threatens to have him lynched in a moment that disrupts the formation of an interracial male bond: "Crooks had reduced himself to nothing. There was no personality, no ego – nothing to arouse either like or dislike. He said, 'Yes, ma'am,' and his voice was toneless."[40] Crooks is silenced in the discourse as well as in the story; any protest at segregation – whether by Crooks himself or the novel itself – can only go so far. The other male characters may lack Crooks's intelligence and his ability to perform, but his self-erasure merely stages their whiteness as natural and normative. Even so, their white identity still has its limitations, based as it is on a core impoverishment that cannot be disguised.

Whiteness might be normative in the novel though even this norm is marginal at best, given the disabilities of the characters. Disability thus operates along a spectrum, with Lennie's inability to control his actions lying at the extreme (eugenic thinking about intelligence noted that among "those classed as normal, vast individual differences have been found to exist in original mental endowment").[41] At the top of the grade, and an apparent exception to the disabled norms of whiteness in the novel, lies the character Slim:

> He held a crushed Stetson hat under his arm while he combed his long, black, damp hair straight back. Like the others he wore blue jeans and a short denim jacket. When he had finished combing his hair he moved into the room, and he moved with a majesty only achieved by royalty and master craftsmen. He was a jerkline skinner, the prince of the ranch, capable of driving ten, sixteen, even twenty mules with a single line to the leaders. He was capable of killing a fly on the wheeler's butt with a bull whip without touching the mule. There was a gravity in his manner and a quiet so profound that all talk stopped when he spoke. His authority was so great that his word was taken on any subject, be it politics or love. This was Slim, the jerkline skinner. His hatchet face was ageless. He might have been thirty-five or fifty. His ear heard more than was said to him, and his slow speech had overtones not of thought, but of understanding beyond thought. His hands, large and lean, were as delicate in their action as those of a temple dancer.[42]

Within this world of seriousness, this world of anguish, loneliness, and cruelty, we encounter a gravity that fails, a moment of characterization so exaggerated and aestheticized that it is difficult not to read it as just a little camp. In her "Notes on 'Camp,'" Susan Sontag famously dismissed work like Steinbeck's (she was referring to Sherwood Anderson's *Winesburg, Ohio* [1919] in particular) as "bad to the point of being laughable" because of its dogged pretentiousness and lack of fantasy.[43] But at this point in *Of Mice and Men*, almost out of nowhere, emerges a figure who is shockingly different and interesting, a figure who exudes codes of identity that – echoing what Slim hears and says himself – are very much off-script and outside of the novel's depressed vision. Rather, like Sontag's idea of naïve or pure camp, we have a character (Sontag calls it "instant character") who is meant in seriousness but is simply "too much."[44] Slim is all stylization and sensuous surface, a figure of flamboyant, theatricalized experience whose aestheticized self is akin to the androgynous, slim, flowing figures in which Sontag locates the campness of pre-Raphaelite painting and Art Nouveau posters.[45] If Slim sits atop a ranking of white masculinity, then his role is to queer the norm with his intensely exaggerated performance.[46]

The hobo jungle, which is the location for the opening and closing scenes of the book, was a space that sustained queer relationships beyond the norms of society. One of the first studies of itinerant life in the United States, Josiah Flynt's proto-anthropological *Tramping With Tramps* (1899), observed the implicitly queer ways that older tramps would "peetrify" young boys into becoming their slaves through carefully told tales that made dreams and adventures seem seductively real.[47] This is of course precisely the dynamic within Lennie and George's dyadic relationship. George seems to control Lennie with hypnotic stories about having a self-sufficient home in which Lennie can tend his rabbits – a little house in which they will have "a room to ourself" rather than separate rooms to themselves.[48] Steinbeck had explored a dyadic male pairing in *In Dubious Battle*. But without the strong social politics of that novel, in which Mac and Jim merge together as part of a politicized collective, the adhesive nature of Lennie and George's relationship seems weakly theorized and thus quietly resonant with sexual explanations, as the other characters suggest in their curious reactions to the relationship.[49]

Placing *Of Mice and Men* in the context of the novel *Waste Heritage* (1939) by the Canadian writer Irene Baird and other counter-narratives from the 1930s, Caren Irr argues that Steinbeck's novel offers a "brief glimpse of an all-male utopia" of affective bonds, one that resists the capitalist ideology of competition by its intimation of "non-productive sexuality," even as the proto-queerness of George and Lennie's relationship places it beyond the book's envisioned possibilities.[50] Yet the trope of queerness in *Of Mice and Men* is ongoing, as is clear at the end of the novel, after George shoots Lennie and is consoled by Slim:

> Slim twitched George's elbow. "Come on, George. Me an' you'll go in an' get a drink."
>
> George let himself be helped to his feet. "Yeah, a drink."
>
> Slim said, "You hadda, George. I swear you hadda. Come on with me." He led George into the entrance of the trail and up toward the highway.
>
> Curley and Carlson looked after them. And Carlson said, "Now, what the hell ya suppose is eatin' them two guys?"[51]

The curious effect of reading Steinbeck is to be in two very different worlds at once. The simplistic dialogue, the purely behaviorist situation of external action embeds us in naturalism's plot to establish the necessity of dealing with Lennie's disability. But within this establishment of norms lies a relationship between men that cannot quite be comprehended or spoken into being, a potentially queer relationship that seems if anything performative.[52] Identities are flipped (here George becomes the passive figure to be led around by Slim the feminized "temple dancer") and relationships seem inherently stagey: as Wilson pointed out in his early overview of Steinbeck, he produces characters with stagey self-consciousness, leaving them like "actors giving very conscientious performances in a fairly well-written play."[53] We cannot quite reclaim moments such as these as camp; the theatricalization of experience here is not flamboyant but, for want of a better word, *wooden.* Codes of melodrama, sentimentality, and naturalist determinism (all compounded in that single phrase, "you hadda") frustrate the reach into the social world that would be necessary to secure our belief in the novel's claims to demarcate norms. What we are feeling here is not just the aesthetic mediocrity that Wilson detects in his reference to a *fairly* well-written play but another in-between state that helps us to understand the curious effect of Steinbeck's book.

Playing with the Novel

Which is to say, *Of Mice and Men* isn't quite a book – or at least, not fully a novel. Steinbeck conceived it as a novel-to-be-played, a play "in the physical technique of the novel."[54] Believing that the novel was dying as a form, and responding to a "waking up" he saw in the theater, Steinbeck described *Of Mice and Men* as an experiment in "a new dramatic form."[55] He believed that employing the form of the novel would make the play easy to read by avoiding awkward and interrupting stage directions and would enable a more vivid picture of scene and characters for the reader/audience, in effect using the novel to fuse a tone into the play as a single, and highly focused, entity. The novel was first performed as a play in a workers' theater, the Theater Union of San Francisco, to support maritime workers in their fight for unionization; the players created their own script from the novel, with Steinbeck reading it aloud to them.[56] Describing the play-as-novel, Steinbeck wrote: "the recent tendency of writers has been to deal in those themes and those scenes which are best understood and appreciated by groups of people." Certain things "cannot be understood in solitude. . . . [T]he thing that is missing is the close, almost physical contact with other people."[57] The curious form of the book, the way that it looks toward a performed collectivity, resonates with its story of lonely individuals in search of affective connection. There is an affect and a politics to the form itself, a search for solidarity that inflects the novel in its emphasis on live performativity.

Here Steinbeck was in good company. Writing against the conventional wisdom that the interiority and aestheticism of the modern novel were born from the failure of writers like Henry James to succeed in the theater, David Kurnick has detected the continuation of the desire for a palpable relation to an embodied public in works supposedly reacting against mass culture.[58] Kurnick is interested in a kind of "high" failure, in which the novel's frustrated desire to be theater – Kurnick calls it a "melancholy of generic distinction" – becomes a "vocationalized" form of failure that lends aesthetic value to powerlessness, marginality, and alienation from an embodied audience.[59] Where Steinbeck is concerned, readers responded with a somewhat different set of aesthetic reactions, noting another kind of failure. The *New York Times* considered the character of Lennie to be improbable,[60] while another critic observed "moments when the tension and brevity of the story make it read like a theatrical script."[61] The critic Mark Van Doren went into more detail: "All is extreme here; everybody is a doll; and, if there is a kick in the story, it is given us from some source which we cannot see, as when a goose walks over our grave, or as when in the middle of the night the telephone rings sharply, and it is the wrong number."[62] Reactions to the implicit theatricality of *Of Mice and Men* were bound up in judgments about its weakness as a work of art.

Rather than the tense, ontological yearning to be something it is not, which Kurnick detects in the modern novels he analyses, *Of Mice and Men* is curiously at home in two worlds simultaneously. Hence the book is divided into six tightly focused scenes (not categorized as chapters) that are simple, sparse, contained, and inherently stage-able, with each scene beginning with a description of how it should look as enclosed space. The novel even has an off-stage space from which voices can emerge, and from which sounds of the shot that kills Candy's dog (a rehearsal for

Lennie's shooting) ring out in a scene that is dramatic in all senses of that word. The novel had an uncanny effect on its readers because of its ontological duality, as if it is two bodies in a single being, thus again formally replicating an aspect of the story: the duality within Lennie and George's co-dependent relationship. Hence Van Doren describes a feeling of being haunted by a controlling force in the "wings" of the novel – another acknowledgment of its saturated determinism but also a recognition of how the work feels wrong as a novel. It has a power to jar us out of ourselves, Van Doren implies, as if we do not quite belong in the world we are experiencing in the act of reading, or that like a ghost we are living in two worlds at once.

The book begins with a typically Steinbeckian description of the Salinas Valley, in which the environment and its flora and fauna are balanced by a narrative voice with omniscient vision and a level of expertise that allows the detection of differences between dog tracks and deer tracks. But then the realism transforms into something else:

> There is a path through the willows and among the sycamores, a path beaten hard by boys coming down from the ranches to swim in the deep pool, and beaten hard by tramps who come wearily down from the highway in the evening to jungle-up near water. In front of the low horizontal limb of a giant sycamore tree there is an ash pile made by many fires; the limb is worn smooth by men who have sat on it.[63]

Two registers are present simultaneously. We have the history of how the path became that way, which reveals the omniscient knowledge of the narrator. But then we also hear the ghostly voice of a playwright or stage manager, presenting to us in real present time how the scene should look: "There is a path," "there is an ash pile" – these are more like descriptions of how the sparse stage should be arranged. The phrase "the limb is worn smooth by men who have sat on it" again combines that present-time description of how the stage should look and the broader sense of the history of its condition as realistic object. Another example is the description of the story's central location:

> The bunk house was a long, rectangular building. Inside, the walls were whitewashed and the floor unpainted. In three walls there were small, square windows, and in the fourth, a solid door with a wooden latch. Against the walls were eight bunks, five of them made up with blankets and the other three showing their burlap ticking. Over each bunk there was nailed an apple box with the opening forward so that it made two shelves for the personal belongings of the occupant of the bunk. And these shelves were loaded with little articles, soap and talcum powder, razors and those

> Western magazines ranch men love to read and scoff at and secretly believe. And there were medicines on the shelves, and little vials, combs; and from nails on the box sides, a few neckties. Near one wall there was a black cast-iron stove, its stovepipe going straight up through the ceiling. In the middle of the room stood a big square table littered with playing cards, and around it were grouped boxes for the players to sit on.[64]

Here we have a description of the bunkhouse in the novel and simultaneously a description of how the stage set should look in the play. The three walls with square windows describe the realistic, room-like stage sets that became conventional by the end of the nineteenth century. The set description even references a "fourth wall" – here though not the fictional convention, the invisible wall that separates actors and audience into separate spheres, but a "real" wall with a door (a solid door, redoubling its realness). Steinbeck gestures toward theatrical conventions while frustrating them, creating a hybrid somewhere *between* novel and play, a space whose generic self-consciousness (the fourth wall) exposes the failure of the novel to translate easily into theater. But then the attention to detail in the passage only emphasizes that these are specific instructions for how the scene should look, with phrases like "a few neckties" serving as directions of quantity aimed at a stage manager and intended audience rather than a reader. By the time we arrive at the big square table at the end of the passage, we are perfectly in the hybrid world of novel and visualized play to the extent that "the players" could refer to both the fictionalized characters about to play a game of cards and the actors (or players) about to act this drama on the stage.

This doubleness defines *Of Mice and Men* and lies at the root of the uncanny qualities critics recognized in the book, the way it "defies analysis."[65] This doubleness places interpretation at a deep level of formal ontology based on transmediation. *Of Mice and Men* is a fictionalized version of reality but also the representation of a representation (the play) of reality. It wants to reach out into the world, but it is kept from that interaction. We are presented with realistically described objects but also props representing real objects. We see fictionalized spaces that are also sets. We encounter characters in terms of imaginary people who are also actors in a drama (their very names describe their physical appearance – Crooks has a crooked back, Curley has curly hair, Slim is thin – as if the names are made to help with the casting of the play). This generic hybridity thus works in two ways. The represented selves are at one level performative in their very being: there is no performer behind the performance in the sense that there is no purportedly "real" character behind the fictionalized version but instead a projection to an actor who will, at some future point, perform the part. This, I would suggest, is the source of the curious formal disability, or ghost-like effect, of the book. The characters are, with one or two exceptions, imagined as disabled in some physical or mental sense. But they are also disabled formally too. Through a combined performativity and resistance to performance, the characters remain impoverished and disconnected as representational objects, as well as socially in terms of the story. Like Lennie, they cannot develop fully but are held in abeyance.

This effect reaches a climax toward the very end of the book, after Lennie's murder of Curley's Wife, when George confronts Lennie in the space of the hobo jungle. Lennie is worried that George will give him hell, which sets into play their dialogue. "Give ya hell?" asks George:

> "Sure, like you always done before. Like 'If I di'n't have you I'd take my fifty bucks – '"
>
> "Jesus Christ, Lennie! You can't remember nothing that happens, but you remember ever' word I say."
>
> "Well, ain't you gonna say it?"
>
> George shook himself. He said woodenly, "If I was alone I could live so easy." His voice was monotonous, had no emphasis. "I could get a job an' not have no mess." He stopped.
>
> "Go on," said Lennie. "An' when the enda the month come – "
>
> "An' when the enda the month come I could take my fifty bucks an' go to a . . . . cat house . . . ." He stopped again.
>
> Lennie looked eagerly at him. "Go on, George. Ain't you gonna give me no more hell?"
>
> "No," said George.
>
> "Well, I can go away," said Lennie. "I'll go right off in the hills an' find a cave if you don' want me."
>
> George shook himself again. "No," he said. "I want you to stay with me here."
>
> Lennie said craftily – "Tell me like you done before."
>
> "Tell you what?"
>
> "'Bout the other guys an' about us."
>
> George said, "Guys like us got no fambly. They make a little stake an' then blow it in. They ain't got nobody in the worl' that gives a hoot in hell about 'em – "
>
> "*But not us,*" Lennie cried happily. "Tell about us now."
>
> George was quiet for a moment. "But not us," he said.
>
> "Because – "
>
> "Because I got you an' – "
>
> "An' I got you. We got each other, that's what, that gives a hoot in hell about us," Lennie cried in triumph.[66]

The sparse dialogue has the feel of an impoverished hollowness even though, for Lennie, this is the only reality he has. This is a moment too of beginning again, of repeating formulas from the start of the novel. The characters speak almost as if they are actors in a rehearsal, repeating and reading their lines. And they are lines that, in effect, mean nothing; there is no hope of some future community at this point in the novel. The characters are in effect waiting, filling the time with formulaic language, as voices are heard in the distance from the eerie "off-stage" space of the novel.

Weak Modernism

At moments like this, it is difficult not to recall two other tramps from the theater, Vladimir and Estragon in Samuel Beckett's 1953 play *Waiting for Godot*. It is possible that Beckett saw a version of the film *Of Mice and Men*, released as *Des souris et des hommes* in France in December 1946, just two years before Beckett began composing his play. There are several parallels between the two works. Steinbeck's book opens in the evening and introduces us to a path through the willows leading to a bare limb of an isolated sycamore tree; Beckett's play opens with a minimalist condensation of this scene: "A country road. A tree. Evening."[67] Steinbeck's novel and Beckett's play share similar themes of existential loneliness, homelessness, exile, and poverty, while other echoes from *Of Mice and Men* can be found across Beckett's oeuvre, for example Lousse's crippled dog in *Molloy*, the co-dependency of Hamm and Clov in *Endgame*, a play in which Clov echoes Lennie when he plans to kill a mouse. (Steinbeck would eventually come to admire Beckett; he lightheartedly planned to write "A Colloquy of Bugs," a conversation between two cockroaches, after seeing *Endgame*.[68]) As Leo Bersani and Ulysse Dutoit argue in *Arts of Impoverishment* (1993), Beckett's work explores failure as an aesthetic of impoverishment, one in which the artwork inhibits our movement toward it through its failure to express and signify (there is nothing to be learned), a failure to *be* an entity with subject matter – a failure that is inherent in the very writing of the work itself.[69] Ultimately, this failure returns to the minimalism of language, a "mobile mosaic of shifting positions and functions of nearly identical elements," one in which relations between words are destroyed just as unrelatedness is prioritized in the implied social world.[70] Quayson ties similar high modernist tropes – the contingency of language, structures of negation, and representational failure – more directly to Beckett's obsessive approach to human disability whose pain he cannot represent.[71] Steinbeck, as every middle-schooler knows, was not a modernist in a comparable sense. Thus, rather than presenting us with disability as hermeneutical impasse, Steinbeck gives us disability as compulsive action, a disability that is not elided but resolutely dealt with. Rather than the resistance to occasion or to narrative sequence that Bersani and Dutoit describe in Beckett, the plot in *Of Mice and Men* speeds us to its dramatic conclusion.

Yet what do we do with the fractured causality of that plot, its partial inability to explain itself? If *Waiting for Godot* is – as one critic quipped – a play in which nothing happens twice,[72] then Steinbeck's original title for *Of Mice and Men* was "Something That Happened,"[73] a title that describes what he would later call non-teleological thinking. Stuff *happens* in *Of Mice and Men*, in ways that it does not in *Godot*, as becomes clear near the end:

> "Go on," said Lennie. "How's it gonna be? We gonna get a little place."
> "We'll have a cow," said George. "An' we'll have maybe a pig an' chickens . . . . an' down the flat we'll have a . . . . little piece alfalfa – "
> "For the rabbits," Lennie shouted.
> "For the rabbits," George repeated.
> "And I get to tend the rabbits."
> "An' you get to tend the rabbits."
> Lennie giggled with happiness. "An' live on the fatta the lan'."
> "Yes."[74]

At one level, this is a moment of delay in the plot, as George moves Lennie into position before shooting him in the head. It is a pause that allows sentiment to flow before the melodramatic climax. But *within* this conventional moment (and this is what makes Steinbeck's novel so strange) lies something else, not unlike the kind of impoverishment that Bersani and Dutoit find in Beckett or the hermeneutic disability that Quayson detects. We are beginning again, again. George is "going on" even as the scripted dialogue circles back to the beginning of the book. The characters have gotten nowhere. What we confront, at this moment of waiting, is the minimalism of language, words sounding only in and for themselves,[75] a compressed almost tactile idiolect ("fatta the lan'") caught in repetitions because nothing can be said, or done, except to start again. The characters are imprisoned in repetitive situations of broken communication. Lennie giggles, despite having just killed a person, because he lives only within these repeated linguistic formulas, in the self-absorption of language itself.

Of Mice and Men approaches the modernist kind of failure that critics consider successful in Beckett, his desire to "fail better," as he put it.[76] But true to Steinbeck's book as a whole, there are limits to this argument. Enter a gigantic talking rabbit. If you don't believe me, it appears in the final chapter, after Lennie has killed Curley's Wife and just before George arrives to shoot Lennie in the head. At first, Aunt Clara (the character who raises Lennie) appears "out of Lennie's head" and berates him for not listening to George. And then this:

> Aunt Clara was gone, and from out of Lennie's head there came a gigantic rabbit. It sat on its haunches in front of him, and it waggled its ears and crinkled its nose at him. And it spoke in Lennie's voice too.
>
> "Tend rabbits," it said scornfully. "You crazy bastard. You ain't fit to lick the boots of no rabbit. You'd forget 'em and let 'em go hungry. That's what you'd do. An' then what would George think?"[77]

The conversation continues for almost a page, with Lennie arguing with the rabbit, which continues to taunt Lennie, not without good reason. After all, the rabbit has a point: Lennie would be an undoubted disaster at tending rabbits. He has already killed a pet mouse or two, a pet puppy, and a woman. If Lennie must confront this rabbit with its waggly ears and crinkly nose, so must we as readers because the rabbit presents us once again with questions of aesthetic quality, perhaps even more fundamental questions about the formal ontology of Steinbeck's book. What is going on? If we want to categorize Steinbeck's aesthetic at this moment – beyond the fact that it seems merely to be bad writing, or at least something deeply incongruous – we might turn to a category that was receiving contemporaneous attention in the writings of Walter Benjamin: the quality of *kitsch*.[78]

Lacking the irony of camp as a form of bad taste, kitsch – as Benjamin understood it – is centered on the object as a form of unadulterated aesthetic immediacy. It is a wallowing in sentiment that is also a regression to the libidinous gratification of childish perception and a submission to the laws of the symbolic order.[79] Rabbits have featured throughout Steinbeck's narrative as symbols of Lennie's desire for stability and domesticity, for freedom from wage labor by living off "the fatta the lan'" and feeding rabbits with alfalfa.[80] This, then, is a moment when the symbolic order steps in to gain a voice and to control the laws of the narrative. This moment of kitsch is also, in a curious but quite literal way, the embodiment of Lennie's disability. The "bad taste" of the moment is a performance of Lennie's childishness, his developmental limitation; we see his regressive fantasy take shape before our eyes almost as though Lennie has written this part of the play himself. As Winfried Menninghaus argues in his essay on kitsch, Benjamin "directly evokes the child's way of touching things at their 'not always seemliest' spot as a model of the adult's contact with 'dream kitsch.'"[81] Rabbits symbolize Lennie's libidinous (and always inappropriate) urge to touch something soft and comforting, his need for immediate emotional connection. His desire for the soft, cute object is – as Sianne Ngai would put it – "an aesthetic response to the diminutive, the weak, and the subordinate," though this cuteness can easily flip from being the object of sentimentalism to a theatricalized figure of the freak.[82] The startlingly kitsch appearance of the rabbit is the formal enactment of a complex, regressive, and ambivalent attachment to cuteness, as if the play-as-novel suddenly and perversely *reaches out to touch us*, its audience, with this big furry presence.

But of course – and this is the point – it does so clumsily, even violently through this gigantic aesthetic blunder, something like a formal equivalence to Lennie's disastrous encounter with Curley's Wife. It is kitsch at one level, though it would be difficult to argue – as Menninghaus does of Benjamin's idea of kitsch – that "it presents no difficulties in interpretation and has absolutely nothing to do with an aesthetics of negativity."[83] This is also a difficult moment (not unlike the fleeting appearance of camp through the character Slim) because it is such a sudden and partial eruption of kitsch into an otherwise naturalist environment. Indeed, we might read the rabbit as the spokes-animal for the book's eugenic determinism: the rabbit is right that Lennie's execution is an ethical necessity, according to the logic of the narrative. But having a gigantic talking rabbit deliver the moral only ironizes the message. In a similar way, we are presented here, for the first and only time in the story, with a character's point of view (an embodiment of Lennie's deep psychological life) rather than the hard-boiled observation of the third-person narrative. But again, placing this psychologizing moment in the body of a gigantic talking rabbit only impedes any reality effect in the enunciation of character. The scene is both kitsch and the inverse of kitsch in its negativity, not least because, if this is meant to be "so scened and set that it can be played as it stands," as Steinbeck described it,[84] then we are presented with a moment that is virtually *un-playable* from a dramatic perspective.

As Steinbeck explained in a 1937 interview with the *New York Times* concerning his experimental "play in the form of a novel": "Despite the fact that it has sold more than 150,000 copies, I don't consider that it was quite a success – as a play. The experiment flopped."[85] The novel approaches a high modernist failure but then fails to maintain that seriousness. This failure is thus different from the glitches that Kurnick has in mind in his modernist novels: marginalized moments that expose a melancholy longing for theatricality. Indeed, Steinbeck was not, like Henry James, a failure in the theater – far from it. He worked with the well-known playwright and director George S. Kaufman to turn the play-as-novel into a more conventional play, which won the New York Drama Critics' Circle Best Play in 1938 (see Figure 6.2). The collaboration with Kaufman led Steinbeck to "do a lot of extensive rewriting of the book itself," as he put it.[86] In other words, there exist two versions of the same essential thing. Steinbeck does not write another work or adapt the novel into a play in three acts, but he rewrites *the book itself.* (Indeed, the book itself is also already a rewrite of an earlier manuscript that is allegedly chewed to bits by Steinbeck's dog.[87]) The play exists in two forms: an earlier version performed in San Francisco, with the script created by the players from the novel, and the Broadway version of the rewritten play. The success of the play, however, only clarified Steinbeck's adherence to failure. "The play M & M went on and is a success," he wrote in his journal, continuing: "And with its success,

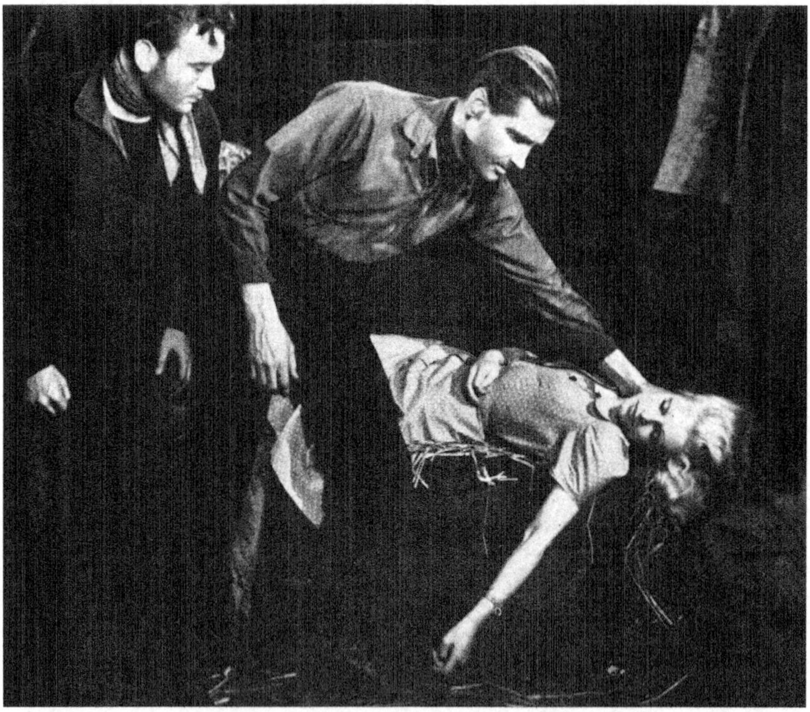

Figure 6.2 Claire Luce as Curley's Wife, in the 1939 London premiere of *Of Mice and Men*, discovered dead by Slim and George. © Lebrecht Authors/Bridgeman Images.

I know there is never to be any ease, any pleasure for me," underscoring how the feeling of failure was crucial to his identity as a writer.[88] His natural condition of writing was more like the feeling he confessed to Louis Paul as he began *Of Mice and Men*: "I have to start [writing] and am scared to death as usual – miserable sick feeling of inadequacy."[89]

If the play-as-novel version is formed by this inadequacy, then Kaufman felt it. "The girl, I think, should be drawn more fully," wrote Kaufman: "she is the motivating force of the whole thing and should loom larger."[90] The play-in-three-acts version of *Of Mice and Men* has much in common with the play-as-novel. Steinbeck makes clear how the scenic descriptions in the play-as-novel are intended as stage-set descriptions specifically.[91] The speech of the characters becomes slightly more normalized in the play ("fatta the lan'" becomes "fat of the land," suggesting how in the novel it represents a tactile use of language beyond mere dialect), while George's attraction to Slim and animosity toward Curley's Wife become starker still.[92] The gigantic talking rabbit naturally disappears. And if the play-as-novel has an inadequacy in its very being because its characters seem performative shells unable to sustain the motivation of the events, then this limitation is partially lifted in the three-act play because greater texture is added to the character of Curley's Wife (though she still fails to gain a proper name). Steinbeck even wrote a letter to Claire Luce, the actress who played Curley's Wife in the original Broadway production, to help establish the character's depth: "She grew up in an atmosphere of fighting and suspicion," Steinbeck mansplains: "Quite early she learned that she must never trust any one but she was never able to carry out what she learned. A natural trustfulness broke through constantly and every time it did, she got hurt. . . . Now, she was trained by threat not only at home but by other kids. And any show of fear or weakness brought an instant persecution."[93]

Steinbeck adds to the play a long interchange between Curley's Wife and Lennie, prior to the murder, a scene in which we learn something more about her background and her victimization. She is an abused child and is thus someone who needs something from Lennie, some human connection; she is no longer the superficial floozy who simply tempts Lennie with her hollow sexuality. "Weakness" thus becomes attached to a deeper characterization, effectively turning Lennie's disability – his compulsive desire for softness – into plausible and mutual attraction, just as our increased sympathy for Curley's Wife makes Lennie's actions seem more starkly wrong. We thus gain a sharper appreciation of the kind of failure represented by the play-as-novel. It is a failure to develop the conventions of plot and character, one that makes disability not a trope for philosophical investigation but a weakness at the level of form, as if we are witnessing a wounded creature that, in its very being, can only behave in limited ways. In the three-act play, the explicit lynch threat is also removed in a revision that critics have viewed as a rejection of the original motivation of the novel "against the racism and sexism that were entrenched in [Steinbeck's] society."[94] It also reduces the uncertainty of motivation that haunts the novel, in which there seems to be some kind of link between the lynch threat and the murder of Curley's Wife but one that is never fully articulated.

The three-act version of *Of Mice and Men* becomes, ironically, more novelistic, and hence it throws into light Steinbeck's curious experimentation in his 1937 novel. In *Of Mice and Men* (the novel), theatricality is baked in at virtually every moment – except, of course, for its gigantic talking rabbit, that big floppy flop. It is a different kind of bad writing, and a truer, less ironized example of failure (the kind of failure that fails, as I've written elsewhere) precisely because of its skewed relationship to a modernist aesthetic.[95] We can flip this on its head and say that *Of Mice and Men* approaches the conditions of modernist discourse, not least in the way it frustrates referentiality by occupying a space between novel and play. But then it retreats from this discursive technique through its sentimentalism and the conventions of naturalism that determine its plot. The novel retreats through other forms of aesthetic badness that directly contravene high modernist thwarted mimesis and that fracture the representational surface in a blundering if equally challenging way. We might call it weak modernism, one that – like Lennie himself – fails to develop fully.

CHAPTER 7

Emergence and Failure: The Middleness of The Grapes of Wrath

Of all his works, Steinbeck's *The Grapes of Wrath* (1939) continues to gain attention and to generate new interpretations, not least because of the ways it seems to mirror social and cultural attitudes during the Great Depression, demonstrated brilliantly in Michael Szalay's reading of the novel as an embodiment of the broader logic of the New Deal.[1] Whatever the reading, critics tend to return to a central question: How consistent is Steinbeck's political vision in the novel? In a thorough account of the complex social values in *Grapes*, Cyrus Zirakzadeh asks whether the novel targets the conditions of modernity in a call for wholesale economic change, or whether it is essentially conservative in its nostalgic yearning for a preindustrial America. He concludes that, ambivalently, it is both. Is *Grapes* a book about a specific community of displaced Oklahomans, or is it attempting to offer a blueprint for a transformation in humanity at large?[2] Steinbeck's novel was written during the early phase of what Mark Greif terms "the age of the crisis of man," a period that begins in the 1930s, intensifies during World War II, and culminates in the social upheavals of the 1960s and early 1970s. During this era, a range of intellectuals and writers responded to the fear "that human nature was being changed, either in its permanent essence or in its lineaments for the eyes of other men. The change would have the same result in either form: the demolition of those certainties about human nature, which had been pillars for optimistic thinkers for two centuries."[3]

It is difficult to think of a writer more central to this discourse of humanistic crisis than Steinbeck, even though he is largely (and, given his current status among academics, perhaps predictably) absent from Greif's study. If Steinbeck attracts criticism for his baggy philosophizing, then it is important to note that the discourse of the crisis of humanity – as Greif describes it – is itself "loose" and curiously "empty": it tends to behave as if it wants to be filled with a single answer yet "in fact generates the continuation of attempts, or tacitly admits to unanswerability."[4]

Grapes is, I would suggest, the quintessential novel of the "crisis of man," not least because of the "looseness" of its ideas. A better question, then, is not how consistent and coherent is Steinbeck's thinking in the book, but what work is being done by that messiness? How does it push readers to make connections or, if those connections somehow do not hold, then what are the implications of the failure to cohere? Approaching these questions, and in turn understanding both the productive and the problematic contradictions of *Grapes*, returns us to a concept central to Steinbeck's imagination – one that we have seen run through his interests in race, ecology, sociality, and states of consciousness. That concept is *emergence*. It lies at the foundation of Steinbeck's peculiar worldview in the novel, his description in particular of characters and things. And it helps us to understand the book's complex social philosophy, its discourse of crisis, and its relation to a public sphere in an age when the arts of manipulating public opinion were gaining attention and theorization following the Great War and the rise of mass media. As we look ahead to Steinbeck's increasingly global concerns in the 1940s, we encounter in this idea of emergence a crucial tension between Steinbeck the big thinker about the direction of the human species and Steinbeck the bearer of a narrower and precarious historical vision.

Characteristic Steinbeck

We saw at the end of Chapter 5 how Steinbeck's minute, naturalistic observation of plants in the first chapter of *Grapes* becomes one of human emergence that answers novelistic needs for narrative progression. It also places the book in a familiar tradition of thinking about the West less as a place than a process.[5] *Grapes* is, first and foremost, a road narrative defined by serial movement. Chapter two, for example, is an exercise in pure seriality: the "listless language of the roadsides" goes on and on; the waitress obsessively returns to explore a lump behind her ear; the driver chews his gum and plays on the slot machine with its whirring cylinders; Tom Joad rolls a cigarette and plays with the visor of his cap, "starting [its] future ruin" – a promise of seriality that will only continue in the novel.[6] According to Michael Denning, this grand narrative of migration is exactly what offers Steinbeck a "way out" of confronting the ideological crisis of the Great Depression; it is a sign of the novel's implicit political conservatism.[7] That may in part be true, but it only begins to recognize the complex process of emergence in the novel: the formation of new and novel wholes, diachronically, from component parts.[8] Steinbeck is most interested in a kind of movement in which parts are *on their way* to becoming autonomous wholes. Take, for example, the first description of Tom Joad in chapter two:

> He was not over thirty. His eyes were very dark brown and there was a hint of brown pigment in his eyeballs. His cheek bones were high and wide, and strong deep lines cut down his cheeks, in curves beside his mouth. His upper lip was long, and since his teeth protruded, the lips stretched to cover them, for this man kept his lips closed. His hands were hard, with broad fingers and nails as thick and ridged as little clam shells. The space between thumb and forefinger and the hams of his hands were shiny with callus.[9]

Here the various parts – eyes (and their component eyeballs), cheeks (and their component lines and curves), fingers (and their component nails) – are only slowly accumulating into something we might call the holistic character of Tom Joad, not least because Tom possesses the anti-linguistic quietness that Jane Tompkins identifies in the archetypal figure of the Western hero. Talk might threaten to "dissipate presence" and make vulnerable the self, writes Tompkins of the logic of masculinity in the genre of the Western.[10] It also here *delays* full presence, just as we as readers can only slowly piece together Tom's backstory from his reticent answers to the successive questions of the truck driver from whom he hitches a ride.

Steinbeck's interest in emergence as process explains the slow care with which he works to introduce the Joads. "Must take time in the description, detail, looks, clothes, gestures," he wrote in the journal he kept while writing the novel (posthumously published as *Working Days*). He must pile on details slowly until "the whole throbbing thing emerges."[11] Steinbeck undertook careful research into the conditions of the Oklahoma migrants as he built his characters, and he was generally detail oriented in his approach. But what we feel here is not just slowness: it is more like a self-conscious *slowing down*. As Steinbeck would write to his agent, Elizabeth Otis, midway through writing the novel: "The new book is going well. Too fast. I'm having to hold it down. I don't want it to go so fast for fear the tempo will be fast and this is a plodding, crawling book. So I'm holding it down to approximately six pages a day."[12] This slowness can be felt in the description itself. Knowing what we do of Steinbeck's writing process – the blisters and calluses he suffered, his adjusted grip owing to the pain caused by the act of writing – we can think of Tom's pick (the object that makes his hands "shiny with callus") as the equivalent of Steinbeck's pen. Rather than moving the character forward, this moment creates a pause of self-reflective contemplation, just as the callus is itself shiny and reflective. Steinbeck seems to be contemplating his own act of production, the emergence of narrative itself. Other points of descriptive pause – for example, the moment of restless anxiety before the western exodus begins – are also instances of writerly self-consciousness: "Soft fingers began to tap the sill of the car window, and hard fingers tightened on the restless drawing sticks."[13] This is a description of a pause in the action. But it is also a moment when we feel the writing slowing down through a metanarrative (the pen is a drawing stick) that stalls the progression of the story, actively decelerating the prose.

This slowness is present everywhere in the book. Think of Steinbeck's famous turtle that plods through chapter three. The turtle is so obviously a symbol, of ecological process, or migration, or folk wisdom and endurance. But the turtle also has a narrative, almost anti-narrative, function: it embodies descriptive slowness and is defined by tiny details. It moves "little by little" and exists in a "long moment." After the turtle is flipped by a speeding truck, it gradually rights itself, and the chapter ends with a line that epitomizes the slow action of Steinbeck's description: "His yellow toe nails slipped a fraction in the dust."[14] The slipping is itself divided into smaller parts (fractions) as if it is calibrated in its gradualness. In a similar way, Steinbeck's characters slowly emerge from parts. Here is Tom Joad Sr.:

> "What do you want?" old Tom mumbled around his mouthful of nails. He wore a black, dirty slouch hat and a blue work shirt over which was a buttonless vest; his jeans were held up by a wide harness-leather belt with a big square brass buckle, leather and metal polished from years of wearing; and his shoes were cracked and the soles swollen and boat-shaped from years of sun and wet and dust.[15]

Tom Sr. is built from details of things that are products of a slow process of ruin and erosion, as if each object has a "live" or temporally resonant quality. Tom Sr. is not just wearing a belt: his jeans are being actively "held up" by it; they exist in tension against a desire to fall. These things or qualities are adding up to a bigger picture of character, but they are also breaking down into separate parts, obstructing holistic characterization. Hence Tom Sr. can barely talk through the nails in his mouth, objects that represent his activity but also effectively undo his complete realization. We might say that Tom Sr. is always *becoming* a character, never quite getting there, because of the individual resilience of the Steinbeckian detail, whereby each detail suggests the slow work of making character. The character Noah, the oldest Joad son, is the ultimate example of this process.

He cannot develop a full social self because he cannot overcome the act of being literally shaped at birth by the hands of his father. He exists in the novel as a sign of being worked over, his emptiness a condition of his own perpetual madeness.

The nature of Steinbeckian description in general often carries this feeling that details are suspended in their own singularity. Physical things gain an interiority or inner dynamism that makes them seem full of movement, as in this description of the scene just before the Oklahomans enter "an organization of the unconscious" and begin their migration west (it is another moment of pause, of slowing down):

> The film of evening light made the red earth lucent, so that its dimensions were deepened, so that a stone, a post, a building had greater depth and more solidity than in the daytime light; and these objects were curiously more individual – a post was more essentially a post, set off from the earth it stood in and the field of corn it stood out against. And plants were individuals, not the mass of crop; and the ragged willow tree was itself, standing free of all other willow trees. The earth contributed a light to the evening. The front of the grey, paintless house, facing the west, was luminous as the moon is. The grey dusty truck, in the yard before the door, stood out magically in this light, in the over drawn perspective of a stereopticon.[16]

We return to Steinbeck the magical realist that we glimpsed at the very beginning of his career in *The Pastures of Heaven* (1932) and *To a God Unknown* (1933): his style is resonant with the "New Objectivist" focus on the uncanny singularity of objects, as if they are magically emerging from the flux of molecules in the background.[17] No wonder Twentieth Century Fox commissioned Thomas Hart Benton to make six lithographs to promote the 1940 film of *The Grapes of Wrath*: Benton's work possesses this aliveness and vibrating motion of the objective world; see Figure 7.1. Objects are not simply represented but they are "over drawn." They are realist details, but then they are more than this. A post or a plant or a tree or a truck is *more essentially* itself: objects are on their way to becoming symbolic embodiments of themselves. They are always dynamically emerging into another, higher, larger, more abstracted condition of their own being. Objects are real and they are also hyper-real representations of their categorical individuality. Hence the language of the technology of vision ("stereopticon," "film of evening light") reflects this enhanced visuality, as if the scene is being projected simultaneously onto a bigger screen, or as if it is seen in a convex mirror in which excess attention makes details seem to bulge. With his inherently scalar imagination, Steinbeck's style of writing is always on the move from part to whole. This writing is thus both

Figure 7.1 Thomas Hart Benton, "Departure of the Joads," 1939. © 2020 T. H. and R. P. Benton Testamentary Trusts/UMB Bank Trustee/Licensed by VAGA at Artists Rights Society (ARS), NY. Photo © San Diego Museum of Art, Gift of Mr. and Mrs. Leslie L. Johnson/Bridgeman Images.

referential in its detail and implicitly theoretical in its self-awareness, leaving us with a quality of space that is hybrid in its fusing together of the low (concrete) and the high (abstraction). The real and the marvelous seem to coexist.

The vibrancy of things in the novel helps to establish what Bill Brown would call the book's object-orientated ontology in which physical things gain a subjectivity, beyond their use-value in a capitalist economy, and come to structure human interiority.[18] We need only think of the relationship between Grampa and his "pilla" (it gains a special name to suggest that it is more than simply a "pillow"), with its picture of an "Injun." "He jus' liked her," we are told: it is a pure emotional bond. In this way, objects resist any sense of having an exchange value – Grampa will blow the goddamn stinking head off anyone who comes for his pilla – because of the way they contain and organize human feelings and desires.[19] Both emotionally and physically, things move people. The Hudson Super Six is the means of transportation for the Joads. But it is also the thing – one could even say the character – that has the most interiority, with young

Al Joad listening so sensitively throughout the journey to its every inner murmur. Selected because its parts are easily attainable and replaceable, the truck is emerging into a holistic condition, becoming a "living principle" around which the characters organize their lives.[20] The truck thus stages a process of emergence that operates as a basic assumption of the novel: that people and things are "more than their analysis." Steinbeck described his characters as an "over-essence of people."[21] Certainly they can possess a cartoon-like exaggeration: Grampa's very being, for example, is defined by the "too much."[22] They are defined by a level of hyper-detail, a condition of the novel's slow writing (think of how Grampa does not simply scratch his testicles, he scratches *under* his testicles: always that piling on or extension of detail). Ma Joad is similarly "thick" and "heavy" with her own slow builtness of character, her morning rituals resonating with the rituals of Steinbeck's unhurried observation and description.[23] Characters exist in an always incomplete process of emergence into their own characterization, the hyper-detail a sign of the characters' own writtenness, or over-writtenness, as if Steinbeck is attempting to conjure up through these parts of description some holistic emergent reality (what he called a "unity feeling") that he can virtually live in himself. Hence that moment toward the end of his journal, when Steinbeck finds himself actually calling out "Tom! Tom! Tom!" thinking for a moment that the character has materialized in his study.[24]

The original review of *Grapes* in the *New York Times* captured well the novel's ambivalent temporality: "It is a very long novel . . . and yet it reads as if it had been composed in a flash, ripped off the typewriter and delivered to the public as an ultimatum. It is a long and thoughtful novel as one thinks about it. It is a short and vivid scene as one feels it."[25] The novel was written quickly, in one hundred days or so, but there is that slowness *within* the compressed period of writing. It is long and thoughtful "as one thinks about it"; there is a self-reflexivity within this act of slow contemplation. The prose-poetic interchapters may be the most obvious "pace-changers," as Steinbeck described them, designed to slow things down, to open readers and leave them vulnerable to a plunging violence of description.[26] Slowness allows for sudden, even violent changes in pace that might make us rethink what critics call Steinbeck's conservatism. Take, for example, the sudden moment of police brutality in chapter twenty,[27] which reflects what Steinbeck described as the "vicious" and "angry" quality of the book.[28] We might likewise understand the slowness of the novel's opening, the way that the gradual emergence of drought eventually leads to the displacement of people, in relation to Rob Nixon's ecocritical idea of "slow violence": a form of attritional violence against the poor that is often difficult to see and describe because it is so delayed and secondary in its action.[29] In certain ways, the slowness *is* the politics. But to understand fully how emergence is an integral part of the novel's politics and philosophy, we need to turn from Steinbeck's descriptive style and his building of character to his faltering attempts to express a social vision that famously runs through chapters fourteen, seventeen, and nineteen of the novel.

The Failing Public Sphere

In his journal, Steinbeck described chapter fourteen as expressing the emergent move from "the I to We," the crucial move from individual parts to a whole greater than their sum.[30] Steinbeck returns to the concern with "Manself" that Greif describes occupying mid-twentieth-century thought, and he does so according to the logic of "over-essence" that creates the idea of people and things somehow becoming more than themselves: "For man, unlike any other thing organic or inorganic in the universe, grows beyond his work, walks up the stairs of his concepts, emerges ahead of his accomplishments."[31] Yet again like the hyper-details that obstruct as much as they enable description, Steinbeck's concept of emergence is always in a state of becoming, one that necessarily precludes holistic completion. Zirakzadeh has grappled in fullest terms with the apparent contradictions of Steinbeck's social philosophy in *Grapes*, concluding that its "call for wholesale economic change rests on socially conservative grounds."[32] Yet to argue for such a pattern in the novel, compelling though the argument is, misses a more basic problem whereby the novel is trying but failing to express its ideas. Indeed, chapter fourteen, the philosophical heart of the book, actually restarts halfway through when its initial attempt to describe man emerging and growing beyond "himself" becomes a recognition of human stumbling into violent slaughter: "This you may say of man – when theories change and crash, when schools, philosophies, when narrow dark alleys of thought, national, religious, economic, grow and disintegrate, man reaches, stumbles forward, painfully, mistakenly sometimes."[33] What begins as a recognition of human growth slips beyond its own ethical frame to become a celebration of violence as a good in itself. The style itself becomes aspirational, as if it is struggling to say and convince ("This you may say and know it and know it"). Any clarity in its philosophical ideas descends into vagueness. A defining quality of "Manself" is that he will "die for a concept." But what is this concept, precisely? And what is "Manself" itself? With the drift into arcane biological terminology in the second part of chapter fourteen ("Here is the anlage of the thing you fear. This is the zygote"), Steinbeck's ideas seem to overreach themselves as they strive for some impossibly grand statement about the origins and meaning of social change.[34]

The language of "slipping back" that defines Steinbeck's turtle and comes to dominate chapter fourteen is not unlike the feelings of failure that occupied Steinbeck when he was writing the novel, trying to maintain his pace through a number of distractions and annoyances, not least with himself. "It's just like slipping behind at Stanford," he writes at one point: "Panic sets in. Can't organize." To read *Working Days* is to realize that *Grapes* was written during a period of intense personal breakdown ("Stomach went to pieces, dizziness, and blind nausea") and overwhelming self-doubt. "The new book goes very fast but I am afraid it is pretty lousy," he writes at one point, adding "I don't care much." And again later on: "but I am sure of one thing – it isn't the great book I had hoped it would be. It's just a run-of-the-mill book. And the awful thing is that it is absolutely the best I can do."[35] We have already encountered some of the ways that formal failure embodies meaning in Steinbeck's work, for example, in *To a God Unknown* and *Of Mice and Men* (1937). But in *Grapes* this relationship to negative feelings becomes particularly close and extreme. "You pages – ten of you – you are the dribble cup – you are the cloth to wipe up the vomit," he writes early in his journal: "Maybe I can get these fears and disgusts on you and then burn you up."[36] He would indeed burn an earlier draft of the project, "L'Affaire Lettuceberg," which Steinbeck described as a vicious manuscript designed to provoke hatred through "partial understanding."[37] Reading narrowly, we might view the muddled social philosophy of *Grapes* as a result of Steinbeck's faltering grasp on himself and his craft. We might see it as another way that the self-conscious experience of writing leaves its mark on the writing itself, as a form of overwork. But there are other uses of "partial understanding" in *Grapes*, ones that link Steinbeck to events in California's Central Valley, and that help us comprehend his central aim in writing the novel – to impact public opinion.

Michael Warner has described a kind of public that comes into being only through written texts, and particularly in response to the reflexive circulation of those texts, which enables a relation between strangers essential to the existence of a public sphere.[38] The newspaper is the most obvious example, but *Grapes* also possessed this power, not just by presupposing a rhetorical addressee but also by having the "worldliness" that

Warner ascribes to the "public" text.[39] Steinbeck's novel had something like an actual destiny, a historical agency that pressured opinions and even policies. It was a reflexively circulating text – or a series of intertexts – demonstrated by the circular relationship among report, novel, photograph, movie, photograph, report that constituted the book's initial life. The documentary reports of conditions in the camps that Steinbeck received from his friend Tom Collins (the manager of the Weedpatch camp),[40] and the photodocumentary images of Horace Bristol (Steinbeck originally intended to write an essay for *Life* magazine, with images by Bristol, with whom he visited the camps), fed the novel's ethic of information found in its detailed descriptions. This then cycled into the movie version of the novel – produced soon after publication of the book – which itself used Collins as a consultant to ensure the movie's fidelity, both to the novel and to the conditions the novel represents. This in turn led Bristol to reprint his original photographs of the Visalia migrant camp alongside stills from the movie, in an article in *Life* magazine – one of a number of contemporary articles about the Okies' plight – to cement further the realism of the film. Bristol even renamed his photographic subjects after characters in Steinbeck's book. And then, of course, the Joads gained their own facticity, feeding into the documentary reports they emerged from, just as what the novel represented entered public opinion as a kind of truth. In a way, *Grapes* tried to specify the life-world of its circulation, to create its own self-authenticating buzz.[41]

"*Grapes* got really out of hand," wrote Steinbeck describing the furor after publishing the book, when his catastrophic sense of personal breakdown only increased. The book became "a public hysteria and I became a public domain."[42] Steinbeck was referring to the intense public reactions it provoked, which ranged from book burnings by enraged local farm owners to vocal support at the national level, most notably from Eleanor Roosevelt. The extremely varied nature of these reactions – the wide spectrum of responses *Grapes* allows – helps us to understand the relationship between the book and the problems that were widely seen as developing within the idea of "the public," problems that explain the kind of failure that seems written into Steinbeck's novel. The "manufacture of consent," wrote Walter Lippmann in his 1922 book *Public Opinion*, made it "no longer possible ... to believe in the original dogma of democracy; that the knowledge needed for the management of human affairs comes up spontaneously from the human heart." For Lippmann, a picture acted upon by a group constitutes public opinion. But the pictures inside people's heads do not necessarily correspond to the world outside because of the insertion between person and world of a "pseudo-environment," a fiction open to propaganda.[43] Taking his ideas further in *The Phantom Public* in 1927, Lippmann described as fanciful the idea of sovereign and omnicompetent citizens, the idea of the people as a superindividual of one will and mind (an "organism with an organic unity of which the individual is a cell"), and the idea of the public having intuition and acting as a natural dispenser of laws and morals. The public was really an abstraction that depended on a "mystical notion of society," he wrote.[44] We must, then, abandon the idea of finding a unity that absorbs diversity because "the public" had come to possess a phantom meaning. Or as C. Wright Mills phrased it a few years later, the public had begun to stand for a "vagueness of policy."[45]

"Writing to a public" argues Warner, "helps to make a world insofar as the object of address is brought into being partly by postulating and characterizing it."[46] Accordingly, *Grapes* is at heart *about* stranger relationality, about how individuals come together into a social whole. Chapter seventeen attempts to draw readers into its theoretical ideal when it describes the family uniting in a deliberative democracy. Worlds are built, from which naturally emerge rights and laws, and eventually a government and (getting more policy driven) a social security program: "a kind of insurance developed in these nights."[47] Yet just as the Weedpatch government camp in *Grapes* is an island in the novel as a whole (as Zirakzadeh points out, other government initiatives are not presented in a positive light) and is no solution for the migrants,[48] so too do Steinbeck's theories and ideas seem more like what Lippmann called the "dogma of democracy": "forms of persuasion we cannot verify" and in which we should no longer believe in the age of propaganda.[49] The characters' techniques of world-making check off virtually all the points of Lippmann's "phantom public": sovereign and omnicompetent citizens become a superindividual of one mind, possessing organic unity, acting as a natural dispenser of laws and morals.[50] The public in the novel seems more like a mythical and mystical democratic fantasy, just as the novel has equally phantom-like designs on the public outside its pages. The novel's other philosophies, which often emerge from the mouths of the characters themselves (take Casy's belief in an Emersonian oversoul), are rendered in vague versions, only partially brought to light by their speakers.[51] But that which is not fully understood still features again and again, as the novel keeps before us its philosophical cloudiness. For example, Steinbeck's image in chapter five of the Bank or the Company as "a monster, with thought and feeling, which had enslaved them"[52] again relates to Nixon's idea of a slow violence that often remains formless and stays out of sight: it is pervasive yet elusive, providing a challenge to narrative and symbolic expression.[53] The vagueness of "the monster" is really the point: we cannot see clearly the forces of global capitalism that are violently abusing the land, reflected in the driver who sits like a zombie on his tractor, a dehumanized individual or "walking dead" controlled by a corporate-capitalist-media empire. A less generous reading might see this idea of the monster as only half a theory, a provocative but incomplete figuration. Take another example, again from the mouth of Casy:

> They's stuff goin' on and they's folks doin' things. Them people layin' one foot down in front of the other, like you says, they ain't thinkin' where they're goin', like you says – but they're all layin' 'em down the same direction, jus' the same. An' if ya listen, you'll hear a movin', an' a sneakin', an' a rustlin', an' – an' a res'lessness. They's stuff goin' on that the folks doin' it don't know nothin' about – yet. They's gonna come somepin outa all these folks goin' wes' – outa all their farms lef' lonely. They's comin' a thing that's gonna change the whole country.[54]

This is one of many descriptions in the novel of characters in the act of thinking, as if Steinbeck is attempting to conjure the weight of public opinion through an accretive logic that brings us into a questioning mode ourselves. But it is usually *thinkin'*, without that final *g*. It is both folksy, in other words, and incomplete, pulling us into experiences that further drive and cloud new thinking. Casy's speech here is an example of almost sublime vagueness. At best, it suggests that his thought is still being worked out. At worst, the clipped words and missing letters embody a process of thinking shot through with holes.

Laurence Buell has shown how the era's mechanics of public relations – its noisy media buzz – became ironically refigured in John Dos Passos's dizzying techniques spanning his *U.S.A.* trilogy of novels (1930–36).[55] Steinbeck's relationship to this public noise, however, seems far less ironic. *Grapes* acts more like the vague and idealized fantasy world that Lippmann described as public opinion. Tom Joad's parting promise to Ma, to be "ever'where" – "Wherever they's a fight so hungry people can eat, I'll be there. Wherever they's a cop beatin' up a guy, I'll be there . . . " – his promise to become what Bruce Springsteen would call "The Ghost of Tom Joad" resonates with this public sphere *as* a phantom, circulating around, supposedly binding people together as a unit but only because its associated emotions are partially understood.[56] Remarkably, immediately after Tom makes this now-famous speech to Ma, both characters admit that they don't understand what he means. "I don' un'erstan'," Ma says: "I don' really know." "Me neither," replies Tom.[57]

Failure, then, is not simply the outcome of the economy's scale and abstraction; failure becomes epistemological, wired into the way characters, and the novel itself, attempt to signify. We are often left in the middle of something to be worked out, potentially from a number of different, even contradictory directions, ranging from Marxist theory to a fascistic celebration of folk and soil.[58] Ambiguity arrives not at the end but at the beginning of political action. It is fruitful ground for a public political possibility, one that seems to depend on failed clarity. We are in a better position now to understand why *Grapes* tends to generate such divergent reactions, and how it serves as a source of critical frustration for readers, especially scholarly readers. We can also better understand two of the most problematic aspects of the novel: its implicit racial politics, which apparently displace nonwhite laborers from the California fields, and, of course, its shocking and mysterious ending.

History while It Is Happening

Chapter nineteen is the final in the sequence of "theoretical" chapters in *Grapes*, one that attempts to manufacture our consent to the novel's political assumptions and vision. The chapter offers a history of how corporate California came into being. It describes the colonization of Mexican lands by American settlers; the gradual capitalization of the land as it falls into fewer and fewer hands, which leads to a decline in personal land-lust among the people; the importation of "slave" laborers – Chinese, Japanese, Mexican, Filipino – who are inevitably killed or driven from the country, only to be replaced by Oklahoman migrants who bring a new hunger, a new energy that will inevitably (according to these laws of history) overthrow the moneyed interests. "We ain't foreign," exclaims their collective voice: "Seven generations back Americans, and beyond that Irish, Scotch, English, German. One of our folks in the Revolution, an' they was lots of our folks in the Civil War – both sides. Americans."[59] These nativist assumptions become clearer still in *Their Blood Is Strong* (1938), the pamphlet collection of journalistic articles in which Steinbeck first exposed the suffering of the Dust Bowl migrants in the Central Valley. The pamphlet featured photographs by Dorothea Lange, including Figure 7.2 on its cover – an image of generational continuity that may also have influenced the final scene of *Grapes*: "Foreign labor is on the wane in California, and the future farm workers are to be white and American," argues Steinbeck in the penultimate chapter of the pamphlet: "This fact must be recognized and a rearrangement and a readjustment of the attitude toward and treatment of migrant labor must

Figure 7.2 Dorothea Lange, "Drought refugees from Oklahoma camping by the roadside," August 1936. Library of Congress, Prints & Photographs Division, FSA/OWI Collection, LC-DIG-fsa-8b38480.

be achieved."[60] This was, indeed, an interesting moment in the history of California agriculture. If the industrial system had previously exploited competing groups from different ethnic, often national backgrounds – importing and exporting them at will – then because of the Dust Bowl white laborers were flowing into the "factories in the field," as Carey McWilliams pointed out.[61]

We can read in various ways Steinbeck's interpretation of this moment as an inevitable and necessary whitening of California labor. We can read it as part of Steinbeck's problematic views of race in general, his partial blindness to questions beyond the pale of white America – a point that several critics have highlighted,[62] and that we have seen already in works such as "The Vigilante." At a stretch, we could read it as a rhetorical move to bring public attention to migrant poverty, the assumption being that a mainstream public would not have cared (or would have found ways to explain it away) if this were the poverty of Mexican Americans or of other nonwhite groups. Alongside Zirakzadeh, we could read this whitening as a result of Steinbeck's interest in the survival of this *particular* group of laborers, a group that embodies the nostalgic values of a preindustrial America.[63] Or, following my larger argument in this chapter, we could read it as another example of the novel's deep investment in the dynamic of emergence, and the kind of failure it presupposes. Steinbeck was aware of this social emergence while writing the novel. In a letter he wrote of California as a "bomb," "an active beginning" toward general revolt.[64] In the novel as a whole, there is a constant feeling that change is on the way; Tom becomes particularly "sensy" and aware of change, even though its nature is unclear. And most famously to his agent Elizabeth Otis, concerning his urgency when writing the earlier draft of *Grapes*, Steinbeck writes: "I'm trying to write history while it is happening and I don't want to be wrong."[65] By taking a historical blip in the labor force and reading it as a racial inevitability, Steinbeck demonstrates the difficulties of writing in a moment of emergence. This is another example of partial understanding, a failure to think through the whole problem, a taking of the part and making it stand for the whole. Steinbeck is writing history while it is happening, in other words, and getting it wrong.

Again, this failed thinking in *Grapes* connects to the way the book imagines its public. Steinbeck's interest in the Okies suggests that he is calling not to a public but to what Warner would call a counterpublic: he is addressing strangers, that is, but not just *any* strangers.[66] The shocking final scene of the novel is another, quite literal study in "stranger relationality":

> For a minute Rose of Sharon sat still in the whispering barn. Then she hoisted her tired body up and drew the comfort about her. She moved slowly to the corner and stood looking down at the wasted face, into the wide, frightened eyes. Then slowly she lay down beside him. He shook his head slowly from side to side. Rose of Sharon loosened one side of the blanket and bared her breast. "You got to," she said. She squirmed closer and pulled his head close. "There!" she said. "There." Her hand moved behind his head and supported it. Her fingers moved gently in his hair. She looked up and across the barn, and her lips came together and smiled mysteriously.[67]

Szalay is surely right in his reading of this scene as embodying the "welfarist" logic of the New Deal; it represents the extending of kin bonds, and sustenance, to strangers. In the words of the philosopher Michael Ignatieff, it recognizes needs as rights.[68] As Szalay argues, the breakup of the family at the end of the novel embodies a move from the private to the public sphere of abstract relations in which motherhood is reinvented beyond the family, thereby naturalizing the idea of social insurance.[69] Yet a thematic reading of this moment – brilliantly revealing though it is – does not quite account for the reverberations from the suddenness of the ending, one that would seem more at home in a short story than a novel, though an ending that Steinbeck may have had in mind from the very beginning.[70] Steinbeck's editor, Pascal Covici, had strong reactions: he wrote Steinbeck that the scene is "not quite satisfying" as an end to the book. The last few pages "need building up," the "incident needs leading up to" and "it needs something else leading away from it."[71] Steinbeck's reaction was equally strong:

> I have your letter today. And I am sorry but I cannot change that ending. It is casual – there is no fruity climax, it is not more important than any other part of the book – if there is a symbol, it is a survival symbol not a love symbol, it must be an accident, it must be a stranger, and it must be quick. To build this stranger into the structure of the book would be to warp the whole meaning of the book. The fact that the Joads don't know him, don't care about him, have no ties to him – that is the emphasis. The giving of the breast has no more sentiment than the giving of a piece of bread.

Again to Covici, defending the balance of the book, Steinbeck writes with characteristically serial compulsion: "One other thing – I am not writing a satisfying story. I've done my damndest to rip a reader's nerves to rags. I don't want him satisfied. / And one more thing – I've tried to write this book the way lives are being lived not the way books are written."[72]

The ending, then, figures the formation of a public, a new relationality between strangers. Predicting Steinbeck's theories that he would work out with Ed Ricketts in *Sea of Cortez* (1941), as we will see in the following chapter, we might read the ending as ultimately non-teleological: it represents a moment of non-blaming love or instant acceptance, designed to move readers toward consent to these emergent relationships. Yet as with Steinbeck's ideas of emergence and his grappling with the idea of the public in general, there is also a feeling here that things are failing to connect. The ending is also a moment of incompletion, of dissatisfaction. What, exactly, are we meant to consent to here? In *Sea of Cortez*, Steinbeck opposes non-teleological thinking to what he calls propaganda, which he describes as being "directed toward change even before the situation is fully understood (maybe as a lazy substitute for understanding)."[73] And here we may want to agree with Leslie Fiedler, that by this point Steinbeck has failed to understand where his subject has taken him.[74] Like the propaganda that was turning the idea of a public sphere into a phantom, there is something in this scene that is simply too much. It seems excessively real, piling it on (or like the actual flood that precedes this scene, flooding us out of our comfort zones), to the extent that the novel breaks down in these moments of partial thinking, just as there seems to be nowhere else for the Joads to go after this scene. It is significant here that *Their Blood Is Strong*, which we can think of as containing some of the information on which *Grapes* is based, repeatedly mentions that malnourished mothers who produce still-born babies lack the capacity to produce breast milk.[75] This final scene, then, cuts against its historical evidence; it is more extreme than anything Steinbeck was likely to have witnessed. We can think of it as a counterfactual moment, designed for propagandistic punch, echoing several other key details in the novel that stretch beyond what was likely from historical accounts.[76]

Steinbeck clearly understood *Grapes* as a kind of propaganda, aimed at the rise of "American Fascism": the formation of a corporate sphere, with the Associated Farmers at its heart, protecting the interests of a wealthy elite through the practice of vigilante violence against non-Californians, and through a strong grip on a conservative news media. Steinbeck described the novel's interchapters as ideally hitting readers below the belt, using poetry to open them up to ideas that they could not otherwise receive. But the propagandistic quality of the novel lies deeper and is akin to the vagueness and incomplete thinking that Lippmann ascribed to the phantom public sphere. Indeed, one of the reasons *Grapes* has passed into the public consciousness it theorizes is that its confused thinking leaves things open ended, partially understandable from different – sometimes incompatible – points of view.

In the letter to Covici, defending the novel's ending, Steinbeck continued:

> I know that books lead to a strong deep climax. This one doesn't except by implication and the reader must bring the implication to it. If he doesn't, it wasn't a book for him to read. Throughout I've tried to make the reader participate in the actuality, what he takes from it will be scaled entirely on his own depth or hollowness. There are five layers in this book, a reader will find as many as he can and he won't find more than he has in himself.[77]

Steinbeck would often claim provocatively that his books operated on multiple levels, without stipulating what they were – a sign of his frustration with the interpretations of critics, perhaps, but also an expression of a desire for his work to have lasting public impact. An aspect of incompleteness lies at the heart of *Grapes*, one that Steinbeck describes as "scaled" according to how it is received by readers. We must supply what the book lacks, and "participate in the actuality" by being captured in an ongoing process of interpretation. It is as if the novel leaves us in the middle of a thought. For Lippmann, partial understanding is an obstacle to the development of public opinion, whereas for Steinbeck it seems an essential characteristic, one that gives his novel a public resonance. If the novel is attempting to manufacture consent – which it clearly is at certain points – then it is moving us all the time to an ill-defined political viewpoint. Hence the inchoate thinking about race in the novel, hence the dissatisfaction of the ending. And hence that constant move to capture some supplementary quality, to make things more than they are. This move, however, ends not in plentitude but inadequacy, underscored by the overall direction of the plot, which culminates in a failure at scale.

We are always in the middle of emergence, never quite arriving at completion. We can now better understand the political middleness of the novel, its simultaneous appeal to different ideologies, as it works to expose problems – poverty, inequality, abuses of political power – rather than to offer clear solutions (and after all, many of the problems Steinbeck describes have still not been resolved). Emergence also explains the curious aesthetic status of *Grapes*, the way that it appeals not despite but because of its limitations as a work of art. *Grapes* is always *on its way* to becoming the Great American Novel, never quite getting there. The book toggles between the deep and the superficial, its middlebrow-ness (as Fiedler realized) resulting from a failed desire to be both highbrow and lowbrow at once. Steinbeck turns partial understanding into the stuff of popular consciousness, and consciousness-raising. Our awakening emerges from what we only partially grasp, what we cannot quite figure out – hence all the nonspecific talk of change. In a novel of strategic mediocrity, confusion and vague theory are what make a public sphere. The phantom public, Steinbeck seems to be saying, is still a public, one that haunts us, like the ghost of Tom Joad.

CHAPTER 8

Borderlands: Extinction and the New World Outlook in Sea of Cortez

With a storm of controversy in his wake following the publication of *The Grapes of Wrath* (1939), and with "powerful voices of hysteria and terror . . . in the air" as the world raced toward war, Steinbeck wrote to his old college roommate Carlton Sheffield about his need for change:[1]

> There are things in the tide pools easier to understand than Stalinist, Hitlerite, Democrat, capitalist confusion, and voodoo. So I'm going to those things which are relatively more lasting to find a new basic picture. I have too a conviction that a new world is growing under the old, the way a new finger nail grows under a bruised one. I think all the economists and sociologists will be surprised some day to find that they did not forsee nor understand it. Just as the politicos of Rome could not have forseen that the social-political-ethical world for two thousand years would grow out of the metaphysical gropings of a few quiet poets. I think the same thing is happening now. Communist, Fascist, Democrat may find that the real origin of the future lies on the microscope plates of obscure young men, who, puzzled with order and disorder in quantum and neutron, build gradually a picture which will seep down until it is the fibre of the future.
>
> The point of all this is that I must make a new start. I've worked the novel – I know it as far as I can take it. I never did think much of it – a clumsy vehicle at best. And I don't know the form of the new but I know there is a new which will be adequate and shaped by the new thinking.[2]

If *Grapes* was an extended essay on the concept of emergence – and the pattern of incompletion it presupposes – then Steinbeck's conviction that "a new world is growing under the old" only increased in the context of impending war. In a letter to Wilbur Needham, Steinbeck expressed his desire to fight in World War II because he viewed it as "part of a species pattern, perhaps a mutation process the results of which are unknown to the individuals. Reasons and causes are then merely symptoms, little flashing lights which do not show causes but merely indicate that the blind tropic movement is underway."[3] *Grapes* was a provocative intervention in a local socioeconomic crisis, but here Steinbeck's interests were moving beyond the political and sociological realm to something he viewed as more fundamental and global. This expansion of perspective required a new kind of observation, one that looks through close attention at small phenomena to produce a way of thinking that sees the species as a whole. This "revolution," as Steinbeck described it in his letter, would require new forms of writing beyond the novel, which had always seemed limiting. Such a new form would flourish in the borderland between poetry and science, particularly biology – a subject of long interest to Steinbeck. Steinbeck's "new thinking" was emerging largely through the influence of Edward F. Ricketts, the marine biologist and eclectic thinker who sought ways to break through the crust of humanity and achieve a deep and transcendent participation in the universe. And as Steinbeck wrote to Sheffield, this new education would center on another kind of borderland, the tide pools of the intertidal zone between sea and land: Ricketts's specialty.[4] This intellectual journey thus involved a physical journey too, toward yet another borderland that would help Steinbeck escape the East-West dialectic in which his work seemed trapped. Steinbeck's literary compass would turn south, toward Mexico, as he worked with Ricketts on the coauthored *Sea of Cortez* (1941): what Steinbeck called the Mexico book.

"Admit that Mexico is your double, that she exists in the shadow of this country, that we are irrevocably tied to her," wrote Gloria Anzaldúa in her classic study of intercultural identity, *Borderlands/La Frontera* (1987): "Gringo, accept the doppelganger in your psyche. By taking back your collective shadow the intracultural split will heal."[5] The shadow of Mexico had hovered over Steinbeck from the earliest days of his career. For the young writer, Mexico was a space of literary experimentation, an opportunity to tackle something truly great – to "remake the novel as it is now understood," as Steinbeck wrote to the book critic of the *Los Angeles Times*,[6] or to "start off the big book which would take a long time and would be a very grave attempt to do a first-rate piece of work," as he wrote to his agent Mavis McIntosh.[7] As early as 1932, he wrote to Elizabeth Otis of a planned trip to Mazatlán and Guadalajara "to do a series of little stories on the road." The plan would involve some typically Steinbeckian desires: to enter a communal mind-set, to explore the road as a space of unfolding narrative, and to discover people on the fringes of society. Something deeper lay in this Mexican plan, a wish to encounter the fundamentals of story itself – its primal conflicts – and to build up from these small units a particular vision, with "color" and "background" that might reveal the spirit of place and "permeate it with the state of mind of its community."[8]

Yet Steinbeck's attempt to take back the "collective shadow" (in Anzaldúa's terms), to see beyond his cultural perspective, would not initially be easy. His plan to collect his Mexican experiences into material for a greater book "gradually evaporated."[9] To produce his ambitious "Mexico book," Steinbeck would have to challenge the idea of story that first attracted him to Mexico; he would have to question the teleology of narrative itself. He would need to take literature into the realm of natural history, to rethink his concept of authorship as a solitary endeavor, and to interrogate more deeply the concept of the human that had occupied him in *Grapes*. As a result, Steinbeck would approach a kind of borderlands consciousness akin to Anzaldúa's, and a type of species awareness necessary to confront the possibility of extinction on a precarious planet. Yet how free could Steinbeck become from the racialized structures of power that must haunt any effort to heal the intracultural split by traveling south? After all, Steinbeck's first trip to Mexico was enabled by the financial success of *Tortilla Flat* (1935), a novel whose Mexican American characters can easily seem, from today's perspective, "grotesque distortions of a people who have been so historically maligned that they have come to be identified as 'forgotten people.'"[10] Forgetting, we shall see, lies at the heart of the possibilities, and also the problems, of Steinbeck's look southward.

Toward the Global South

Steinbeck's interest in the Global South is present from the beginning of his career. His first novel, *Cup of Gold* (1929), is a swashbuckling tale of Captain Henry Morgan's adventures as a pirate in Central America. Steinbeck would disown the book as an "atrocity," yet it contains in its very failures key concerns that would develop in subsequent literary journeys south.[11] Growing up in a mythic Wales haunted by the ghost of King Arthur, Morgan is a figure of insatiable colonial desire whose shadow-self is drawn to the colonies to make it whole. From his initial status as indentured servant, Henry emerges as a leader not unlike William Faulkner's Thomas Sutpen in *Absalom, Absalom!* (1936): he is able to perform his mastery because of an intimate involvement with slavery and with states of subjection.[12] Yet this engagement with the contradictions of colonialism quickly degenerates into a romantic quest narrative, leaving Henry – and the reader – in a confused state by the end of the novel. Steinbeck's focus on Panama reflected a strong interest in the Central American country following the opening of the Panama Canal in 1914, when Steinbeck was twelve. As a boy, Steinbeck visited the Panama-Pacific International Exposition in San Francisco, which celebrated the canal's joining of East and West, and of North and South[13] – a dream of continental wholeness reflected in early studies of Latin American culture and history.[14] But the global concerns of *Cup of Gold* would contract by the mid-1930s into a local concern with another aspect of the Global South, the group of Mexican Americans that Steinbeck called *paisanos* and would write about in his novel/short story cycle, *Tortilla Flat*.

At best, we can understand Steinbeck's episodic narrative involving Danny and friends as an attempt to imagine a kind of existence on another plane, one free from the norms and ideologies of capitalist society. "The biologists are on the verge of new discoveries that make a new world outlook," observed Steinbeck in an interview about *Tortilla Flat*, leaving his interviewer struck by Steinbeck's mystical, other-worldly quality.[15] Steinbeck was turning toward Mexican American culture in that search for wholeness that had failed in *Cup of Gold*, a search that would combine a biological inquiry into behavior with a desire to cross a borderland of cultural difference. Steinbeck vowed never to write about his *paisanos* again following criticism he received for his seemingly apolitical, "curiously childlike natives."[16] *Tortilla Flat* as a whole is an exercise in forgetting, or the revelation of a gap in Steinbeck's imagination. Both the socioeconomic conditions and the racial dynamics that lend this group of characters its antimodern power are reduced to deracinated episodes of comic melancholia, as the group seems unaware of its own cultural identity. In this regard, the purported innocence of Steinbeck's characters – their ideal freedom from the disease of capitalism – corresponds to Steinbeck's own innocence: that his ascription of premodernity to a group of Mexican Americans could be seen as anything but romanticized, soft racism.

However problematic, Steinbeck's engagement with Mexican American characters in *Tortilla Flat* was part of a growing recognition of the importance of Mexico and peoples of Mexican descent within the borders of the United States. In 1934, the year before *Tortilla Flat* appeared, the Berkeley economist Paul S. Taylor published *An American-Mexican Frontier*, a study of Nueces County, Texas, that charted the development of a Mexican American identity as something new and different, an identity becoming more assertive following the involvement of Latinos in World War I.[17] Taylor, who published a multivolume study of Mexican labor in the United States,[18] focused mostly on whites' attitudes toward their Mexican American neighbors, who were typically positioned between Black and white on a racial scale, even as they were beginning to resist many of the social discriminations they faced.[19] George I. Sanchez's *Forgotten People* (1940) suggests how Steinbeck's trope of forgetting in *Tortilla Flat* was a problem even within pioneering accounts of Mexican America. Highlighting how New Mexicans had been forgotten by the political process in a situation of internal colonization, Sanchez believed that the New Mexicans' only hope for success was to participate in a mainstream business culture.[20] Sanchez also placed strong emphasis on Spanish rather than indigenous heritage: the Mexican American's "language, his customs, and his technology remained those of sixteenth century Spain," he wrote.[21] Carey McWilliams's *North from Mexico: The Spanish-Speaking People of the United States* (1949) was more mixed in its response. The study emphasized the diversity of Spanish speakers, the group's strong link to the environment of the Southwest, and its particular way of life – a Spanish colonial heritage deeply intertwined with Indian and Mexican traditions – not molded by modern industrialism.[22] Above all, McWilliams developed the idea of the "borderlands" not as a geographic zone of division but as an expansive and shifting flow of traditions, a living and organic fusion of two distinct cultural systems.[23] McWilliams's work was an important step toward what Anzaldúa would, some four decades later, describe as a "consciousness of the Borderlands." Anzaldúa's idea was a political one, a development from her subject position as a *mestiza*. Borderlands consciousness opposes the capitalist modernity of the industrial world's inbuilt patterns of exploitation, prejudice, and discrimination. But this consciousness was also a kind of perception, a process of thinking, and a way of being, especially in relation to the species-life of humanity on the planet. *Sea of Cortez*, I suggest, is an important – if finally problematic – step toward what Anzaldúa called "cosmic" consciousness.[24]

Borders of Consciousness

Anzaldúa's predominant image for such pluralistic, borderless thinking is the sea. A powerful trope, the sea acts as a metaphorical state of fluid thought (border thinking is "floundering in uncharted seas"); a geopolitical zone that resists the division of national boundaries; and a biological, ecological space that places the individual at the very edge of the human world:

> Wind tugging at my sleeve
> feet sinking into the sand
> I stand at the edge where earth touches ocean

where the two overlap
a gentle coming together
at other times and places a violent clash.[25]

The space where land meets sea, where earth touches ocean – the intertidal zone – was the space of expertise of marine biologist Ricketts. *Sea of Cortez* is fundamentally a recognition of a borderland, an ecological zone running from Southern California (more or less from Point Conception) down through Baja California and beyond, an area marked by a "blending of the temperate and tropical faunas."[26] "Transcending species differentiations," Steinbeck and Ricketts write, "there is a deeply real distinctiveness which is valid both scientifically and in factual common sense, although difficult to state."[27] This was not a trip to just anywhere to conduct biological research. Ricketts and Steinbeck had good reason to travel to Lower California: a desire to study the life-forms of a neglected area, what they called, with colonial undercurrents, a "fairly virginal collecting ground."[28] They sought to recognize a border area between North and South, captured in the etymology of naming practices for a "greater California" – or, from another perspective, a "greater Mexico."[29] *Sea of Cortez* is an important work of environmentalist writing, an ecological manifesto of sorts,[30] and an exercise in locating an intercultural and geographical borderland. But it is still primarily a book about Mexico, written in the tradition of works that emerged in the 1920s and 1930s partly in response to the ideals and questions raised by the Mexican Revolution, which seemed an ongoing revolution for many intellectuals even into the 1930s.[31] At times, Steinbeck and Ricketts fall (perhaps showing Ricketts's influence) into quite conventional and generalized idealizations of the Mexican people as free from the various neuroses and commercial expedients that plague North American society. The Mexicans purportedly seek another kind of profit: they bargain in feelings, pleasures, and simple contacts; they do not think of time as a medium of exchange.[32] Here Steinbeck and Ricketts are on familiar ground. Stuart Chase's *Mexico: A Study of Two Americas* (1931) focused on time in particular – the Mexicans were allegedly a people without clocks[33] – while Waldo Frank's *America Hispana* (1931) recognized the new cultural borderland in mystical terms: "Across the frontier of Rio Grande, two cultures face each other. Both are incomplete, wanting some crucial element of wholeness; both, in varying degrees, long for completion." Although he viewed the Mexican Revolution as an important step toward modernization, Frank was keenest to explore how the heightened spirituality of Mexico – and of Latin America more broadly – could answer needs within the Protestant-capitalist-materialist-pragmatist culture and society of the North.[34]

Sea of Cortez is an exercise in border thinking not least because it finds its center in a sea that denies boundaries, and specifically in a gulf that offers a unique "pattern" of consciousness that obliterates the subjective-objective divide.[35] The Gulf of California is apparently borderless in its peculiar optical effect of mirage that makes this southern region the space of magical realism, returning Steinbeck to one of his fundamental interests and techniques. This hallucinatory quality, in which outlines of reality merge into miraculous dimensions, seemed partly a product of a colonial, racialized encounter with different belief systems.[36] It is the "hazy Gulf, with its changes of light and shape" that establishes the conditions for the philosophical core of *Sea of Cortez*: the concept of "non-teleological thinking" that Steinbeck takes directly from the writings of Ricketts.[37] As a whole, *Sea of Cortez* is a coauthored text, with Ricketts presumably responsible for the bulk of the "Phyletic Catalogue" (a taxonomy of species according to their evolutionary development, which comprises the second half of the book), and Steinbeck for the log of their travels, with Steinbeck incorporating aspects of Ricketts's writing into the text, and passing completed sections to the marine biologist for correction and revision.[38] Ricketts wrote of the "dual structure of thought and beauty" in *Sea of Cortez*: "Contributions from the one side are largely mine, from the other, John's. The structure is a collaboration, but shaped mostly by John."[39] (Given that *Sea of Cortez* was coauthored, I generally ascribe its authorship to Steinbeck and Ricketts, abbreviated to S&R.) Ricketts was a pioneering ecologist whose ideas would have resonated with and expanded upon Steinbeck's own ways of thinking that developed at Stanford University and elsewhere, and that we have seen operating in a number of works, most recently in the concept of emergence in *The Grapes of Wrath*. Ricketts's ideas were fundamentally relational: he was interested in how individual animals group together, how this interdependence contributes to evolution, and how the suprapersonal organization of the group or colony influences the units within it.[40] As Steinbeck noted in "About Ed Ricketts," the sketch he wrote after Ricketts's death and included in 1951 as an introduction to *The Log from the Sea of Cortez* (the travelogue section of the book, without the scientific material that comprises the second half), Ricketts was especially pleased with "commensal" animals, "groups of several species contributing to the survival of all."[41] Ricketts's ideas were thus also holistic: he was interested in how the individual animal (whether human or nonhuman) relates to the community, to the environment, to the planet, and out to the universe. Nature was thus a single indivisible entity combining all things animate and inanimate.[42] Ricketts was what we would today call a deep ecologist who questioned our values down to their root causes, as he sought a "unified field hypothesis" based on a radical interdisciplinarity that fuses literature, philosophy, music, and science.[43] In essays such as "The Philosophy of 'Breaking Through,'" Ricketts sought "moments of transcendence, of integration, and deep participation in the universe" that would overcome the obstacles of inward horizons to reveal our complete existence and place within a universal pattern.[44]

Writing from his position of expertise in the intertidal zone, Ricketts was attempting a kind of borderlands thinking in a more philosophical sense, one that becomes clear from the parallels between Ricketts's (and implicitly Steinbeck's) ideas and Anzaldúa's transcendental and ecological concepts in *Borderlands*. Like Ricketts, Anzaldúa called for a new kind of perception whereby "the senses become so acute and piercing that we can see through things, view events in depth, a piercing that reaches the underworld (the realm of the soul)." This new perception is a living and seeing *into* experience, one that recognizes and accepts our animal impulses – the mythic archetypes of our pre-humanity that lie deep in our unconscious – and that brings our human selves into a deep spiritual connection with "the wind and the trees and the rocks." Anzaldúa describes the need to move away from "convergent thinking, analytical reasoning that tends to use rationality to move toward a single goal (a Western mode), to divergent thinking, characterized by movement away from set patterns and goals and toward a more whole perspective, one that includes rather than excludes."[45] Borderland consciousness is thus a dismantling of causal, goal-directed thinking, an acceptance of what *is*, whereby nothing is rejected or abandoned. Ricketts called this "non-teleological thinking," which Steinbeck and Ricketts theorize in chapter fourteen of *Sea of Cortez*.[46] Chapter fourteen is something of an exception to the coauthored pattern of *Sea of Cortez*. Steinbeck revises an initial section from Ricketts's journal entry and then includes, without revision, Ricketts's entire "Essay on Non-teleological Thinking."[47] Like Anzaldúa's idea of an inclusive, holistic, and divergent mind-set, non-teleological thinking is an attempt to escape the imposition of human causal logic and instead to reveal patterns through relational thinking that establish larger and larger pictures of reality by scalar increase, or fractal expansion, rather than by causal chains of connection: "In the non-teleological sense there can be no 'answer.' There can be only pictures which become larger and more significant as one's horizon increases."[48] The scalar logic of non-teleological thinking enables the ecological understanding of interconnection and the radically democratic, even deconstructive, interrelation between small and large: "Those residua, those most minute differentials, the 0.001 percentages which suffice to maintain the races of sea animals, are seen finally to be the most important things in the world, not because of their sizes but because they are everywhere. The differential is the true universal, the true catalyst, the cosmic solvent."[49] Like Anzaldúa's consciousness of the borderlands, Ricketts's (and Steinbeck's) idea is at once a way of seeing and being (a "living into," a deep participation in things), a theory of observation, a critique of the ideologies of capitalism, and a fundamentally biological understanding that reaches a "cosmic" consciousness by deconstructing the logic of racial difference.[50] Anzaldúa termed this a "(r)evolution," a change (or "morphogenesis") that is at once a shift in political consciousness and a mutation in a "malleable species" toward a racial hybridity.[51]

Much remains problematic in Ricketts's (and Steinbeck's) idea of non-teleological thinking, for example, its sexist targeting of women as most resistant to this higher mode of argument (Carol Steinbeck accompanied them on the voyage but is not once mentioned in the log).[52] The argument ironically seems to be divided into its own rigid taxonomies and teleologies, and it self-consciously realizes its own looseness of method and failure to find a language to embody higher reasoning.[53] Nevertheless, the close parallels with the work of Anzaldúa deserve attention, particularly the common effort to deconstruct the instrumental reasoning of capitalist society, and the common grounding of these ideas in the space of Mexico.[54] S&R and Anzaldúa share an attempt to enter a planetary consciousness in which the very concept of the human is transformed (or reborn: the non-teleological chapter of *Sea of Cortez* takes place on Easter Sunday) by decentering its presence and recognizing the fundamental importance of the nonhuman. Ricketts and Steinbeck would have gained much of their interest in the nonhuman from the poetry of Carmel neighbor Robinson Jeffers, whose sense of place emerged from "many sources – physics, biology, the beat of blood, the tidal environments of life."[55] As Jeffers wrote in his well-known poem "The Roan Stallion" (1925), humanity itself is "the mold to break away from, the crust to break through."[56] Jeffers called for a decentering of the human, an acceptance of "inhumanism," or what we would today call post-humanism: an escape from solipsism by emphasizing the "not-man" and recognizing the fundamental "beauty of things."[57] To Steinbeck and Ricketts, the gulf seemed the natural place to resist the human because of its relatively sparse population.[58] Steinbeck wrote to his uncle in 1940 about his hopes for the Mexico book:

> The new work must jump to include other species beside the human. This is why my interest in biology and ecology have become so sharpened. . . . The bio-ecological pattern, having at its conception base and immeasurable lengthened time sequence, does not admit the emphasis of such crises as human unemployment, except insofar as they vitally threaten the existence of the species.[59]

Informed by the Darwinian tradition but also predicting more recent calls for the necessity of human self-understanding as a species, *Sea of Cortez* is an exercise in creating a species sensibility, one that recognizes humanity as a species among other species, and, in so doing, S&R create a response to a question that every species must face, including our own: the question of extinction.[60]

Describing the Species

The creation of this species sensibility takes us to another borderland in *Sea of Cortez*, a borderland of literary form. Steinbeck claimed that *Sea of Cortez* was "a new kind of writing" not simply because it was collaboratively written in the first-person plural (by the entity I am calling S&R).[61] It was also an attempt to find a borderland between what C. P. Snow in the 1950s called the "two cultures" – the obstructive division of knowledge into the sciences and the humanities – and hence discovering "great poetry in scientific writing."[62] S&R's primary technique was one essential to our recognition and understanding of species themselves: the technique of description. In this regard, S&R's work is continuous with what Rachel Bolten outlines as a long American "practice of description" that takes many forms but that emerged in part from attempts by natural historians and artists to preserve endangered species from environmental loss.[63] Indeed, S&R's idea of non-teleological thinking is already a theory of description. Such thinking is not concerned with how a thing fits into a narrative order but with understanding what it is, in the greatest depth, through the accumulation of description, and hence building by accretion toward a picture of the whole. Description, in other words, has a power to enact an understanding of the world, one that returns not to causes but to highly significant relational aspects that become clear only in the process of description.[64] It is a necessary practice of engagement that differentiates a deep and participating understanding, a focused interest, from shallow dismissals couched in the very same words: "It's so because it's so."[65] The neglected second half of *Sea of Cortez*, consisting mostly of a "Phyletic Catalogue" of the animals they encounter, continues this exercise in species determination, description, and classification. Criticizing the overspecialization of scientists and the current state of scientific writing, S&R seek a "toto-understanding" (presumably Ricketts's term) of their animals and compile their list of references accordingly:[66]

> It has been considered more important to list references which have full descriptions and synonymies, and, most of all, which carry adequate photographs or drawings of the *entire* animal. The method of identification by pictures may be both superficial and primitive, but it still remains not only the most popular, but by far the fastest method for the layman, or even for the specialist out of his own field.[67]

S&R turn mostly to the tradition of nineteenth-century collectors, natural historians (including Charles Darwin), and "field naturalists" to discover, in somewhat unexpected places, written specimens of vernacular and thorough encounter with animals that achieve a "literary charm" transcending time and subject matter – "a quality of universalness."[68]

The discovery of species and the discovery of nuggets of descriptive prose are hence parallel exercises, suggesting how the idea of a species depends on its description (just as the word *species* evolves from the Latin "to look," "to behold") and, indeed, on the work of the collector-describer.[69] S&R's plan of procedure, outlined in the introduction to the Phyletic Catalogue, is to move from discrimination (the act of finding a specimen in the field), to differentiation on the grounds of species type, and finally to naming. This process is followed by a second act of discovery, that of the "original description" of the animal, whose historical course they chase through the literature with the aim of achieving a familiarity with the separate species without losing sight of the whole picture.[70] These acts of heightened description, based on pure moments of holistic encounter and ideally performed across time through a slow-paced accumulation of sight and thought, become an aesthetic "joy" for the describers.[71] In turn, these descriptions enable access for the layperson – the common observer – to the realm of common beach fauna, hence exposing an alternate process of colonization: a colonization by animals that is successful and ongoing, "the whole welded into a fairly coherent, mutually interrelated society in a more or less stable state of equilibrium."[72] The authors make their intentions in *Sea of Cortez* clear: to give access to an ecological mode of thinking through acts of "thick description" – in the Geertzian sense, giving context to make meaning for the outsider – or "toto-picture," as S&R call it, that lays "a path straight through the wilderness," traversable by "average travelers whose interests or businesses justify the expenditure of no great or special effort."[73]

This is a special encounter with Mexico through a kind of description that opposes the nonspecific and inherently prospective description of colonial exploration and exploitation.[74] The ideal description in this regard is found in one of S&R's favorite natural historians, the nineteenth-century conchologist Philip Carpenter. It is a giving of voice *to* the animals, beholding them "on the very threshold of the promised continent," held in stasis.[75] Description is thus more than mere recording. It is an ideal human activity that clarifies our own species distinctiveness through the practice of collecting, observing, and describing other species holistically. Collecting thus merges with the "thinking-speculating activity," and it shares something with the spirit of collecting theorized by Susan Stewart: its privileging of a self-in-reverie, an identity "capable of transcending the accidents and dispersions of historical reality."[76] Hence the obsession in the Phyletic Catalogue with the original describers who overcame the limitations of human effort (not least the finitude of time and money) to offer toto-descriptions and specific names to which subsequent specialists would inevitably return.[77] "One wonders how a single worker could find time in a life-span to digest, co-ordinate, and present all this information," they write.[78] The human becomes an animal of pure collection and description, entering a new state of consciousness through these activities. And if the true nature of species has been captured and fixed by a heroic band of amateur naturalists, then the ideal of description is captured in the color photographs, black-and-white photographs, and many drawings that precede the Phyletic Catalogue. Clifford Geertz theorized description as the act of preserving things, fixing them from perishing conditions.[79] Likewise, the second part of *Sea of Cortez* begins with a detailed description of how to kill and preserve specimens in their original form. The correct determination of species is dependent on these techniques of death and stasis, again tying description to the earlier tradition that Bolten detects.[80] Thinking here of Georg Lukács's classic distinction between the methods of narration and description, we can understand the formal change in the second part of the book as a shift away from the story of the voyage toward a non-narrative catalogue of species, one in which – to paraphrase Lukács – we are presented with the power of description to create still lives that inherently lack humanity.[81]

The descriptive work within the Phyletic Catalogue occurs throughout *Sea of Cortez* and corresponds to a special knack of Steinbeck's. "Jon [*sic*] can make better descriptions than have ever been made," wrote Ricketts concerning their work together on a handbook of marine life along the California coast that they began in preparation for the Mexico book.[82] At one level, this urge to describe species seems to be a fundamental characteristic of human curiosity and desire for possession.[83] At its most ideal, it reaches a kind of transcendent empiricism, a "specification" as a process of observation supposedly free from the influence of social conditioning, an observation closely related to the living animal.[84] At another level, this long watching, naming, and describing of other species lead to the recognition that we "do not objectively observe our own species as a species, although we know the individual fairly well."[85] Description thus affords the opportunity to think about species and to think, self-consciously, *as* a species. This allows S&R to enter into an interspecies relationship that they capture by juxtaposing the image of an observer counting the spines on a preserved fish in a laboratory with an image of a fisherman struggling to land a fish on his boat, in which "a whole new relational externality has come into being – an entity which is more than the sum of the fish plus the fisherman."[86] This species consciousness is thus tantamount to a self-forgetting established in descriptions often marked by an anti-narrative listing:

> With *Heliaster* were a few urchins, but not many, and they were so placed in crevices as to be hard to dislodge. Several resisted the steel bar to the extent of breaking – the mouth remaining tight to the rock while the shell fell away. Lower still there were to be seen swaying in the water under the reefs the dark gorgonians, or sea-fans. In the lowest surf-levels there was a brilliant gathering of the moss animals known as bryozoa; flatworms; flat crabs; the large sea-cucumber; some anemones; many sponges of two types, a smooth, encrusting purple one, the other erect, white, and calcareous. There were great colonies of tunicates, clusters of tiny individuals joined by a common tunic and looking so like the sponges that even a trained worker must await the specialist's determination to know whether his find is sponge or tunicate. This is annoying, for the sponge being one step above the protozoa, at the bottom of the evolutionary ladder, and the tunicate near the top, bordering the vertebrates, your trained worker is likely to feel that a dirty trick has been played upon him by an entirely too democratic Providence.[87]

The resistance of urchins to being dislodged by human tools corresponds to a more general resistance to the human in which species are related to one another so densely that the human is pushed out of the picture altogether. Again like Stewart's idea of collecting as a self-forgetting in which "all time is made simultaneous or synchronous within the collector's world," the "swarming" effect of species encounter eats up time, and even the concept of identity is lost in the process of deep observation.[88] Yet this is not the result of the process of classification that Stewart inscribes with a power to contain and control ephemeral objects.[89] Rather, classification is resisted at such moments, just as the Sally Lightfoot crab remains elusive, beyond human intention and power.[90] The human capacity to define and to differentiate collapses when different species become confused: "Indeed, as one watches the little animals, definite words describing them are likely to grow hazy and less definite, and as species merges into species, the whole idea of definite independent species begins to waver, and a scale-like concept of animal variations comes to take its place."[91]

S&R's descriptive method is geared toward an increase in scale because it works through accumulation, with pictures becoming "larger and more significant as one's horizon increases."[92] Hence S&R use the image of the plateau to describe their idea: definitive cause-and-effect explanations occur only on a plateau that, upon further investigation, will yield to further plateaus that successively reveal more adequate and larger explanations. The idea is at heart ecological because everything "impinges on everything else."[93] The notion of the "cosmic" (whether it is figured as identity, consciousness, or solvent) is enabled by this shuttling between extremes of space and time, moving from "the tide pool to the stars and then back to the tide pool again," just as, with energetic observation, "the tide pool stretches both ways, digs back to electrons and leaps space into the universe and fights out of the moment into non-conceptual time. Then ecology has a synonym which is ALL."[94] This profound interrelationship, this melting of groups and ecological units into one another, ultimately evades the human attempt to create distinctive categories.[95] In its place we discover what scholars such as Gayatri Spivak, Wai Chee Dimock, and Ursula Heise call *planetarity*. This planetarity substitutes what Dimock calls "deep time" for the standardized time of the nation and marks our species imprint as "one species among others, inhabiting a shared ecology, a shared continuum," thus involving us in an ethic of collective responsibility for the earth as a speck in the cosmos.[96] In *Sea of Cortez*, this consciousness returns to an awareness of the precarious balance of the planet owing to the scalar importance of even the smallest changes. These ideas come together early in the book:

> We take a tiny colony of soft corals from a rock in a little water world. And that isn't terribly important to the tide pool. Fifty miles away the Japanese shrimp boats are dredging with overlapping scoops, bringing up tons of shrimps, rapidly destroying the species so that it may never come back, and with the species destroying the ecological balance of the whole region. That

> isn't very important in the world. And thousands of miles away the great bombs are falling and the stars are not moved thereby. None of it is important or all of it is.[97]

S&R return elsewhere to the impact of overfishing (in the gulf specifically) on "the eventual welfare of the whole human species." The book's ecological vision returns to this recognition of how the smallest changes, such as the disappearance of microscopic plankton, "would probably in a short time eliminate every living thing in the sea and change the whole of man's life, if it did not through a seismic disturbance of balance eliminate all life on the globe."[98] But in the passage quoted earlier, the connections are crucially *not* causal. The relationship between the collecting of soft corals, the Japanese overfishing, and the war in (presumably) Europe is not part of a teleological narrative but rather a scalar increase that brings to light a species sensibility, founded on the ways that humans act together, collecting, fishing, or bombing.[99] Or rather, it brings to light a species inevitability: a movement toward extinction. S&R's collecting activity, their technologies of extraction, observation, and description, are *part* of this move toward self-destruction. Just as they return to the United States with thousands of little dead animals in the hold, *Sea of Cortez* is punctuated by death scenes, for example, the long deaths of a sea turtle and, later, of a shark, or the pleasurable killing and preservation of sand dollars.[100] The descriptive energy at such moments suggests the crucial point about the descriptive urge as a whole: its aim not to preserve life but to produce *still* life. It is bound up with acquisition and murder. To practice description is to recognize death as a process, a living in death – life as the long death.

While formulating the plan that would become *Sea of Cortez,* Steinbeck had another idea, to write two theses, "Phalanx" and "The Death of the Species," for John Cage to set to percussion music.[101] Though the project was never realized, *Sea of Cortez* can be understood as uniting these two theses, combining Steinbeck's great theme of individuals merging into a common body, which runs through so many of his works, with a second theme less noticeable but extremely important to *Sea of Cortez*: extinction. Much of S&R's interest in species is directed at our "pre-humanity," the unconscious memories of sounds and visual symbols, "a group psyche-memory which is the foundation of the whole unconscious."[102] This interest in pre-humanity also admits the possibility of a post-humanity, a radical change in the direction of the species. It admits the possibility, indeed inevitability, of extinction as a result of a diagnostic species trait of self-destruction exacerbated by contemporary conditions of collectivization and war.[103] These conditions suggest a mutation in the species away from the instinct of survival based on hope in a progressive future, as human desires become rerouted to things outside ourselves, "a tendency that can end only in extinction."[104] Accordingly, the central running joke of *Sea of Cortez* – that their unpredictable outboard motor, the Hansen Sea-Cow, has developed a mind and soul of its own – marks a serious concern that industrial society has reached its peak and has suddenly mutated to produce something "more than a species. It is a whole new re-definition of life," a new machine-life that spells the doom of humanity.[105] Recognizing both the damage humans have wreaked on the planet and the capacity of the "trees and creeping plants, ice and erosion" to remove our marks "in a fairly short time," S&R end their vision with an ironic image of humankind, "not a species, but a triumphant race," approaching a moment of "perfection":

> And perhaps when that occurs – when our species progresses toward extinction or marches into the forehead of God – there will be certain degenerate groups left behind, say, the Indians of Lower California, in the shadows of the rocks or sitting motionless in the dugout canoes. They may remain to sun themselves, to eat and starve and sleep and reproduce. Now they have many legends as hazy and magical as the mirage. Perhaps then they will have another concerning a great and godlike race that flew away in four-motored bombers to the accompaniment of exploding bombs, the voice of God calling them home.[106]

S&R's point that humankind has come to admire the "progressive" forces that will bring its own extinction returns us to a racial distinction that cuts across the desire to understand humans at a species level, while reminding us of the importance of Mexico as context for this thinking.[107] It also returns us to both the possibilities and the problems of race in Steinbeck's work more generally. To some degree, S&R's interest in race is part of their urge to change the species away from the destructive values of capitalism, their attempt to change the "world-picture," the "pattern of all life" – a transformation based on the possibility that the "species is not set, has not jelled, but is still in a state of becoming."[108] The racialized condition of the indigenous Mexicans thus promises a reversal of perspective, an ideological shift away from the progressive values of Western modernity and Americanization, toward a holistic consciousness, a valuing of the natural world, and a merging with the reality of the cosmos. These ideas are practiced on a small group of impoverished Indians they meet in a canoe at Pulmo Reef:

> They seemed to live on remembered things, to be so related to the seashore and the rocky hills and the loneliness that they are these things. To ask about the country is like asking about themselves. "How many toes have you?" "What, toes? Let's see – of course, ten. I have known them all my life, I never thought to count them. Of course it will rain tonight, I don't know why. Something in me tells me I will rain tonight. Of course, I am the whole thing, now that I think about it. I ought to know when I will rain."[109]

A possibility of a different kind of extinction is offered here, not the death of the species but the extinction of certain traits within the species – revealed in the collapse of the "I" into the environment itself – that seem to be advancing it to its own destruction.

S&R's construction of the indigenous population returns to central ideas within US encounters with Mexico beginning in the 1920s. According to Waldo Frank in *America Hispana*, the diseased individuals of the mechanized North could rediscover an awareness of self as "a purposive integer in the cosmos" by accepting a key condition of Mexican culture, stretching back to the Aztecs, that offered both possibilities and problems: the goal of "blotting out of the differentiated person and of the personal will and of all human value." For Frank, Mexico was at heart a "person-denying culture," one dominated by a "cult of personal extinction."[110] S&R's Mexican Indians resonate with the ideas of Frank, Stuart Chase, and others: for example, the idea that they have "a different time sense – 'time-world' would be the better term – from ours," one that seems to "trail an expanding universe, or perhaps to lead it."[111] These indigenous people embody a cosmic, or borderlands, consciousness. They are ultimately passive and egoless. They live *into* the planet, their bodies are indistinguishable from their material surroundings, and hence they reflect the aphorism that S&R glean from John Elof Boodin's *A Realistic Universe* (1916): "Somehow the laws of thought must be the laws of things if we are going to attempt a science of reality."[112] In a very specific and ultimately problematic way, the stasis of these Indigenes offers an alternative to the worries and neuroses of modernity. We can understand their purported self-extinction alongside more recent ideas of what humans must do to survive the carbon-fueled capitalism that is inescapably plunging the earth into climatic catastrophe. Roy Scranton calls it "learning to die," an anti-capitalistic, anti-teleological revolution in mind-set.[113] Writes Scranton:

> Learning to die as an individual means letting go of our predispositions and fear. Learning to die as a civilization means letting go of this particular way of life and its ideas of identity, freedom, success, and progress. . . . Learning

> to die means learning to let go of the ego, the idea of the self, the future, certainty, attachment, the pursuit of pleasure, permanence, and stability. Learning to let go of salvation. Learning to let go of hope. Learning to let go of death.[114]

According to S&R, these indigenous people live a non-teleological existence. They supposedly cannot link cause and effect but can only understand the unfolding of external events through their own bodies' connection to the physical universe. They are part of the fauna of the gulf, waiting for the tide to pick them up.[115] If the human imagination of ourselves as a species facing extinction has tended to stress narrative – the stories we tell – as Ursula Heise has argued recently,[116] then for Steinbeck this species sensibility lies in a kind of description that allows passive contemplation and holistic encounter. Scranton also suggests a kind of descriptive solution to impending human extinction: "We must inculcate ruminative frequencies in the human animal by teaching slowness, attention to detail, argumentative rigor, careful reading, and meditative reflection."[117] The Phyletic Catalogue can be understood in this regard. It is an enormous multispecies network of the diverse flora and fauna of the gulf, with humans implicitly present as the observing, collecting, and describing animal. "Surely what being a 'species' means, from a biological and ecological as well as a social perspective," writes Heise in response to skepticism toward species-thinking, "is to be situated in a network of lived, existential relations with other species and with the inanimate environment (soil, water, atmosphere, weather patterns)."[118] The Phyletic Catalogue can be understood as precisely this networked act of species description.

However, who gets to describe? As objects to be collected, the native population are also victims *of* description; like specimens or empty "shells," they wait to be described. We are reminded again of Lukács's critique of description aimed at the naturalism of Emile Zola, its reduction of humans to animals that for Lukács signaled not simply an act of debasement but also an essentially static mind-set, unable to understand the forces of history or the inner vitality of human development.[119] The impoverished Mexicans S&R encounter in San Lucas, the morose young men who hang about waiting for something to happen, live in an anti-narrative space ("We told funny stories, knowing they wouldn't be enjoyed, tiring of them ourselves before the point was reached") that is more like a racially specific silent suffering, a frustration and hopelessness, and a profound lack of social or political agency.[120] Ironically, to achieve species consciousness is to be isolated and abject. Like the anecdote S&R glean from the eighteenth-century Jesuit historian of Lower California, Francisco Javier Clavigero, in which the native population repeatedly eat, regurgitate, and re-consume a piece of meat on a string, this anti-narrative repetition is a sign of impoverishment but also the register of a degree of racialized disgust at difference.[121]

Sea of Cortez seems to end with an ideal moment of borderland consciousness, an entry into the ecology of the gulf through a close relationship to the little animals it contains.[122] The urge to describe enables a species consciousness. Yet it also ends in failure when the power differentials of race come to haunt the universalized understanding of humankind.[123] S&R cannot finally reach the ideal, hybridized borderland consciousness of Anzaldúa. In lines drawn more or less directly from Ricketts's "Verbatim Transcription": "One can go from race to race. It is coming back that has its violation."[124] Writing of Steinbeck's affection for the boat and the unspoiled sea, Steinbeck's biographer Jackson Benson writes that Steinbeck "appears to have drawn a distinction in his attitude between the technology of discovery and the technology of exploitation, and he does not seem to have been particularly concerned with the usual process whereby one leads to the other."[125] Yet the book is aware, at least, of some of the contradictions that discovery creates. For example, S&R idealize the practice of slow observation and description while also noting how it requires the introduction of hunger and competition in animal groups for which these destructive forces had not existed before.[126] There is a violence within description, just as observation becomes exploitation. In the end, a tragic vision marks *Sea of Cortez*, as the indigenous population cannot finally sustain the theory of non-teleological living they are made to carry. They cannot escape the "civilizing web"; high-tension wires destroy their culture.[127] We can only long for the simplicity of the indigenous person's condition, write S&R, if we remain in ignorance of the complications of poverty and misery.[128] And through this irony, the steady drift into human extinction.

We might finally read these various contradictions in a pivotal moment of *Sea of Cortez*, the first plate, "Pink Murex" (see Figure 8.1), in the book's series of illustrations. It is a dialectical image, one of relationality, perhaps creating a yin-yang effect in its double-sidedness. Here the shell is the crust to break through, on one side, and the revelation of interiority on the other, as if a fleshy entry into the body itself (in the original color plate, the inside of the shell is a fleshy pink). It is a moment of pure observation and description (the murex seemingly floats in space, detached from everything but itself), a revelation of the inner life of the animal, both physical and

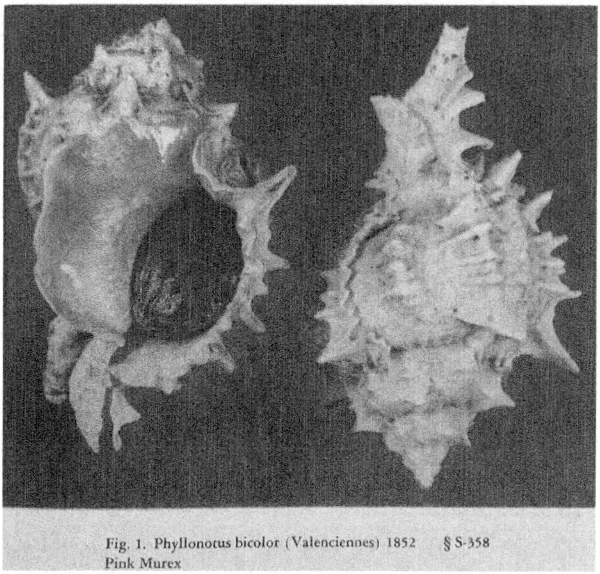

Fig. 1. Phyllonotus bicolor (Valenciennes) 1852 § S-358
Pink Murex

Figure 8.1 "Phyllonotus bicolor (Valenciennes), 1852. Pink Murex." John Steinbeck and Edward F. Ricketts, *Sea of Cortez: A Leisurely Journal of Travel and Research, with a Scientific Appendix Comprising Materials for a Source Book on the Marine Animals of the Panamic Faunal Province* (New York: Viking, 1941), plate 1.

mystical – a "living into" it. We could read this plate as the ultimate non-teleological moment, unconnected from narrative. It just "is." Or is it? Responding to this eye looking back at us, we can read the photograph as a moment of species intersectionality, a breakdown of the hierarchy between human and nonhuman animal, the kind of intersectionality idealized by theorists of the post-human such as Donna Haraway. Yet as Haraway also notes: "*Species* reeks of race and sex."[129] Beneath the photograph is the name of the original describer of the species, Achille Valenciennes, who worked with Alexander von Humboldt classifying the flora and fauna of New Spain. It reminds us that many of the zoologists and other scientists who gave our shells (and plants and animals in general) their names were involved in missions not merely scientific but also commercial and colonial in their aims. Libidinous men, we are told, are the best describers – hence the anecdote regarding John Xantus, a zoologist and collector but also an agent of the government, an imperialist presence who fathered children with the native population.[130] Our very nomenclature is shot through with such power differentials, and any act of description must bear this burden. Tremendous irony therefore lies in that apparently innocent act of changing the Gulf of California to the Sea of Cortez, "a better-sounding and more exciting name" – its colonial name.[131] An effort at one level to change the very meaning of the colonial, from a structure of human power and exploitation to the cosmic relationality that binds animals together into groups in which the whole is greater than its parts, *Sea of Cortez* is haunted by this history of colonial acquisition, just as the collecting of animals mimics the process of exploitation.

CHAPTER 9

Mexican Revolutions: The Forgotten Village, The Pearl, *and the Global South*

Mexico provided Steinbeck with a space to explore the borderlands of human consciousness in *Sea of Cortez* (1941). It also brought home to him the deep social and economic suffering in the Mexican countryside. The indigenous people who offer Steinbeck the possibilities of post-human, passive living in synch with the needs of the planet are close to self-obliteration in another sense. They are also stunned into inaction by the disasters of colonial contact: "So much evil the white man had brought to their ancestors: his breath was poisonous with the lung disease; to sleep with him was to poison the generations. Where he set down his colonies the indigenous people withered and died. He brought industry and trade but no prosperity, riches but no ease."[1] Steinbeck had famously confronted the poverty of Dust Bowl migrants amidst the greed of capitalism in *The Grapes of Wrath* (1939). *Sea of Cortez* expands this concern into a networked understanding of Northern industrialism and Southern poverty on an international scale. In a social and economic sense – beyond being a zone of cultural contact – Steinbeck's Mexico is part of what scholars term the Global South.

As the compass of American studies has pointed beyond the nation in recent years, this Global South has come into view as a means to relate the literature of American modernity to global distributions of capital that divide Anglo from Latin America but that unite many writers from these different regions in a common project of postcolonial representation and critique. Hence even the obstinately local work of William Faulkner, centered on what he called his "own little postage stamp of native soil,"[2] has gained new significance as scholars have searched for the "Latin American Faulkner" whose South is hemispheric in scope.[3] Drawing in particular on the Mississippian's influence on Gabriel García Márquez and on the so-called Boom writers of the 1960s and 1970s, scholars have reevaluated the nature of Faulkner's modernism, or what Márquez called the "'Faulknerian' method," and its effectiveness as a lens onto Latin

American reality.[4] Episodes such as Thomas Sutpen's journey to Haiti in Faulkner's *Absalom, Absalom!* (1936) have moved scholars into analyses of colonial and postcolonial identity formation – one inherently fragmented, hybrid, and ambivalent – and a vision of history at once cyclical, recursive, and traumatic.[5]

The aim of this final chapter is not to unseat Faulkner from his position in the Global South. His influence on Latin American writers was undoubtedly profound, impacting their techniques and analyses of modernity. But still, it does not quite seem correct to speak of this relationship as a "dialogue," at least if we understand dialogue as multidirectional exchange.[6] Apart from the case of Sutpen in Haiti (which in any case features Sutpen quelling a rebellion of enslaved people decades after slavery had ended in Haiti, in an otherwise chronologically obsessive book)[7] and the occasional references to Mexican ancestry in *Light in August* (1932),[8] scholars have resorted to implication and speculation to establish Faulkner's awareness of and interest in Latin American history, identity, and literature.[9] Ironically like the version of history that writers have discovered in Faulkner, the relationship between Faulkner and Latin America can seem one of uncertain directions and secondary echoes.

The purpose of my chapter, instead, is to uncover an alternative version of this Global South – one far less dependent on the established channels of a modernist aesthetic, or on the dynamics of reception – in the writings of Steinbeck. The case for Steinbeck's relevance could be based on quantity alone: Steinbeck's biographer, Jackson Benson, estimates that Mexican or Mexican American subjects comprise one-third of Steinbeck's published work.[10] We have encountered this Latin presence already in his first novel, *Cup of Gold* (1929), and in *Tortilla Flat* (1935). In addition to his Mexican travelogue of scientific exploration, *Sea of Cortez*, even works set in Steinbeck's Salinas Valley, such as *The Wayward Bus* (1947), had Mexican origins. If Faulkner was silent on the Mexican Revolution, then Steinbeck researched and wrote a path-breaking history of its revolutionary leader, Emiliano Zapata, and a screenplay of the classic movie of the revolution, *Viva Zapata!* (1952).[11] Beyond the sheer quantity of Steinbeck's southern engagements, it is their quality that impresses most. Steinbeck may not have influenced Latin American writers to the same degree as Faulkner, but he did share directly in the cultural dialogue that scholars attempt to conjure in the proprietor of Yoknapatawpha County.[12] This is particularly true of two projects that returned Steinbeck to the social inequalities and the dependency he had glimpsed in *Sea of Cortez*: Steinbeck's experimental documentary film *The Forgotten Village* (1941) and his narrative *The Pearl* (1947), which exists variously as anecdote, magazine story, novel, and film. These works are some of Steinbeck's most overtly political, as Marijane Osborn has pointed out.[13] Through the various dialogues that constitute their creation, they also provide new ways to think about the opportunities and the limits of transamerican literary relations, ones very different from the Faulknerian method and the recursive nature of its implied temporality.

Participatory Documentary

The Forgotten Village, like *Sea of Cortez*, was born from the difficult moments following the publication of *The Grapes of Wrath*. Badly shaken by the fierce reactions to his Dust Bowl classic, his first marriage failing, and his career now indelibly stamped by the expectations of success, Steinbeck turned his confused anger on the form of the novel itself. This led Steinbeck to the "new thinking" and experimental science writing in *Sea of Cortez*. It also inspired him to new experiments in social involvement, driven by the hope that world war, and its accompanying social chaos, would bring a profound shift in the human species.[14] Steinbeck had already experienced something like the immediacy of participation, writing *The Grapes of Wrath* while history "is happening," as he put it.[15] His feelings in the early 1940s, however, drove him away from the novel as he returned to the public motivations that had inspired earlier forays into drama through the hybrid form of *Of Mice and Men* (1937). If Steinbeck felt that the novel had lost its ability to move a public, then cinematic images had a power to make audiences participate in and accept the projected world, because of what Steinbeck described as humanity's "built in mechanism of illusion, closely tied to his glands and his cortex."[16] Steinbeck was in search of new media and new literary forms to enact his desires. He was looking for a revolution, and he turned to Mexico to find it.

The Forgotten Village project began when Steinbeck was approached by Herbert Kline to write a documentary feature about a possible Fascist uprising in Mexico. Kline had already directed a number of successful documentaries about Adolf Hitler's conquest of Europe. He turned to the possibility of a similar threat far closer to home, as supporters of the right-wing general Juan Andreu Almazán sought to overthrow the progressive left-wing government of Lázaro Cárdenas and his successor Manuel Ávila Camacho. Mexico was a cauldron of opposing political forces, the promises of the revolution still in the air following the leftward shift under Cárdenas, even as those promises seemed imminently vulnerable to a totalitarian threat, heightened by the Fascist takeovers in Europe. According to Kline, Steinbeck's original story featured a group of silver miners who become entangled in these left/right political conflicts.[17] But on the ground in Mexico, Steinbeck's attention shifted to a favorite subject, water – specifically to the presence of bacterial disease in the water supply of isolated villages, and to the challenge faced by modern science and medicine to improve the health of Mexico's impoverished rural citizens living under traditional ways. Attention shifted, in other words, from political conflict narrowly understood to the more basic conflict between indigenous cultures and the forces of modernization.

The Forgotten Village was conceived simultaneously with the writing of *Sea of Cortez.* Kline and his team were already working in Mexico when Steinbeck sailed to the Gulf of California with Ed Ricketts; later, Steinbeck came and went from Mexico as he wrote his sections of the marine travelogue. Steinbeck wrote to Kline from Loreto, Baja California, suggesting the degree to which his attention was directed to Mexico's political situation as much as it was to the world of marine invertebrates. In an unpublished letter, Steinbeck noted his frustration on meeting poor fishermen who seemed to favor a Fascist dictatorship and American-style modernization, rather than the collectivist motivations that had fueled the revolution.[18] Steinbeck responded to what he saw with a desire for direct participation in the struggle of ordinary people for a better life. "You must try to direct this, Herb, as I try to write," Kline recalled Steinbeck saying about *The Forgotten Village*, "on one top level for our peers, those who know as much as we like to think we know – and on another level to keep it simple and true for people with little or no education so they can understand and be moved by our story."[19] Steinbeck was attempting to write a kind of revolutionary literature by turning to the medium of film as an agent of grassroots social change.

Marijane Osborn has explored Steinbeck's "participatory aesthetic" in his three movies about Mexico (*The Forgotten Village*, *John Steinbeck's "The Pearl,"* and *Viva Zapata!*), particularly his use of irresolution and moral ambiguity as means to engage the cinema audience with the political struggles of impoverished and neglected populations.[20] But the real participation in *The Forgotten Village* involved not its audience but the makers of the film themselves, through their deep immersion in a moment of potential social change during what many saw as a long revolutionary era.[21] In the preface to a book version of *The Forgotten Village*, in which photographic stills from the movie are juxtaposed with a brief and simple narrative, Steinbeck described the unique and patient working method of the documentary film. The crew entered the pueblo of Santiago with a "very elastic story" – at base just a question, Why do so many children die? – and then they let the story unfold as it would, through their conversations and interactions with the villagers. The actors were real versions of the roles they played in a story that rapidly became a dramatic conflict between "medicine and magic."[22] Steinbeck's desire to impact the complex culture he encountered was nothing new. A decade earlier, in his study *Tepoztlán, a Mexican Village: A Study in Folk Life* (1930), the anthropologist Robert Redfield similarly considered which aspects of modernization would improve the lives of impoverished populations while leaving the organic foundation of village life unaltered.[23] What makes *The Forgotten Village* so interesting is that this humanitarian dilemma – how to improve living conditions through modernization while avoiding the American cultural hegemony that typically accompanied such interventions – has a formal correlative all the more fraught because Steinbeck was using a medium, film, tied to the potentially negative aspects of modernization. Steinbeck wanted to inspire an inherent thrust toward social improvement both within and against an indigenous culture already impacted by a prior colonization. The method he chose was dialogic. The crew would participate in a culture in a descriptive sense, not seeking to "editorialize, attack, or defend anything," filming what they found and then "only arranging it to make a coherent story."[24] *The Forgotten Village* is formed from this dynamic of observation and arrangement. A non-teleological encounter with a social situation confronts the desire for teleology, in the sense of both narrative movement and social development through collective action.

The story centers on the village school, the space of participatory democracy lauded by John Dewey during his visit to Mexico, and described by another observer as a beacon of hope in a dark landscape, being run "not from the outside, but from the inside, so to speak. It has fitted into the village democracy and become a source of stimulus and strength to that democracy."[25] With the school, rather than a charismatic revolutionary leader (or ideology) at the center, the aim of the film was to turn the villagers into actors in two senses. First, they would be actors on the movie set, playing a version of their own lives. We meet Trini the *curendera*, or traditional native healer; Juan Diego, the young boy who strives to educate his village and then himself; his friend the schoolteacher; and so on. And second, they would be actors in a deeper sense, stepping onto the stage of history by helping to create a narrative of social betterment for themselves through collective action. The former met with some success, though the latter proved much more difficult to achieve. The tension within this experiment is hinted at in Steinbeck's preface to the book version of *The Forgotten Village* and becomes explicit in Kline's recollection of the film. Kline describes the mistrust that developed between the villagers and the film crew, especially when they were forced to stop filming to save women and children from being harmed by Trini's traditional medicinal "cures." Kline also describes the crew's failed efforts to make the villagers aware of their position in a system of inequality and injustice, and their failed attempts to make the villagers feel collective grief for lost loved ones, against their acceptance that "sickness and death" were "God's will."[26] But ironically, the villagers only lost their self-consciousness (a self-consciousness clearly on display in still photographs taken during the filming; see Figure 9.1), and hence only became effective actors in the film, through their absorption in the Aztec rituals and

Figure 9.1 Dance scene from *The Forgotten Village*. Papers Relating to the Production of Steinbeck's *The Forgotten Village*, 1941, Stanford University Libraries, Department of Special Collections, M1350, Box 1.

indigenous medical practices that – at least as Kline and Steinbeck saw it – prevented them from becoming historical actors in a narrative of emergence from poverty.[27] Aesthetics and politics thus collide as the villagers' resistance to modernization inflects the story itself. During a key scene in the democratic schoolhouse, the villagers violently reject the technology of vision that tells of the "little animals" living in the water and promises to cure cholera through vaccination.[28] They smash to the ground the borrowed film projector, putting in jeopardy the move toward modernization and indeed the technology of mass communication underpinning the making of *The Forgotten Village* itself.[29]

Buried in Stanford University Libraries' Special Collections lies an incomplete, holograph manuscript of *The Forgotten Village* (subtitled "El Pueblo Olvidado"), in Steinbeck's hand in a ledger presumably purchased in Mexico and composed during the making of the film. The ledger manuscript describes certain scenes as they appear in the film but also contains scenes that remain unwritten because the film footage has not yet been edited. The manuscript also records instructions for that editing. In other words, it describes the dynamic process of give-and-take in which the narrative is emerging from the nature of the footage, just as that footage is being edited according to the needs of the story. The ledger manuscript ends at the point when the villagers reject the photographic evidence of bacteria in their water supply. This moment of interaction with the villagers is clearly crucial in the overall plot development, in which Juan Diego moves away from the community of the village, rejected even by his own family owing to his belief in modern methods. He travels to Mexico City to receive an education. The possibility of social change is thus pushed toward a vague future, as the story finally repeats the claim that change "will come, is coming." The film's final line, "I am Juan Diego" (a line not present in the ledger manuscript), marks an ultimate recognition of how the film has abandoned the narrative of participatory democracy and replaced it with a conventional one of individual growth, in which the hero emerges against the backdrop of a static people.[30]

The film suggests the failure of progressive efforts to intervene in another culture to encourage the benefits of modernization, efforts based on belief in an indigenous will to democratic action, all the while avoiding the ills of an encroaching, Americanized modernity. The significance of the *Forgotten Village* project lies in the way that the medium, form, and process of the documentary film are directly wired into the situation the film attempts to represent and alter. Itself a technology of modernization, the film, and the film*ing* are both medium and agent of would-be change, just as Steinbeck the solitary writer is himself seeking emergence into both artistic and social collaboration. At the end of Steinbeck's ledger manuscript is a loose, typed sheet, presumably from Steinbeck to Kline, which speaks volumes about the nature of their interaction with the villagers:

> Please ask Trini whether she knows either of the following words but do it casually.
>
> 1. YEHYECAME (this is the disease she is supposed to have been treating, in the nahuatl language)
> 2. xxxxxxxxxxxx [*sic*] YEHYECATZITZIN. (These are the little gods which are supposed to cause it.[31]

The filmmakers were striving to understand an indigenous culture on its own terms, to learn its language and to understand its systems of belief and traditional medicine. Steinbeck's injunction to "do it casually" hints at the tensions surrounding the inquiry, the degree of indigenous opposition to Steinbeck and Kline's intentions (the film crew were allegedly stoned by the villagers at one point of tense relations). This breakdown of intercultural dialogue suggests its own story of failed communication and intervention. The film features no direct dialogue, in part because the technical challenges of recording sound on location were too great, and in part because many of the villagers spoke an indigenous language (Nahuatl) not Spanish. In the ledger manuscript, Steinbeck notes that the resulting voiceover (eventually performed by Burgess Meredith) "should be persuasive in factual matters while, in matters of story, it should attempt the caressing, almost reverie tone of a thing remembered and retold."[32] In the preface to the photo-text book *The Forgotten Village*, Steinbeck further comments that the voiceover should embody "a spoken story so natural and unobtrusive that an audience would not even be conscious of it," with each scene advancing the story in a significant way.[33] The voiceover thus bears the weight of teleology imposed on an intervention gone awry. The voice should at once participate in historical facts as they unfold while carrying the retrospective tone of a story already formed: the demands of the narrative *as* narrative. The voiceover is a sign of the imposition of narrative, and simultaneously a stand-in for a broader cultural dialogue that the film fails to record.

The finished film contains another glitch, almost unnoticeable but again resonant with meaning. During Juan Diego's first journey to Mexico City to seek the help of doctors to save his village from cholera, an unexplained moment breaks into the narrative. "The streets were quiet, for order was restored and the day of fighting was over," speaks the voiceover, to a scene of Juan Diego virtually alone, crossing an unpeopled street, surrounded by automobiles, his bundle pointing up to the sky, echoing the new building being constructed to the right, with Mexico City's Monument to the Revolution in the background; the moment is suggested in another still photograph taken during the filming (Figure 9.2). Filming in the city on election day, Kline and crew had captured scenes of fighting between supporters of the right-wing Almazán and their opponents (Figure 9.3). Impressed with the footage taken in his absence, Steinbeck initially planned another ending to the film, "one in which Juan Diego and the teacher would take up

Figure 9.2 Juan Diego in *The Forgotten Village*. Papers Relating to the Production of Steinbeck's *The Forgotten Village*, 1941, Stanford University Libraries, Department of Special Collections, M1350, Box 1.

Figure 9.3 Demonstration during the Mexican electoral campaign of 1940. Papers Relating to the Production of Steinbeck's *The Forgotten Village*, 1941, Stanford University Libraries, Department of Special Collections, M1350, Box 1.

arms to help fight the Fascist take over."[34] Steinbeck's ledger manuscript, which ends at the pivotal moment when the villagers reject the filmed evidence of cholera and its cure (following a scene in which Juan Diego is left on the floor, "holding the projector almost as though it were a baby"),[35] contains this final note:

> This is the end of the written and cut film. From the approach to the military camp, through the election scenes, to the doctors, to the coming of the doctors to the village. Hence I will write the scene, and comment tentatively. Then it can be changed if necessary. This is how I see it anyway.
>
> Furthermore – the soldier's speech will be the longest in the whole picture. The election sequences must be carefully cut carefully [*sic*]. I leave it to you how often to cut back to the soldier in order that the audience will be constantly aware that it is he doing the talking.[36]

None of this is present in the completed film (the soldier does make a brief cameo appearance in the photo-text of *The Forgotten Village*, even if his voice is missing). Steinbeck may have wanted the schoolteacher and Juan Diego to become involved in this mass political action. In an undated letter, Steinbeck accordingly writes to Kline of his dissatisfaction with the ending: "It should not go without a hitch. There must be consistent and constant conflict right up to the end."[37] But the soldier's lesson is about the problem of collective action in light of the growth of a political class peddling empty words, and about the need for improvement through education.[38] With the riots suppressed, Steinbeck persuaded Kline and company to eliminate the scenes of violence and keep to the storyline of the fight against "ignorance" and "superstition," and the fictionalized story of Juan Diego's journey to the city and his progressive education. Ironically, the original idea for the story – silver miners caught in left/right conflicts – does emerge in a different form during the filming of *The Forgotten Village*, only to be edited out of the final version. The confusing reference to unrepresented political action is an ultimate sign of Steinbeck's confused and thwarted intentions in his experimental documentary. The glitch implies fundamental questions, about intervention; about the ability to understand another culture in dialogue; about the desire to find something in Mexico akin to the ideals of the revolution; and about the struggle to find a form capable of capturing, even creating, this revolutionary urge.

Steinbeck's friend and collaborator on *Sea of Cortez*, Ed Ricketts, wrote an "anti-script" to Steinbeck's screenplay, in which he opposed the narrative, linear logic of progress with a "Region of Inward Adjustments" that he attempted to capture in static, descriptive vignettes of cyclical action and deep personal harmony with the environment.[39] Criticizing both the message and the medium of *The Forgotten Village*, Ricketts dreads the emergence of new roads leading the young inhabitants of Mexico's countryside into town to watch a movie.[40] Ricketts's script attempts to describe a de-colonial humanity free from what recent scholars have called "Americanity," a series of values defined by "coloniality, power, ethnicity, racism, and newness, or instrumentalized scientific progress."[41] It throws into sharp relief the problems of *The Forgotten Village*: how its transamerican encounter fails not despite but because of a desire for the teleology of narrative – a narrative of the development of the individual subject. Following *The Forgotten Village*, it would have been easy for Steinbeck to turn away from the difficulties he encountered in Mexico, and to abandon film as the always already problematic medium of modernization. But Steinbeck would face again head-on the dynamics of cross-cultural collaboration and the potential of art to make a social difference in the novel and the film of *The Pearl*.

The Pearl of the World

Steinbeck met Emilio Fernández in Mexico City in February 1944. Shell-shocked from his experiences as a reporter in Europe,[42] Steinbeck was in Mexico at the invitation of the Russian Embassy to celebrate the twenty-sixth anniversary of the founding of the Soviet Army.[43] A rising star of the burgeoning Mexican film industry, Fernández would go on to a long career in Mexico and in Hollywood. He worked closely with the cinematographer Gabriel Figueroa to develop a distinctly Mexican film style, known for its low-angle shots and dialectical composition of elements, and showing the influence of the Mexican muralist tradition of the revolutionary era.[44] Steinbeck was immediately intrigued by Fernández's identity as what he called an "ex-cowboy actor, ex-revolutionary leader": "He is really an Indian Zapotec I think and he knows that level of life and is passionate about wanting to put it down." Steinbeck told Fernández and Figueroa the pearl story he had heard during his travels in the Gulf of California and included in *Sea of Cortez*, and they formed a plan to collaborate and – as Steinbeck put it – to "make it straight without any concessions to Hollywood."[45] Based on this conversation, Steinbeck would write a story, "The Pearl of the World," published in *Woman's Home Companion* in 1945, and simultaneously a movie script of the same name. He would subsequently work closely – at times fractiously – with Fernández on producing a bifurcated film, one version in English and one in Spanish, both released in 1947, *John Steinbeck's "The Pearl"* and *La Perla*, all made with Mexican financing, Mexican actors, and a Mexican crew. *The Pearl* was the first Mexican film to receive general release in the United States, not least because of Steinbeck's strong involvement with it. The screenplay of *The Pearl/La Perla* was written by Steinbeck, Fernández, and Jack Wagner, a friend of Steinbeck who had grown up in Mexico (in the Spanish-language version of the film, Fernández's name would receive top billing for the screenplay). To coincide with the release of the movie, Steinbeck would republish "The Pearl of the World" as a novel, *The Pearl* (1947), including five drawings by José Clemente Orozco, whose name lies directly below Steinbeck's, in smaller font, on the title page ("it is the only book he has ever consented to illustrate and that to me is a very great compliment," wrote Steinbeck).[46] With customary idealism, Steinbeck wanted to give something to Mexico, and to give something of Mexico to an American audience. In the latter aim, he was on firm ground, walking in the footsteps of those US visitors from the 1920s and early 1930s who saw a heightened spirituality and a fresh political promise in Mexico. In the former aim, he was on much more experimental, and problematic, ground as he sought to create a new form, or series of forms, to carry his intentions.

The story of the pearl lies at the center of a remarkable series of transnational and intercultural collaborations, just as it undergoes a series of radical shifts across media, from folktale, to short story, to film, to novel – even to a sequence of artworks, if we count Orozco's five drawings as another version of the story. If we term this broader transmedia and collaborative phenomenon of the story THE PEARL, then it began in chapter eleven of *Sea of Cortez*, following an encounter with an indigenous fisherman who sings the praises of General Almazán. The moment is passed off with ironic humor in *Sea of Cortez*, but Steinbeck's letter to Kline, as we saw, suggests that Steinbeck was much more concerned about the almost universal popularity of the right-wing Almazán on the peninsula. Steinbeck moves from this encounter with contemporary politics to an account of the necessity of developing an explanation for their unusual practice of collecting specimens, which they describe as valuable "curios" to satisfy the suspicious inquiry of locals.[47] The subsequent discovery of the pearl story in La Paz – one of the few towns on the gulf to be successfully colonized, Steinbeck observes, owing to its lucrative industry of pearl fishing – is thus a particularly self-conscious moment in which a tale about the chance uncovering of wealth at the bottom of the sea is equivalent to the discovery of a perfectly formed, parable-like narrative, seemingly ready-made for literary exploitation. The kernel of the story remains the same across the different formats of THE PEARL: a man (or boy in the folktale) discovers a pearl of great value, is cheated by the racketeering of the pearl buyers, and is assaulted by mysterious strangers, from whom he flees to the mountains, only to return to La Paz to renounce his potential wealth by throwing the pearl into the sea. Steinbeck describes the story as a parable because the final renunciatory action of the boy is far too "reasonable" to be true, and lies "contrary to human direction."[48] The future of this story, as it unfolded on page and on the big screen, would bring a fleshing out of character and a thickening of event. Most important, it would involve a move from the moral parameters of the folk story – the boy wants his newfound wealth for disreputable purposes at the beginning, but after a series of punishments he emerges, through relinquishment of the pearl, a happy and free man – to a much more political story as Steinbeck collaborates with the "ex-revolutionary" Fernández.

It is difficult to say how much Fernández impacted Steinbeck's early conception, or rather revision, of the pearl story. The 1945 film script of "The Pearl of the World" – presumably written simultaneously with the story of the same name that appeared in *Woman's Home Companion*, both bearing Steinbeck's name alone – suggests that there were two *Pearls* at the outset, the film script and the story, both speaking to each other in different media languages. "The Pearl of the World" script suggests some close collaboration between American novelist and Mexican filmmaker. Though rudimentary in its camera directions, the script begins with the kind of low-angle shots and the de-centered perspective for which Fernández and Figueroa were becoming known. There is a more forceful role for the *curandera* figure, who seems responsible for curing Kino's baby son Coyotito (following a scorpion bite) with her traditional medicine, suggesting an explicit rejection of the logic of *The Forgotten Village* through this new indigenist perspective.[49] (Steinbeck uses the term *indigene* in the novel version of *The Pearl* to describe the Native Americans of Mexico, an unusual word in English that suggests again the influence of the Mexican, Spanish-language context, in which *indígena* is a more common term.) The early script also contains the scenes that may have been added to the film to resonate with the *macho* interests of the Mexican audience, for example, the long scene in which Kino gets drunk in a local bar with two dubious characters and even has a failed engagement with a local prostitute.[50] The 1945 script also contains the scene in which a wealthy woman seeks to procure an abortion from the doctor, just prior to his refusal to help Kino, a scene removed from the US version of the 1947 film, presumably owing to Hollywood's Production Code. It would not be unreasonable to assume that the moments when the story in the film differs from the story in the novel reveal Fernández's direct influence, though Kino's character at such moments also seems much more like the figure from the folktale recorded by Steinbeck in *Sea of Cortez*. It is thus more productive and probably more accurate to think of THE PEARL as a creative dialogue between multiple auteurs.

The choice of Orozco to illustrate *The Pearl* further complicates these relationships and suggests another kind of collaboration. In his anti-script to *The Forgotten Village*, Ricketts referred to Orozco's *Catharsis* (1934; fresco, Palace of Fine Arts, Mexico City) as "a mural in which a mechanical man is shown strangling the Mexican race," thus opposing the modernizing logic of Steinbeck's film.[51] Further countering this logic, the integration of Orozco's work into *The Pearl* places the novel in direct lineage with the art of the Mexican Revolution, an art designed to communicate political ideas directly to the public, simply and on a massive scale. Significantly for Steinbeck's project, Orozco was known for his indigenist perspective, and for his alter-modern representations of the perils of industrialization and the abuses of political power.[52] He was also known for his refusal to idealize the revolution, his recognition of its destructive violence, and for his skepticism regarding a harmonious democratic future in Mexico.[53] Taken in series, the five charcoal sketches in *The Pearl* also present their own narrative interpretation of Steinbeck's story. The first drawing, in its merger of Kino, Juana, and Coyotito, represents the wholeness of the family unit. The second drawing, in its de-centered, slanted perspective, represents the introduction of a gendered inequality, a reflection of the power imbalance in society at large. Typical of the oblique perspectives and diagonal composition of Orozco's murals, which tend to mark divisions and disharmony through spatial imbalance,[54] this drawing also suggests Orozco's influence on the visual style of Fernández and Figueroa. According to the film scholar Charles Ramirez-Berg, the rejection of centered and linear perspective, the preference for transversal over parallel lines in Fernández's and Figueroa's films, mark divisions between classes and races imposed by the colonial system: the visual representation of an unbalanced ideology that Fernández's protagonists battle against.[55] The third Orozco drawing represents the victimized, pressured male body, forced to the very bottom of society, attempting to earn a living by extracting it from the seafloor. The fourth image represents gendered inequality and abuse again, as the family unit bears the pressure of the social realm. The final drawing, in which Kino throws the pearl back into the sea, represents the rise of the female character to occupy a space equal to that of the male, even if the female character is mere border without content, a minimalist or unfinished self. Steinbeck's work is full of such "unfinished" selves.

This final drawing in the Orozco series is significant in another way. It directly predicts the first striking shot of the film, *John Steinbeck's "The Pearl,"* in which veiled female figures stand in silhouette facing the sea. Not only, then, do these Orozco drawings embody the intercultural relations between Steinbeck's PEARL project and the legacy of the Mexican Revolution. They also mark an important site of *transmediation*: a translation of written narrative into picture series on the one hand but also – in this final image – a bridge toward the film, as if the book is imagining its own imminent visualization as moving picture.

The PEARL, of course, was not the first time Steinbeck had played with genre and transmediation. As we saw in Chapter 6, *Of Mice and Men* was a play in the form of the novel whose generic hybridity embodies a feeling of human fragility. As the mirroring between the final Orozco drawing and the first scene of the film suggests, *The Pearl* is another of Steinbeck's hybrid genres – a novel that looks toward its life as a film – though in ways notably different from *Of Mice and Men*. *The Pearl* (novel), for example, features very little dialogue – at times, Kino seems afraid of his own voice – though it is highly self-conscious of sound, particularly musical sound. This engagement with music is one of the experimental qualities that Steinbeck mentioned in a letter about *The Pearl* written to his agent from Cuernavaca in 1945, concerning his work with Gwyn Conger, Steinbeck's second wife: "It was so full of experiments and I had no idea whether they would come off at all. Gwyn made some recordings of the basic music – the Family and Pearl themes. The Evil music is not finished. Gwyn is going to try to have a pressing sent to you. These themes are ancient Indian music long preceding the Conquest. And I think they are beautiful."[56] Steinbeck would often claim that his books were primarily aural, their techniques emanating from the forms of music.[57] The soundtrack of *John Steinbeck's "The Pearl"* thus bears witness to Steinbeck's and Conger's deep ethnographic involvement with their subject during the making of the film, their interest in indigenous memory and continuity with precontact culture. At one point, production of the film was halted because Steinbeck wanted more of this indigenous music.[58] When this music is referenced in the novel it again evokes a feeling of cultural wholeness and racial history, but its effect on the novel does not stop there. In an odd but meaningful way, the novel can be said to have a soundtrack:

> The music had gone out of Kino's head, but now, thinly, slowly, the melody of the morning, the music of evil, of the enemy sounded, but it was faint and weak. And Kino looked at his neighbors to see who might have brought this song in.[59]

The reference to music here reads almost like instructions on how to create the soundtrack, or notes on where the music should change to reflect the drama of the action. At times these instructions are quite detailed and intimate. For example, when Kino hears the music of evil, it "was not large and overwhelming now, but secret and poisonous, and the pounding of his heart gave it undertone and rhythm."[60] These are meta-filmic moments but, curiously, meta-filmic moments *in a novel*, as if Kino is suddenly becoming aware of the soundtrack of the movie in which he will play a part. Through this musical sensibility, Kino reacts to the tension of the situation, but he also reacts to the music he would hear "in" the movie, or at least in a projected movie in which the soundtrack is literally being heard by the actors rather than added thereafter. The effect here is to place us both intimately inside the character but also outside the character, listening to an overwhelming soundtrack that calls out the drama at a public level of sound.[61]

These moments suggest an understanding of dialogue that sets *The Pearl* apart from Steinbeck's earlier works. During the scene that exposes the underhand collusion of the pearl buyers to keep the villagers in a state of perpetual dependency, reported speech suddenly contravenes the conventions of realism (that we are meant to be overhearing people actually talking to one another) when one of the buyers speaks thus to his servant: "Boy, go to such a one, and such another one and such a third one. And ask them to step in here and do not tell them why."[62] Like a hangover from a poorly told folktale, the moment suggests just how unimportant spoken dialogue is in the novel. Instead, communication occurs at another level, represented by the background music that links characters into a community of felt knowledge. Hence the novel presents an ecology of the human:

> A town is a thing like a colonial animal. A town has a nervous system and a head and shoulders and feet. A town is a thing separate from all other towns, so that there are no two towns alike. And a town has a whole emotion. How news travels through a town is a mystery not easily to be solved. News seems to move faster than small boys can scramble and dart to tell it, faster than women can call it over the fences.[63]

We are no longer in the behaviorist worlds of *Of Mice and Men* and *The Red Pony* (1933, 1936), in which virtually mechanical humans move in response to external stimuli. *The Pearl* presents a different philosophy of mind. Consciousness seems an embodied reality closely related to the environment, as we glimpsed at times in *The Grapes of Wrath*. Objects seem to have their own consciousness that is intertwined with the human, just as human cognition leaks out into the physical world. Mind depends as much on what people do as what they think. The novel thus offers a social constructivist viewpoint in which humans gain their understanding not directly from natural forces but from communicative interchange and conflict.[64] The social group is key, but Steinbeck's ideas in *The Pearl* differ significantly from the concept of the "phalanx" that he explores in stories such as "The Vigilante" and in his novel *In Dubious Battle* (1936). If the phalanx is a holistic mind-set partly independent of the individuals who comprise it, then *The Pearl* is more interested in the power of the individual to disrupt that conservative wholeness: "But let one man step out of the regular thought or the known and trusted pattern, and the nerves of the townspeople ring with nervousness and communication travels over the nerve lines of the town."[65]

The pearl buyer's garbled dialogue also marks a bigger point: this moment, like many others, seems less important for its realism, and more important as a draft instruction for the film-to-be. The moment behaves rather like Orozco's final sketch in *The Pearl*: it links the two media together. It has a built-in or implied futurity, looking forward to the film. In other words, the dialogue exists at another level, as a dialogue *with Fernández* – a dialogue about soundtrack, as we have seen, but also about the novel's incipient visuality. Early in the novel, Kino's perspective on the clouds of the gulf flaming high in the air (the kind of cloud scene common in Fernández's pictures of Mexico) is superseded by an image of protean cinematic projection and sound, of words about to become film: "Behind him Juana's fire leaped into flame and threw spears of light through the chinks of the brush-house wall and threw a wavering square of light out the door. . . . The Song of the Family came now from behind Kino." Later we read of characters walking on their own shadows, and of a glowing sun throwing bunched shadows of people on the wall, as if somehow the characters are getting in the way of the projection in a moment that predicts a major criticism of the novel: this cinematic point of view becomes intrusive, with the techniques of vision distracting us from the telling of the tale.[66] But this is not just cinematic effect. It is also self-conscious *intercultural* conversation between auteurs.

The pearl as represented object focuses this cinematic self-consciousness. Like pearlescent cinema screens, which are ideal for lower-output projectors, the pearl is defined by its ability to reflect: "It captured the light and refined it and gave it back in silver incandescence." The "surface of the great pearl" is the space on which Kino can see his "dream forms" – his hopes for the future – just as the discovery of the pearl exposes the "whole structure" of unfair capitalism, rendered in brilliantly simple terms in the novel, that works to keep the indigene in poverty and subjection.[67] The most important pictures that Kino sees in the incandescent pearl, pictures seen too in the movie in another meta-filmic moment, are images of Coyotito in school, learning to read, and becoming assimilated to Americanized ways (Kino sees Coyotito wearing "a blue sailor suit from the United States"), particularly the image of him sitting in a schoolroom, writing on a big piece of paper. The pearl begins to function like an ideology for Kino. It guarantees a future of comfort and security, it "closed a door on hunger," primarily through a faith in education that holds the promise of freedom and full subjectivity along avenues of modernization. But the pearl vision also holds other implicit messages. The 1945 film script instructs that Coyotito (named Juanito in the film) should be "his present size" (a baby) when in the imagined schoolroom. This optic is respected in the film, which makes such moments appear almost comic. Such ironizing humor is hinted at in the novel too, when Kino dreams of Coyotito "reading from a book as large as a house, with letters as big as dogs."[68] These meta-filmic moments thus emphasize the illusion of the medium to establish the delusiveness of an ethic of individual self-improvement that only keeps unequal power relations firmly in place. In a similar way, Kino's individualistic claim, "I am a man!" – echoing the tradition of the emancipation of enslaved people – is accompanied by his physical abuse of Juana.[69]

The lobby posters advertising *John Steinbeck's "The Pearl"* emphasize this theme of vision that ties novel and film naturally together. They feature the scene in which the pearl buyers hand Kino a magnifying glass to confront him with the strange-looking surface of the pearl, a moment that suggests how our normal vision is the illusive one: we cannot see closely enough. The posters also feature the climactic scene at the end when Kino is able to slay his pursuers owing to his superior manipulation of point of view (Figure 9.4). Steinbeck wrote to a friend that *The Pearl* is "made for a picture because of the possibility of space," which comes to fruition in the panoramic latitude of the film's many shots of the Mexican landscape.[70] There are ways too that space offers "possibility" not despite but because of the unclear and uncertain quality of vision in the novel. We glimpse this in the novel's underwater scenes, in which the murky undersea space – a space of colonial exploitation – suddenly by chance reveals the valuable pearl to Kino. These scenes are rendered in the film through some remarkable underwater photography, showcasing the technical expertise of the Mexican film crew at a time when the mysterious underwater world was just beginning to be explored and recorded.[71] The novel theorizes a consciousness extended into the environment and intertwined with surrounding minds, but this situation is complicated by a fundamental uncertainty: things are never quite things in themselves because vision is so unreliable. In this regard, the pearl is the ultimate phenomenological object. It is defined by the shifting desires of those who view it – murky desires because of the "black distillate" it throws up.[72] The undersea in works such as William Beebe's *Beneath Tropic Seas* (1928) was described as

Figure 9.4 *The Pearl* (aka *La Perla*), US poster, 1947. Pedro Armendariz, top left; in box from left: Maria Elena Marques, Pedro Armendariz. Photo by LMPC via Getty Images.

a space of enchantment and hallucination.[73] Steinbeck reverses these usual tropes by describing the topside world as a hazy mirage in which sights are unreal and vision is untrustworthy: "There was no certainty in seeing, no proof that what you saw was there or was not there."[74]

The climactic scene of the novel again returns us to the theme of vision and the critical importance of point of view. Kino has fled the village with Juana and Coyotito after he kills a man in a fight over the pearl. The extended scene is distinctly reminiscent of Steinbeck's earlier story, "Flight" (1938; included in *The Long Valley*), the story of Pepé Torres, one of Steinbeck's Mexican American characters who like Kino kills a man in a fight and is tracked into the mountains by mysterious vigilantes.[75] "Flight" is an example of Steinbeck's full-blown naturalism, in which Pepé is inevitably defeated by powerful natural forces that overwhelm him. *The Pearl*, however, offers a remarkably different outcome precisely because of the visual uncertainty within the novel. The climactic fight scene in both novel and film is a mirror image of the moment when Kino discovers the pearl; rather than diving down into the reef, Kino slithers down the mountainside (in the film, he is wearing a swimsuit and his body appears wet) from his position beside a tiny pool teeming – in typically Steinbeckian fashion – with interdependent "colonial" life.[76] Kino seems almost like a documentary photographer in a murky world, attempting to capture a stable vision of the pursuers beneath him, at one moment receiving a flashed glimpse of the men from the light of a match that "left a picture on Kino's eyes." He attempts from uncertain visual information and partial perspective to triangulate his pursuers' exact positions without exposing his own (again this is implied in the lobby card; see Figure 9.4).[77] Given another glimpse of the watcher's face by match-light and by the uncertain illumination of the moon, Kino leaps at another flash of exposure – "the gun crashed and the barrel-flash made a picture on his eyes" – that leaves him victorious in slaying his pursuers but also leaves him standing with uncertainty when he realizes that Coyotito has also been killed by a simultaneous gunshot during this moment of rolled dice.[78] In this world of obscure vision, a fundamental uncertainty governs actions, with Coyotito's death an outcome of that random variation.

Steinbeck's politics in *The Pearl* are, at one level, clear and simple. Colonialism has been a disaster for the Mexican people and, indeed, for the environment. The invading European powers have left a legacy of racism and depleted resources in the country. In the film versions, this colonizing presence is made more explicit (in the Spanish-language version, the doctor and the patron, who controls the economy of pearl buying, have European accents). The market economy is a scam that keeps the rural Mexicans in a state of poverty and dependency. In the film versions, they are close to starvation. At one level, *The Pearl* can be read as a moral parable built on this theme of injustice, a parable locked in a cyclical pattern of repetition – a story, we are told in the prologue, told and retold so that "it has taken root in every man's mind."[79] As we saw at the outset of this chapter, Steinbeck's Global South is very different from Faulkner's, though here perhaps *The Pearl* shares in that same cyclical, traumatic historical sensibility that Latin American writers found so appealing in Faulkner.

But on another level, *The Pearl* is extremely complicated in its political meanings and its implied temporality. The prologue tells us that there are only "good and bad things . . . and no in-between anywhere," but then it also introduces a third term, "good *and evil* things," hence upsetting any binary logic by introducing a tension between social bad and moral evil, which plays out in the book's precarious politics, which lie insecurely between moral parable and political manifesto.[80] This uncertainty, built into theme and form, is precisely what unlocks this novel from an inevitable vision of inequality and dependency. Kino's character shares in this uncertainty. At times subservient, at other times driven by race-conscious rage, he has a "dangerous" potential.[81] As Fernando Sánchez has pointed out, Kino is very like the figure of the "sensitive, fearful, distrustful" Mexican rural hero described by the sociologist Roger Bartra.[82] At the end of the novel, alongside Juana and with their dead baby in their arms, Kino famously tosses the pearl back into the sea in an act of renunciation that marks a rejection of the ideologies of modernization, education, and self-improvement. What will happen next? Of course it is impossible to say, though the unresolved problems that critics have pointed to at the end of the novel and film are perhaps really the point.[83] Alongside its representation of brutal social inequality, the novel has developed a logic of random variation together with a theory of extended consciousness and mutual interdependence which lay the groundwork for a feeling that anything *could* happen. At the end Kino has lost all of his projected material hopes, with the exception of one. He holds a rifle, a Winchester carbine, the weapon of choice of Emiliano Zapata and the army of the South – a rifle that has the potential to break down barriers, we are told, to burst whole horizons.[84] We know from earlier in the novel that the "doctor was of a race which for nearly four hundred years had beaten and starved and robbed and despised Kino's race."[85] If we date the beginning of colonization in Mexico to 1519 (the Cortez expedition), then the "nearly four hundred years" leaves us potentially on the verge of the Mexican Revolution, just as Kino's song, part of the novel's "soundtrack," has by the end become "a battle cry."[86]

The picture left in Kino's eyes when he slays his pursuers is of course another cinematic image, one that captures Steinbeck's hope that his own movie project will likewise impact the minds of its viewers in a lasting way. In typically self-conscious fashion, the novel seems to contain a desire for its own impact as a film. "Things projected are experienced," says the narrator concerning Kino's plan while seemingly sanctioning the public power of film itself: "A plan once made and visualized becomes a reality along with other realities."[87] The film was certainly popular in Mexico; writing to his friend Jack Wagner, who collaborated on the screenplay, Steinbeck was impressed that "nearly everyone in Mexico" had seen it, even if he remained doubtful that "a good thing" will come out of it.[88] Doubts were inevitable when the book-to-film project had such radical intent: to encourage a rejection of

"Americanity," to decolonize the minds of the Mexican people. Steinbeck was again at his most idealistic in his hope to reach across cultures in the name of social change; he lies in the tradition of a Ralph Waldo Emerson or a Henry David Thoreau at their most reformist. Perhaps he was also at his most naïve in using a medium, film, that embodied the very modernity he was proselytizing against. At least one critic considers Fernández's film a successful "indigenist text" that urges separation and protectionist isolation from the capitalist economy, with the ending leaving Kino at a moment of "politicized clarity" as he throws the pearl with potential "radicalism and resistance."[89] Other viewers might respond differently to a film marked by inconsistent characterization, melodrama, slow pace, and what one critic describes as a "conflict between an excess of ingrained Mexican artistry and Hollywood commercialism."[90]

This conflict may mark the failure of the PEARL project overall, but it is also curiously its point. Across its broadest reach, the story attempts to link the world of the *Woman's Home Companion* – where "The Pearl of the World" first appeared in 1945, in columns of text running between glossy advertisements for irons, pressure cookers, and new instant desserts – and a Mexican post-revolutionary indigenism. Steinbeck was striving to rebuke his middle-class American readers for their growing materialism with his tale of Mexican poverty, while also reaching out to Mexican viewers to provoke a reassessment of encroaching Americanization. The inequality Steinbeck targeted was systematic and global, stretching from the American living room to the Mexican pueblo. Perhaps the story was most efficacious in chiding its American readers about their lifestyles, though the place where Steinbeck saw the most potential was south of the border. Returning there to conduct historical research for his screenplay *Viva Zapata!*, Steinbeck noted that after the revolution another revolt took place, "the revolt of the dispossessed against the group which held the resources of Mexico, and that revolt has continued during all Mexican history and still continues."[91] This revolt embodied an ongoing desire for the redistribution of land and resources among Mexican people, one that Steinbeck hoped he could tap into. Steinbeck would become interested in the revolutionary figure of Zapata because his revolution was a homegrown agrarian reform, community based and democratic, not Marxist and ideological.[92] *Viva Zapata!* is one of the few Hollywood films of the 1950s in which the Indians are the good guys – indeed, the good gals too, with Steinbeck recognizing the important role of the *soldaderas* in the Mexican Revolution. Zapata appealed to Steinbeck too for the way he finally renounces power rather than letting it corrupt him; the film's message is ultimately anti-totalitarian. If *Viva Zapata!* looks back on the revolution, then the PEARL looks forward in its temporality. Unlike Zapata's, Kino's renunciation lies at the beginning and not the end of action.

The Forgotten Village, with its formal faltering and its fraught change of direction, is a story of the failure of progressive intervention. *The Pearl* attempts to freeze in place a different, if equally ideal moment immune to the demands of a modernization narrative. The novel theorizes an ecology of the human in which the individual can become free from the deterministic forces of history (whether natural or social) through a combined process of random variation and willful action. Moreover, that individual can communicate a new mind-set to impact and change the form of the collective whole. When Kino and Juana return to the village at the end of the novel to cast the pearl into the sea, we read, "everyone hurried to see them. The sun was settling toward the western mountains and the shadows on the ground were long. And perhaps that was what left the deep impression on those who saw them."[93] With Kino viewing recent events in the surface of the pearl and apparently hearing the distorted and insane soundtrack that accompanies him, the ending of the novel is also again an inherently cinematic moment. Here the political and formal motives of the novel lock together. By representing a moment in which a revolutionary mind-set is being communicated from individual experience to collective group, the novel is again implicitly imagining the process of its transmediation from book to film, from private reading experience to public recognition and action.

With projected light making their shadows long, Kino and Juana become mythical, larger-than-life cinematic characters who are capable of gathering an audience and making a deep impression on the public, transforming their dangerous revolutionary potential into "an event that happened to everyone."[94] Here lies the curious temporality of *The Pearl*. At the formal level, in its encoded filmic aspiration, it has a built-in futurity. The novel finally positions us in a moment of what Hannah Arendt describes as revolutionary time, an ongoing moment of pure emergence that breaks with cause and effect – an event that seems to abolish "the sequence of temporality itself."[95] We are not locked into a cyclical history, but we are on the pivot of a moment of social transformation. The effect is carried by an incipient *literary* revolution, as the novel imagines a crossing of cultural and media borders through a process of collaboration with Fernández and crew to produce a public art capable of transforming a political sphere. Always in tension with the novel as a genre, Steinbeck builds into its form a process of media transformation that encapsulates an always-becoming emergence of structural change, as experimental as it was idealistic.

EPILOGUE

The Aftertaste of Cannery Row

Written in New York City in a prelude to Steinbeck's more permanent move East, *Cannery Row* (1945) marks the end of the first half of Steinbeck's career as a writer, a period defined by direct involvement with the history and the environment of the West. *Cannery Row* also embodies the variety of that career, one that had seen Steinbeck play the part of short story writer, novelist, and playwright; marine biologist, relief worker, and government propagandist; non-teleological philosopher, war journalist, and filmmaker. For good reason, the experience of reading Steinbeck can seem bewildering, a series of shifting centers that are difficult to hold in steady view. Steinbeck actively encouraged that feeling of de-centering in *Cannery Row*. Recalling comments he made about *The Grapes of Wrath* (1939), Steinbeck claimed to his friend Carlton Sheffield that *Cannery Row* is "written on four levels and people can take what they can receive out of it," and again to the critic Joseph Henry Jackson he claimed that it "is written on several levels of understanding and people can take out of it what they can bring to it but even on the thinnest level of understanding I think it is fun."[1] In a letter to his editor, Steinbeck observed, "no critic has discovered the reason for those little inner chapters in C.R. . . . Mostly all lay readers know. Only the critics don't."[2] The critics certainly did not understand this most fragmented of novels, loosely centered on the countercultural group of Mack and the boys and their efforts to throw a party for Doc, another Ed Ricketts stand-in. Orville Prescott described *Cannery Row* as "a trivial and seemingly meaningless and purposeless novel," while Malcolm Cowley described the writing as cynical, "as if the author were trying to protect his emotions, which nevertheless escaped him. The aftertaste is a little unpleasant, as if you had eaten a poisoned cream puff."[3] As Cowley's strange image suggests, confusion seems written into *Cannery Row*, but it is a confusion we need to understand to confront the central questions raised in this book. How do we read Steinbeck? How does he fit into literary history? And what does an interest in Steinbeck say about our own critical "taste"?

These are difficult questions because a problem of audience haunts Steinbeck's work, work that seems at times mired in the contradictions of local history while at other points it looks to the stars to philosophize about the future of humanity. Who was Steinbeck writing for? Looking back on his short novels in 1953, Steinbeck claimed that *Cannery Row* was a peculiar kind of war narrative, a book written not about but for the troops, a book "written for a group of soldiers who had said to me, 'Write something funny that isn't about the war. Write something for us to read – we're sick of war.'"[4] At one level, the book self-consciously generates the kind of nostalgia that draws critical disdain, as we encountered in my Introduction. The story of Mack and the boys' experience with Lee Chong's Ford Model T truck seems pitched as pure nostalgia to the homesick boys abroad (Steinbeck described the novel in general as "born out of homesickness").[5] *Cannery Row* seems written for the troops in multiple ways. The camaraderie of Mack and the boys is resonant with military experience, while the group's live-in-the-moment mind-set resonates with a way of thinking that Roy Scranton describes as necessary in combat situations: the act of "learning to die," letting go of progressive narratives or any sense of the future, to live only in an ongoing present.[6] The book is shot through with more conventional trauma narrative, embodying, perhaps, the violence Steinbeck had experienced recently as a war correspondent in Europe. *Cannery Row* is by far Steinbeck's most gruesomely violent book. We see his favorite themes – for example, the tide pool as the space of species interrelationship – reflect the chaos of witnessed battle: "The smells of life and richness, of death and digestion, of decay and birth, burden the air."[7] If the theme of wartime disillusionment becomes a lowbrow form of "fun" in *Cannery Row*, then there are other ways that Steinbeck's serious concerns jostle with moods of parody and play, placing the reader again in a confused position. The violence of *Cannery Row* can seem at times like a self-destructive violence turned against the key concerns of an entire literary career.

The novel places familiar demands on our political reactions to Steinbeck's work as well. When Doc confronts a dead girl floating face up in a La Jolla tide pool, her hair washing gently about her head and her lips slightly parted, it is an unresolved shock (one of Ricketts's interests was "wave-shock," the impact of traumatic action on marine life) that recalls all those women characters who float problematically through Steinbeck's work, whether they are superficial like Curley's Wife, sentimental like

Ma Joad, or repressed like Elisa Allen. At the heart of Steinbeck's ecological interests, focused on Doc's collecting trip in *Cannery Row*, lies a female presence whose representation is shockingly inadequate. In addition to the problem of gender, *Cannery Row* also embodies the problems of race we have faced throughout Steinbeck's work. We have seen how Steinbeck is capable of complex examinations of the "race psychopathology" of white culture but then fails to examine critically the crimes of racism. We have likewise seen his indigenous characters vacillate between roles, as revolutionary alternatives to modernity on the one hand, and as passive victims of unequal social structures on the other. Onto this difficult terrain steps Lee Chong in *Cannery Row*, a novel described by Colleen Lye as "the first serious literary work by a major American writer to include an Asian American in its character ensemble."[8] Lye argues for a constitutive Asian presence in Steinbeck's work more generally, defining his view of agricultural labor conditions in California: "In a way the Okie is simply the name for the Asiatic who won't go away," writes Lye.[9] Drawing on Steinbeck's ecological thinking and his interest in Eastern philosophy, Lye views Chong and his general supply store as a solution – through the exchange they facilitate between social and natural worlds – to the class conflicts and market crisis of the Great Depression. Lye argues that Chong together with the more resolutely Orientalist "Old Chinaman" who haunts the novel represent an "insertion of the Asiatic into a local ecology, and a strategy of the alien's indigenization."[10]

This is surely right – to a degree. With Steinbeck, both alternatives can be present simultaneously, again making the center difficult to find. Lee Chong bears traces of the "Yellow Peril" discourse of the previous decades (his teeth flash aggressively at his customers), just as the Old Chinaman who walks mysteriously into the novel seems an Orientalist fantasy, passive and exotic. Yet the Old Chinaman nevertheless reacts to the racism he attracts, confronting prejudice with unassimilable racial difference.[11] Lee Chong similarly seems both alienated from and directly connected to the narrative logic of the book as a whole. To the extent that there is anything like a plot in this digressive novel, it is enabled by the power of Lee Chong's "credit" to fund the plans of the characters. And as a credible and significant character, Lee Chong does – as Lye argues – materialize an Asian presence in Steinbeck's fictional world. But if Steinbeck's disclaimer at the beginning of *Cannery Row* describes the book as both a "fiction" and a "fabrication," then Lee Chong is both a believable character and a symbolic, mythical presence – indeed, he is something like a process, even a theory, of narrative itself:

> The Word is a symbol and a delight which sucks up men and scenes, trees, plants, factories, and Pekinese. Then the Thing becomes the Word and back to Thing again, but warped and woven into a fantastic pattern. The Word sucks up Cannery Row, digests it and spews it out, and the Row has taken the shimmer of the green world and the sky-reflecting seas. Lee Chong is more than a Chinese grocer. He must be. Perhaps he is evil balanced and held in suspension by good – an Asiatic planet held to its orbit by the pull of Lao Tze and held away from Lao Tze by the centrifugality of abacus and cash register – Lee Chong suspended, spinning, whirling among groceries and ghosts.[12]

We have seen throughout this book how Steinbeck's work can swing between the fantastic and the realistic, how it can move between different genres and different media, forming hybrids even as it dismantles them. Lee Chong is part of this process of meaning-making, this shuttling between the linguistic and the material that leaves us both with the realized world of Cannery Row (after all, the neighborhood in Monterey takes its name from the book) and a metafictional realm of the symbolic and mythic order. The problem of race, in *Cannery Row*, is also then a problem of form. Lee Chong is a credible Asian character but, like Fedallah in Herman Melville's *Moby-Dick* (1851), he is also a linguistic construct, an amalgam of myth, philosophy, and stereotype. Steinbeck would use another divided Asian character – Lee in *East of Eden* (1952) – to represent the values of universalism, as Heidi Kim has argued convincingly.[13] Lee in *East of Eden* is a code-switching character, but he is also a metafictional device. He is a servant in the story and also in the discourse itself. He is a means to move other characters from place to place, thus making the story happen, and a mouthpiece for authorial opinion. In both *Cannery Row* and *East of Eden*, Steinbeck includes racial difference but then dissipates that difference by making readers aware of its fictional construction. Embodied in characters like Lee and Lee Chong, metafiction is never an encompassing explanation of Steinbeck's work but merely one among competing alternatives. Accordingly, we can read Lee Chong in *Cannery Row* as a simple grocer giving credit to his customers, or as a ghostly presence akin to the literary power that makes fictional worlds seem credible to their readers.

The difficulty deciding what *Cannery Row* is, precisely – a realist novel? a symbolist fantasy? a metafictional experiment? – returns us to another thread we have seen running through Steinbeck's career. We can read *Cannery Row* as a non-teleological novel that resists the idea that it has any progression or ultimate meaning. Or rather, that lack of progression *is* the meaning because it also defines the ethos of its central group of characters,

Mack and the boys, who live in the abandoned pipes of a sardine cannery and simply gaze on the "flow and vitality of Cannery Row."[14] Flow is that feeling of total immersion in a moment, an energized absorption, a perpetual emergence. Predicting the Beat and the counterculture movements of the 1950s and 1960s, Mack and the boys represent the "cosmic Monterey"; they have turned on, tuned in, and dropped out.[15] According to Doc, Mack and the boys remain healthy and clean by living beyond the nervousness of modernity. Their rejection of the success ethic makes them kind, open, honest, and understanding. Like the primitivist notion of the "Fellahin" idealized by Beat writers such as Jack Kerouac and William S. Burroughs – a tribe stretching across the equatorial belly of the world and incorporating the American underclass[16] – Doc describes these individuals as part of a global tribe: "I've seen them in an ice-cream seller in Mexico and in an Aleut in Alaska."[17] The Beats' ideas of the Fellahin drew from Oswald Spengler's *The Decline of the West* (1918, 1923), which described the lives of the Fellahin as "a planless happening without goal or cadenced march in time, wherein occurrences are many, but, in the last analysis, devoid of significance."[18] Combined with the Daoist philosophy of non-action and flow with the moment, such ideas permeate *Cannery Row*. The novel features a series of planless happenings that bring happiness because of their isolation and self-sufficiency, for example, Mack and the boys' trip to collect frogs as specimens, the organization of the party for Doc, and the moments of working together when an influenza outbreak coincides with a large sardine catch. Such happy moments have a carnivalesque feel, offering a liberation from the utilitarian and the practical, a merger of the individual into the collective, and a release from the rigidity of time.[19] They are serendipitous examples of the process of emergence that occupied Steinbeck throughout his career.

These moments of happiness are formalized in the episodic structure of the narrative. Episodes, writes Matthew Garrett, "insist upon the question of the part's relationship to the whole and in so doing they unsettle any easy assumption about interpretive prioritization." If plot tends to emphasize causality and determinism, then the episode stresses contingency and freedom.[20] In general, novelistic narrative stages a battle between a sense of the whole, the overall meaning of the text, and the individual unit episodes that threaten to attract significance to themselves and hence fragment the work. *Cannery Row* perhaps goes as far as possible in the direction of pure contingency and fragmentation while still roughly satisfying the progression of a novel. Take chapter thirty-one, the penultimate chapter, which instead of preparing us for the conclusion of the novel presents us with an episode about a gopher, an episode that even contains its own mini-episode when the gopher reaches a moment of pure contentment only to see it destroyed by a desire for domesticity. Episodes within episodes, episodes following episodes – *Cannery Row* is almost all digression. The novel follows a number of haphazard or apparently meaningless journeys, and irrelevant or unrelated incidents, as characters simply wander away or pursue conversations merely for the sake of flow. This digressive quality finds a focus in the figure of the artist Henri, a character named for the Ashcan school practitioner of social realism but whose ideas about art are more aligned with values just beginning to emerge in the mid-1940s – values that rejected representation to emphasize the action, struggle, and process of painting itself. It may seem too much to call Henri an abstract expressionist, though he is certainly on the way to becoming one:

> Henri had suddenly decided that the old-fashioned pin-cushion was an art form which had flowered and reached its peak in the Nineties and had since been neglected. He revived the form and was delighted to see what could be done with colored pins. The picture was never completed – you could change it by rearranging the pins. He was preparing a group of these pieces for a one-man show when he heard about the party and he instantly abandoned his own work and began a giant pincushion for Doc. It was to be an intricate and provocative design in green, yellow, and blue pins, all cool colors, and its title was Pre-Cambrian Memory.[21]

Earlier in the novel Henri had experimented with his media, moving among glue, iron-rust, colored chicken feathers, and nutshells; he became obsessed with the movements of a local attraction, a man roller-skating on an elevated platform, and "thought of doing a huge abstraction called Substratum Dream of a Flag-pole Skater."[22] His proposed pincushion for Doc is the culmination of Henri's interest in abstraction – the elimination of recognizable imagery – and in the material process rather than the completion of artistic creation. His interest in "Pre-Cambrian Memory" recalls Wolfgang Paalen's essay "Totem Art" (1943), which called for an art based on action, ritual, and prehistoric memory.[23] The point at which Henri becomes distracted from his project by news of the party for Doc directly links this abstract expressionism to the form of *Cannery Row* by suggesting that the book's many digressions can be thought of as swooshes of paint (or lines of pins) on a flowing and always unfolding canvas.

Of course it would be going too far to call *Cannery Row* a work of abstract expressionism. This would take Steinbeck's experiments too "seriously," although the humor of the book is reminiscent of an Ad Reinhardt cartoon from the mid-1940s, in which the abstract canvas looks back at a mocking viewer who questions what the canvas represents only to hear the reply: "What do you represent?"[24] As Steinbeck claimed to Joseph Henry Jackson in his comments on the book's "several levels of understanding," *Cannery Row* is simply "fun" though it also asks deeper questions of the reader: "people can take out of it what they can bring to it." *Cannery Row* is an experimental novel in its extreme episodicity even as it offers an easy parody of avant-garde art, one apparently aimed at the middlebrow reader. But if a middlebrow aesthetic sanctions middle-class values by making readers secure in their level of taste,[25] then nothing could be less true of *Cannery Row*, which at every turn lambastes the sterility and hypocrisy of middle-class life. Perhaps after all we should view the book as written for the troops, as Steinbeck claimed: it contains such contradictory "classes" of understanding, smashing together the high, the middle, and the low, because it is aimed at a particular group with experiences and needs that transcend the conventional values of social class. There is a battle-worn weariness to the novel that gives it the poisoned aftertaste Cowley detected. It evokes a free frolicking in the moment, a digressiveness that, in a curious way, is an irresponsible desire to leave things behind and to forget. Early in the novel, when the minor character William – a low-status, depressed "pimp" – takes his own life, the narrative simply replaces him with another character and moves on without a second thought.[26] It doesn't matter. Life is just an episode anyway. Who cares?

Ross Posnock has identified a strong tradition of renunciation that runs through American literature, art, and philosophy. "Undoing their own authority, refusing exemplarity," Posnock's renunciants "gain most of what they need – including joy and energy and certainty – not by explaining, not by knowing, nor even by thinking – but rather by finding freedom in logics of abdication."[27] In its combination of Zen principles of the relinquished self with an episodic structure that constantly leaves things behind, *Cannery Row* is a novel of renunciation. Its combination of joy and violence is a sign of farewell, just as the novel's exhaustive rehearsal of Steinbeck's major themes signals a tired departure from the West Coast location that made Steinbeck seem an outlier to the literary establishment. Renunciation has run as a binding theme throughout Steinbeck's career as a whole. We have encountered his uneasy relationship to the literary conventions he was taught, a partial resistance to realism that can make his work difficult to categorize. We have encountered his move away from the centrality of the human to explore other forms of consciousness, and we have seen an interest in emergence lend his works a powerfully disturbing affect of recoil. We have met Steinbeck's rejection of modernity and his ethic of extinction in his treatment of the species. And we have experienced renunciation operating formally too. Each of Steinbeck's productions can seem like a rejection of what has come before – a rejection often fueled by a lingering dissatisfaction with the novel as a genre. Yet lacking the purity of Posnock's abandoners, Steinbeck's renunciations seem only partially complete, as if renunciation itself is being renounced, leaving Steinbeck again in a middle position that critics find discomforting. We have also thus encountered the failures, weaknesses, limitations, and contradictions of Steinbeck, which make his work hard to position in a political framework. His continuing appeal to readers, combined with his ongoing neglect by critics, only makes the point – one that I have tried to address throughout this book – that Steinbeck is a writer so difficult, but so necessary, to understand.

Notes

Introduction: Loving and Hating Steinbeck

1 Leslie Fiedler, "Looking Back After 50 Years," *The Devil Gets His Due: The Uncollected Essays of Leslie Fiedler*, ed. Samuel F. S. Pardini (Berkeley, CA: Counterpoint, 2008), 162–71.

2 Edmund Wilson, *The Boys in the Back Room: Notes on California Novelists* (San Francisco, CA: Colt Press, 1941), 48, 52. The original essay, "The Californians: Storm and Steinbeck," appeared in *New Republic* in December 1940.

3 Arthur Mizener, "Does a Moral Vision of the Thirties Deserve a Nobel Prize?" *The New York Times* (December 9, 1962): 4, 43–45.

4 Robert Gottlieb, "The Rescue of John Steinbeck," *The New York Review of Books* (April 17, 2008), www.nybooks.com/articles/2008/04/17/the-rescue-of-john-steinbeck/. For a strong response to Gottlieb, see Michael J. Meyer (ed.), *The Grapes of Wrath: A Re-Consideration* (Amsterdam: Rodopi, 2009), viii. See also Jackson J. Benson, "John Steinbeck: The Favorite Author We Love to Hate," in Donald R. Noble (ed.), *The Steinbeck Question: New Essays in Criticism* (Troy, NY: Whitston, 1993), 8–22.

5 The best overview of Steinbeck's earlier career remains, in my view, Peter Lisca, *The Wide World of John Steinbeck* (New Brunswick, NJ: Rutgers University Press, 1958). For a balanced view of Steinbeck, see Louis Owens, *John Steinbeck's Re-vision of America* (Athens: University of Georgia Press, 1985). For an excellent, recent collection of essays, see Cyrus Ernesto Zirakzadeh and Simon Stow (eds.), *A Political Companion to John Steinbeck* (Lexington: University Press of Kentucky, 2013). *The Grapes of Wrath* continues to generate compelling readings; see, for example, Michael Szalay's brilliant chapter four, "The Vanishing American Father: Sentiment and Labor in *The Grapes of Wrath* and *A Tree Grows in Brooklyn*," in *New Deal Modernism: American Literature and the Invention of the Welfare State* (Durham, NC: Duke University Press, 2010), 162–200.

6 According to Steinbeck's biographer, the "chances of reading Steinbeck in an English class in a major university are very low, and in the Ivy League practically zero." Benson, "John Steinbeck," 11.

7 See www.wired.com/2016/10/president-obama-reading-list/.

8 See www.pbs.org/the-great-american-read/results/. PBS used the polling service "YouGov."

9 I am thinking here of Michael Denning's *The Cultural Front: The Laboring of American Culture in the Twentieth Century* (London: Verso, 1997), in which Steinbeck fares poorly in comparison to Woody Guthrie, Carlos Bulosan, and Ernesto Galarza, not least because *The Grapes of Wrath* was a "cultural success" (266).

10 In "Dregs of Wrath," Jonathan Yardley writes in *The Washington Post Book Review*: "The faults noted in the past by some critics seem all the more glaring now that his fiction has lost much of its extra-literary urgency: the solemnity, the sentimentality, the heavy-handed irony, the humorlessness, the labored colloquialisms, the clumsiness, the political naivete" (October 9, 1994).

11 Wilson, *Boys in the Back Room*, 42, 52.

12 For example, Susan Beegel, Susan Shillinglaw, and Wes Tiffney (eds.), *Steinbeck and the Environment: Interdisciplinary Approaches* (Tuscaloosa: University of Alabama Press, 1997); Hannes Bergthaller and Peter Mortensen (eds.), *Framing the Environmental Humanities* (Leiden; Boston: Brill Rodopi, 2018), specifically chap. 9; Lloyd Willis, *Environmental Evasion: The Literary, Critical, and Cultural Politics of "Nature's Nation"* (Albany: State University of New York Press, 2011), specifically chap. 4; Paul B. Thompson, *The Agrarian Vision: Sustainability and Environmental Ethics* (Lexington: University Press of Kentucky, 2010), specifically chap. 4; and Meyer (ed.), *The Grapes of Wrath: A Re-Consideration*, Section V.

13 See for example Colleen Lye, *America's Asia: Racial Form and American Literature, 1893–1945* (Princeton, NJ: Princeton University Press, 2005), and Heidi Kim, *Invisible Subjects: Asian America in Postwar Literature* (Oxford: Oxford University Press, 2016).

14 Mizener, "Does a Moral Vision," 4.

15 Wilson, *Boys in the Back Room*, 52.

16 Fiedler, "Looking Back," 168.

17 Wilson, *Boys in the Back Room*, 42.

18 Fiedler, "Looking Back," 171.

19 Elaine Steinbeck and Robert Wallsten (eds.), *Steinbeck: A Life in Letters* (New York: Penguin, 1989), 162.

20 See Kathryn S. Olmsted, *Right Out of California: The 1930s and the Big Business Roots of Modern Conservatism* (New York: The New Press, 2015), 102–5; and Sarah Wald, *The Nature of California: Race, Citizenship, and Farming Since the Dust Bowl* (Seattle: University of Washington Press, 2016), 53–65.

21 Fiedler, "Looking Back," 165.

22 John Steinbeck, *The Grapes of Wrath and Other Writings, 1936–1941*, ed. Robert DeMott (New York: Library of America, 1996), 373.

23 After all, he begins *Grapes* with "The Battle Hymn of the Republic" – a Civil War song – and wrote to his agent that "There's Civil War making right under my nose" when he confronts the plight of California's migrant laborers. See Susan Shillinglaw, *On Reading The Grapes of Wrath* (New York: Penguin, 2014), 100.

24 Ann Douglas, *The Feminization of American Culture* (New York: Farrar, Straus, Giroux, 1998). Douglas writes that sentimentalism "provides a way to protest a power to which one has already in part capitulated. It is a form of dragging one's heels. It always borders on dishonesty but it is a dishonesty that for which there is no known substitute in a capitalist country" (12).

25 Jane P. Tompkins, *Sensational Designs: The Cultural Work of American Fiction, 1790–1860* (New York: Oxford University Press, 1985). Tompkins argues that the function of sentimental scenes "is heuristic and didactic rather than mimetic, they do not attempt to transcribe in detail a parabola of events as they 'actually happen' in society; rather, they provide a basis for remaking the social and political order in which events take place" (xvii).

26 Eric J. Sundquist, *New Essays on "Uncle Tom's Cabin"* (New York: Cambridge University Press, 1986), 11.

27 Steinbeck, *Grapes of Wrath*, 380; emphasis added.

28 Steinbeck, *Grapes of Wrath*, 382.

29 John Steinbeck, interview by Diana, Lady Avebury, reprinted in Thomas Fensch (ed.), *Conversations with John Steinbeck* (Jackson: University Press of Mississippi, 1988), 66; see also Shillinglaw, *On Reading*, 65.

30 John Steinbeck, "Breakfast," *The Grapes of Wrath and Other Writings, 1936–1941*, ed. Robert DeMott (New York: Library of America, 1996), 58.

31 John Steinbeck, "A Primer on the Thirties," *America and Americans, and Selected Nonfiction*, eds. Susan Shillinglaw and Jackson J. Benson (New York: Penguin, 2003), 21, 23; Mizener, "Does a Moral Vision," 4.

32 See Svetlana Boym, *The Future of Nostalgia* (New York: Basic Books, 2001), 34. "Gastronomic and auditory nostalgia were of particular importance," Boym writes (4).

33 Roland Barthes, *S/Z*, trans. Richard Miller (New York: Hill and Wang, 1974), 4.

34 Steinbeck, "Breakfast," 59.

35 Steinbeck, "Breakfast," 60.

36 Steinbeck, "Breakfast," 60.

37 Barthes, *S/Z*, 5. As Barthes writes, "the writerly text is *ourselves writing*" (5).

38 Jackson J. Benson, *John Steinbeck, Writer: A Biography* (New York: Penguin, 1990), 298.

39 Steinbeck, "Breakfast," 58.

40 Ella Winter quoted in Benson, *John Steinbeck*, 297.

41 Steinbeck, "Breakfast," 58.
42 Boym, *Future of Nostalgia,* 8.
43 Steinbeck, "Breakfast," 60.
44 Boym, *Future of Nostalgia,* 21. Boym equates this modern nostalgia with the work of Charles Baudelaire.
45 Boym, *Future of Nostalgia,* 21.
46 Wilson, *Boys in the Back Room,* 41.
47 William Faulkner, *The Paris Review Interviews,* vol. 2 (New York: Picador, 2007), 57.
48 Malcolm Cowley (ed.), *The Portable Faulkner,* revised and expanded edition (New York: Penguin, 2001), ii.
49 Not only have critics tended to neglect the presence of race in Steinbeck's writing; Steinbeck has been positioned – even by his antagonists – as someone who inherently resists racial paradigms. Leslie Fiedler's harsh condemnation of *The Grapes of Wrath,* for example, implies just such an evaluation in its comparison of Steinbeck's novel with Margaret Mitchell's contemporaneous *Gone with the Wind* (1936). Mitchell's novel may be even more "flagrantly sentimental, stereotyped, didactic and melodramatic" than Steinbeck's, argued Fiedler, but it still possesses an "archetypical resonance" and "mythopoeic power" that implicitly emerge from Mitchell's subject of slavery and its aftermath. Fiedler, "Looking Back," 167.
50 Alexandra Minna Stern, *Eugenics Nation: Faults and Frontiers of Better Breeding in Modern America* (Berkeley: University of California Press, 2005), 20, 25.
51 Wilson, *Boys in the Back Room,* 42.
52 Benson, *John Steinbeck,* 48. Although he successfully convinced his English department advisor, the medical school would not admit him on the necessary special-study basis.
53 Alfred Kazin, *On Native Grounds: An Interpretation of Modern American Prose Literature* (New York: Harcourt, Brace & World, 1942), 395.

1 Short Stories in School and Lab: "Tularecito" and "The Snake"

1 Jackson J. Benson, *John Steinbeck, Writer: A Biography* (New York: Penguin, 1990), 193–94. See also Richard Astro, *John Steinbeck and Edward F. Ricketts: The Shaping of a Novelist* (Minneapolis: University of Minnesota Press, 1973).
2 John Steinbeck, *The Pastures of Heaven, Novels and Stories, 1932–1937,* ed. Robert DeMott (New York: Library of America, 1994), 3.
3 Steinbeck, *Pastures of Heaven,* 3–4.
4 Steinbeck, *Pastures of Heaven,* 4.
5 Susan F. Riggs, "Steinbeck at Stanford," *Stanford Magazine* 4 (Fall-Winter 1976), 17.

6 Mark McGurl, *The Program Era: Postwar Fiction and the Rise of Creative Writing* (Cambridge, MA: Harvard University Press, 2011).
7 Benson, *John Steinbeck*, 55.
8 Benson, *John Steinbeck*, 53.
9 Andrew Levy, *The Culture and Commerce of the American Short Story* (Cambridge: Cambridge University Press, 1993), 36, 38.
10 Levy, *Culture and Commerce*, 40.
11 Levy, *Culture and Commerce*, 98.
12 John Steinbeck, "Preface to the Compass Edition," in Edith Ronald Mirrielees, *Story Writing* (New York: Viking, 1962), vi.
13 Mirrielees quoted in Levy, *Culture and Commerce*, 52.
14 Steinbeck, "Preface to the Compass Edition," vi, vii.
15 Levy, *Culture and Commerce*, 96.
16 Edgar Allan Poe, "Twice-told Tales," *Graham's Magazine* 20.5 (May 1842), reprinted in John L. Idol Jr. and Buford Jones (eds.), *Nathaniel Hawthorne: The Contemporary Reviews* (Cambridge: Cambridge University Press, 1994), 63–68.
17 Mirrielees, *Story Writing*, 59.
18 Benson, *John Steinbeck*, 48.
19 Levy, *Culture and Commerce*, 49.
20 For Steinbeck's deep interest in Anderson, which began when he heard Anderson speak at Stanford University, see Brian Railsback and Michael J. Meyer (eds.), *A John Steinbeck Encyclopedia* (Westport, CT: Greenwood Press, 2006), 15.
21 Anon., "Shorter Notices," *Nation* 135 (December 7, 1932), in Joseph R. McElrath Jr., Jesse S. Crisler, and Susan Shillinglaw (eds.), *John Steinbeck: The Contemporary Reviews* (Cambridge: Cambridge University Press, 1996), 18.
22 E. B. C. Jones, "New Novels," *New Statesman and Nation* [England] 5 (June 10, 1933), in McElrath, Crisler, and Shillinglaw (eds.), *Contemporary Reviews*, 19.
23 Cyrilly Abels, "Keeping Up with the Novelists," *Bookman* 75 (December 1932), in McElrath, Crisler, and Shillinglaw (eds.), *Contemporary Reviews*, 17; Anon., "*The Pastures of Heaven*," *Times Literary Supplement* [London] (June 15, 1933), in McElrath, Crisler, and Shillinglaw (eds.), *Contemporary Reviews*, 19.
24 André Gide, quoted in Jay Parini, *John Steinbeck: A Biography* (London: Heinemann, 1994), 262.
25 Long Le-Khac, "Transnarrative: Giving Form to Diversity, Community, and Migration in Asian American and Latina/o Literature," Ph.D dissertation, Stanford University, May 2015.
26 Steinbeck, *Pastures of Heaven*, 5.

27 Steinbeck, "Preface to the Compass Edition," vii.
28 Steinbeck, *Pastures of Heaven*, 36.
29 Steinbeck, *Pastures of Heaven*, 35.
30 For references to Hop-Frog gritting and gnashing his powerful and repulsive teeth, which are associated with his "maniacal rage," see Edgar Allan Poe, "Hop-Frog," *Selected Tales*, ed. David Van Leer (Oxford: Oxford University Press, 1998), 314, 317.
31 D. H. Lawrence, *Studies in Classic American Literature* (New York: Penguin, 1977), 56; emphasis in original. Lawrence discusses the moment when Caliban, free from Prospero, surrenders into willing slavery to Stephano. To be masterless is to be mastered in new ways.
32 Levy, *Culture and Commerce,* 89–90.
33 Steinbeck, *Pastures of Heaven*, 35.
34 Steinbeck, *Pastures of Heaven*, 42.
35 Steinbeck, "Preface to the Compass Edition," vii.
36 Benson, *John Steinbeck*, 53–54.
37 Benson, *John Steinbeck,* 379.
38 Parini, *John Steinbeck*, 176.
39 Benson, *John Steinbeck,* 75.
40 Steinbeck, *Pastures of Heaven*, 38.
41 Steinbeck, *Pastures of Heaven*, 37.
42 Steinbeck, *Pastures of Heaven*, 41.
43 Steinbeck, *Pastures of Heaven*, 43.
44 Benson, *John Steinbeck*, 79, 92.
45 Franz Roh, "Magical Realism: Post-Expressionism," in Lois Parkinson Zamora and Wendy B. Faris (eds.), *Magical Realism: Theory, History, Community* (Durham, NC: Duke University Press, 1995), 15–32; Stephen M. Hart and Wen-chin Ouyang (eds.), *A Companion to Magical Realism* (Woodbridge, UK: Boydell and Brewer, 2005), 32.
46 Alejo Carpentier, "On the Marvellous Real in America," in Zamora and Faris (eds.), *Magical Realism*, 88.
47 Patricia C. Rice and Ann L. Paterson, "Anthropomorphs in Cave Art: An Empirical Assessment," *American Anthropologist* 90.3 (1988): 664–74; Enrico Comba, "Mixed Human-Animal Representations in Palaeolithic Art: An Anthropological Perspective," *Bulletin de la Société Préhistorique Ariège-Pyrénées* LXV–LXVI (2010–11): 1853–63.
48 Steinbeck, *Pastures of Heaven*, 43.
49 Steinbeck, *Pastures of Heaven*, 44.
50 Frank O'Connor, "The Lonely Voice," in Charles E. May (ed.), *Short Story Theories* (Athens: Ohio University Press, 1976), 86.
51 O'Connor, "Lonely Voice," 84, 86–87.

52 Steinbeck, *Pastures of Heaven*, 43–44.
53 Steinbeck, *Pastures of Heaven*, 46.
54 Le-Khac, "Transnarrative," 11, 14.
55 Henry James, *The Ambassadors* (New York: Charles Scribner's Sons, 1909), xii.
56 Steinbeck, *Pastures of Heaven*, 42.
57 Steinbeck, *Pastures of Heaven*, 168.
58 Mirrielees, *Story Writing*, 147.
59 Vivyan C. Adair, "Of Home-makers and Home-breakers: The *Deserving* and the *Undeserving* Poor Mother in Depression Era Literature," in Susan C. Staub (ed.), *The Literary Mother: Essays on Representations of Maternity and Child Care* (Jefferson, NC: McFarland & Co., 2007), 59; Nellie Y. McKay, "'Happy [?]-Wife-and-Motherdom': The Portrayal of Ma Joad in John Steinbeck's *The Grapes of Wrath*," in David Wyatt (ed.), *New Essays on "The Grapes of Wrath"* (New York: Cambridge University Press, 1990), 47–69; Michael Szalay, *New Deal Modernism: American Literature and the Invention of the Welfare State* (Durham, NC: Duke University Press, 2010), 170–71.
60 See Edward F. Ricketts, *Renaissance Man of Cannery Row: The Life and Letters of Edward F. Ricketts*, ed. Katharine A. Rodger (Tuscaloosa: University of Alabama Press, 2002). Some figures with whom Ricketts and Steinbeck exchanged ideas include John Cage, Henry Miller, and Joseph Campbell.
61 The standard account of the relationship of Steinbeck and Ricketts is Richard Astro, *John Steinbeck and Edward F. Ricketts: The Shaping of a Novelist* (Minneapolis: University of Minnesota Press, 1973).
62 John Steinbeck, *The Log from the Sea of Cortez, The Grapes of Wrath and Other Writings, 1936–1941*, ed. Robert DeMott (New York: Library of America, 1996), 732.
63 Edward F. Ricketts, *Breaking Through: Essays, Journals, and Travelogues of Edward F. Ricketts*, ed. Katharine A. Rodger (Berkeley: University of California Press, 2006), 23.
64 The sentence continues, "but it is I guess an indication of a staggered mind." John Steinbeck, *Working Days: The Journals of "The Grapes of Wrath," 1938–41*, ed. Robert DeMott (New York: Viking, 1989), 127.
65 Steinbeck, *Log from the Sea of Cortez*, 711.
66 Edward Weston, *The Daybooks of Edward Weston*, vol. 2: *California*, ed. Nancy Newhall (New York: Horizon Press, 1966), 32.
67 Modotti quoted in Weston, *Daybooks*, 31.
68 Steinbeck, *Log from the Sea of Cortez*, 712.
69 John Steinbeck, "The Snake," *The Grapes of Wrath and Other Writings, 1936–1941*, ed. Robert DeMott (New York: Library of America, 1996), 48.
70 Steinbeck, "The Snake," 50.
71 Mirrielees, *Story Writing*, 112.

72 Steinbeck, "The Snake," 52.
73 Steinbeck, "The Snake," 56, 57.
74 Steinbeck, "The Snake," 56.
75 Steinbeck, "The Snake," 58.
76 Steinbeck, "The Snake," 50, 51, 57.
77 Steinbeck, "The Snake," 57.
78 Julio Cortázar, "Some Aspects of the Short Story," in Charles E. May (ed.), *The New Short Story Theories* (Athens: Ohio University Press, 1994), 245–55. Cortázar writes that short stories/photographs are thus capable of acting on their viewer/reader beyond the visual/literary anecdote they embody.

2 Drought, Climate, and Race in the West: *To a God Unknown*

1 John Steinbeck, "Fingers of Cloud: A Satire on College Protervity," *Stanford Spectator* 2.5 (February 1924): 149, 162–64. "Protervity" – peevish, petulant behavior – may refer to the story's tone, which occasionally descends into the absurd.
2 This has perhaps motivated critical views of Gertie's mental deficiency; see for example Jay Parini, *John Steinbeck: A Biography* (London: Heinemann, 1994), 54, and Jackson J. Benson, *John Steinbeck, Writer: A Biography* (New York: Penguin, 1990), 62.
3 Inexplicably, Pedro stores severed horses heads in the camp's fire barrel.
4 Parini, *John Steinbeck*, 54.
5 For a collection of essays on Steinbeck's environmentalist interests, see Susan F. Beegle, Susan Shillinglaw, and Wesley N. Tiffney Jr. (eds.), *Steinbeck and the Environment: Interdisciplinary Approaches* (Tuscaloosa: University of Alabama Press, 2007).
6 Gertie is a symbol of whiteness – "her hair, as white as a washed sheep's wool" – and rain, as she becomes associated with a Norse thunder-god (149).
7 Margaret Cheney Dawson, "Some Autumn Fiction," New York *Herald Tribune* (September 24, 1933), in Joseph R. McElrath Jr., Jesse S. Crisler, and Susan Shillinglaw (eds.), *John Steinbeck: The Contemporary Reviews* (Cambridge: Cambridge University Press, 1996), 23.
8 Anonymous review in *Forum* (November 1933), in McElrath, Crisler, and Shillinglaw (eds.), *Contemporary Reviews*, 26.
9 Pritchett, "Fiction," *Spectator* (April 5, 1935), in McElrath, Crisler, and Shillinglaw (eds.), *Contemporary Reviews*, 27.
10 Dawson, "Some Autumn Fiction," in McElrath, Crisler, and Shillinglaw (eds.), *Contemporary Reviews*, 26.
11 Franz Roh, "Magical Realism: Post-Expressionism," in Lois Parkinson Zamora and Wendy B. Faris (eds.), *Magical Realism: Theory, History,*

Community (Durham, NC: Duke University Press, 1995), 22; emphasis in original.

12 Zamora and Faris (eds.), *Magical Realism*, 6.

13 Rawdon Wilson, "Metamorphoses of Fictional Space," in Zamora and Faris (eds.), *Magical Realism*, 220, 225. See also Roh, "Magical Realism," 26.

14 Alejo Carpentier, "On the Marvelous Real in America," in Zamora and Faris (eds.), *Magical Realism*, 88.

15 John Steinbeck, *To a God Unknown, Novels and Stories, 1932–1937*, ed. Robert DeMott (New York: Library of America, 1994), 257.

16 This inheritance is secured, early in the novel, by a bizarre ritual blessing in which Joseph places his hand on his father's genitals.

17 Steinbeck, *To a God Unknown*, 193.

18 Steinbeck, *To a God Unknown*, 297.

19 Dawson, "Some Autumn Fiction," in McElrath, Crisler, and Shillinglaw (eds.), *Contemporary Reviews*, 23.

20 Steinbeck, *To a God Unknown*, 207.

21 Steinbeck, *To a God Unknown*, 244.

22 John Steinbeck, ledger, including "Second Version" (of *To an Unknown God*). The John Steinbeck Collection, 1902–1979, Stanford University Libraries, Department of Special Collections, M0263, Box 18. Emphasis in original. "Man is said to come out of his environment," Steinbeck continued: "He doesn't know when."

23 Steinbeck quoted in Nathan Valjean, *John Steinbeck, The Errant Knight: An Intimate Biography of His California Years* (San Francisco, CA: Chronicle Books, 1975), 123.

24 Steinbeck to Carlton A. Sheffield, June 21, 1933, in Elaine Steinbeck and Robert Wallsten (eds.), *Steinbeck: A Life in Letters* (New York: Penguin, 1989), 74–77. The original typescript of the letter contains explicit references to "racial physiology" that are removed from the published version.

25 Much of "Argument of Phalanx" is reprinted in Richard Astro, *John Steinbeck and Edward F. Ricketts: The Shaping of a Novelist* (Minneapolis: University of Minnesota Press, 1973), 64–65.

26 John Steinbeck, typescript letter to Carlton A. Sheffield, June 21, 1933. The John Steinbeck Collection, 1902–1979, Stanford University Libraries, Department of Special Collections, M0263, Box 5.

27 Steinbeck to Sheffield, June 21, 1933, in Steinbeck and Wallsten (eds.), *A Life in Letters*, 75.

28 Steinbeck to Sheffield, June 21, 1933, in Steinbeck and Wallsten (eds.), *A Life in Letters*, 76–77. The published version omits the explicit reference to "race psychopathology" found in the original typescript.

29 Steinbeck to Sheffield, June 21, 1933, in Steinbeck and Wallsten (eds.), *A Life in Letters*, 75.
30 Steinbeck quoted in Benson, *John Steinbeck*, 266–67.
31 Zamora and Faris (eds.), *Magical Realism*, 10.
32 Steinbeck, *To a God Unknown*, 318, 247, 182, 199–200.
33 Steinbeck quoted in Benson, *John Steinbeck*, 222.
34 Steinbeck quoted in Benson, *John Steinbeck*, 173.
35 Ellsworth Huntington, *The Secret of the Big Trees: Yosemite, Sequoia and General Grant National Parks* (Washington, DC: Department of the Interior, 1913), 3, 8.
36 See Robert DeMott, *Steinbeck's Reading: A Catalogue of Books Owned and Borrowed* (New York: Garland, 1984), 57.
37 Huntington, *Civilization and Climate*, 1–2.
38 Alexandra Minna Stern, *Eugenic Nation: Faults and Frontiers of Better Breeding in Modern America* (Berkeley: University of California Press, 2005), 120–28.
39 Steinbeck, *To a God Unknown*, 182.
40 Huntington, *Civilization and Climate*, 52.
41 Wallace Stegner, *Where the Bluebird Sings to the Lemonade Springs: Living and Writing in the West* (New York: Random House, 1992), 46–47, 54.
42 Adam Trexler, *Anthropocene Fictions: The Novel in a Time of Climate Change* (Charlottesville: University of Virginia Press, 2015), 24, 80. In Octavia Butler's *Parable of the Sower* and Doris Lessing's *Mara and Dann*, continues Trexler, "not drought but broken rule of law and crazed, dehumanized ransackers are the real impetus to flight" (80).
43 Trexler, *Anthropocene Fictions*, 14.
44 Steinbeck, *To a God Unknown*, 179.
45 See Louis Owens, *John Steinbeck's Re-Vision of America* (Athens: University of Georgia Press, 1985), 16.
46 The character Willie, for example, dreams he is in a bright place that is dry and dead, and people come out of holes and pull off his arms and legs; he eventually kills himself when this world of hard dust is realized in a vision of the moon (Steinbeck, *To a God Unknown*, 189, 351–52).
47 "The hills were turning grey as the covering of grass wore off, and the white flints stuck out and caught the light. When December was half gone, the clouds broke and scattered. The sun grew warm and an apparition of summer came to the valley" (Steinbeck, *To a God Unknown*, 304–5).
48 For a reading of Rothstein's "Steer Skull" photograph, stressing its dual documentary and aesthetic motivations, see James Hewitson, "Documenting Disasters: Rothstein's 'Steer Skull' and the Use of Photographic Evidence in Environmental and Political Narratives," in Marlene Kadar, Jeanne Perreault,

and Linda Warley (eds.), *Photographs, Histories, and Meanings* (New York: Palgrave Macmillan, 2009), 43–58

49 Steinbeck, *To a God Unknown*, 362–63, 315, 260.

50 H[arold] B[righouse], "Pan in California," Manchester *Guardian* (March 27, 1935), in McElrath, Crisler, and Shillinglaw (eds.), *Contemporary Reviews*, 27. Pritchett, on the other hand, described Joseph as "a gigantic piece of half-baked mysticism" ("Fiction," 27).

51 French quoted in Rodney Rice, "Circles in the Forest: John Steinbeck and the Deep Ecology of *To a God Unknown*," *Steinbeck Review* 8.2 (December 2011), 36. Clearly the language and concept of magical realism were not always available to critics, even when they felt the book's failure on magically real grounds; referring to the strange character of the animal-sacrificing, cliff-dwelling old man of the West, Edmund Wilson called *To a God Unknown* a "mixture of seriousness and trashiness." See Wilson, *The Boys in the Back Room: Notes on California Novelists* (San Francisco, CA: Colt, 1941), 52.

52 As Rice points out in a useful reassessment of the novel from an ecocritical perspective, recent criticism has remained divided over Joseph's death: "heroic readings" explain it as "an attempt to move outward toward God and transcendent truth, while ironic interpretations see his demise as part of a bewildering movement inward toward man and human understanding." "Viewing Joseph narrowly using dualistic classifications that assign him a role either as an exotic hero or a confused mortal is probably too restrictive" ("Circles in the Forest," 36, 37).

53 Steinbeck, *To a God Unknown*, 207.

54 Steinbeck, *To a God Unknown*, 305.

55 Steinbeck, *To a God Unknown*, 307.

56 Steinbeck, *To a God Unknown*, 313.

57 Steinbeck, *To a God Unknown*, 317–18.

58 Steinbeck, *To a God Unknown*, 366.

59 Boehmer, quoted in Stephen M. Hart and Wen-chin Ouyang (eds.), *A Companion to Magical Realism* (Woodbridge, UK: Tamesis, 2005), 6.

60 Hart and Ouyang (eds.), *A Companion to Magical Realism*, 3.

61 Virginia Barney, "Symbols of Earth," *New York Times Book Review* (October 1, 1933), in McElrath, Crisler, and Shillinglaw (eds.), *Contemporary Reviews*, 25.

3 Race and Revision: "The Vigilante" and "Johnny Bear"

1 Details about the Hart kidnapping and the Thurmond and Holmes lynching are drawn from James P. Delgado, "The Facts Behind John Steinbeck's 'The Lonesome Vigilante,'" *Steinbeck Quarterly* 16.3–4 (1983), 70–77; Brian McGinty, "Shadows in St. James Park," *California History* 57.4 (Winter 1978–

79), 290–307; and Ken Gonzales-Day, *Lynching in the West: 1850–1935* (Durham, NC: Duke University Press, 2006), 105–11.

2 John Steinbeck, "The Vigilante," *The Grapes of Wrath and Other Writings, 1936–1941*, ed. Robert DeMott (New York: Library of America, 1996), 87. See Delgado, "The Facts," 75.

3 Delgado traces these various parallels ("The Facts," 75–76).

4 The Long Valley ledger, Martha Heasley Cox Center for Steinbeck Studies, San Jose State University.

5 Gonzales-Day, *Lynching*, 206.

6 John Steinbeck, "Flight," *The Grapes of Wrath and Other Writings, 1936–1941*, ed. Robert DeMott (New York: Library of America, 1996), 34, 47.

7 My transcription of Steinbeck's notes in the Long Valley ledger, 80.

8 Ernest Hemingway, "Soldier's Home," *The Short Stories* (New York: Scribner, 1995), 145–53.

9 The conversations on this topic between Doc Burton and the other characters in Steinbeck's *In Dubious Battle* (1936) is another good example.

10 Steinbeck, "Case History," Long Valley ledger, 82.

11 In "Case History," the victim of the lynching is accused of kidnapping and murder, as were Thurmond and Holmes.

12 Steinbeck, "Case History," Long Valley ledger, 81–82, 85.

13 Steinbeck's note in the Long Valley ledger, 126.

14 In the ledger version of "The Vigilante," we read "on south 10th between Jones and Santa Rosa" (124); the actual streets would be John and Santa Clara.

15 We learn that the bar Mike visits closes at midnight; the actual lynching took place at 11:15 p.m.

16 See Delgado, "The Facts," 74.

17 Steinbeck, "The Vigilante," 86.

18 Take, for example, the exhibition that became James Allen's *Without Sanctuary: Lynching Photography in America* (Santa Fe, NM: Twin Palms Publishers, 2000).

19 Steinbeck, "The Vigilante," 87.

20 See Gonzalez-Day, *Lynching*, 97; Shawn Michelle Smith, "The Evidence of Lynching Photographs," *Lynching Photographs*, eds. Dora Apel and Shawn Michelle Smith, (Berkeley: University of California Press, 2007), 14.

21 Dora Apel, "On Looking: Lynching Photographs and Legacies of Lynching after 9/11," *American Quarterly* 55.3 (September 2003), 458.

22 According to Gonzales-Day, someone produced a multi-card set of images depicting the journey from prison cell to hang tree (*Lynching*, 115).

23 See Brian McGinty, "Shadows in St. James Park," *California History* 57.4 (Winter 1978–79), 304. McGinty also notes that the community had effective law enforcement.

24 As we will see again in the next chapter, Steinbeck's ideas often resonate in curious ways with those of the philosophers Gilles Deleuze and Félix Guattari, who were fascinated with states of becoming and "pack" action, for example, the move toward assemblage that they describe as the war machine: "a pure and immeasurable multiplicity, the pack, an irruption of the ephemeral and the power of metamorphosis." See Gilles Deleuze and Félix Guattari, *A Thousand Plateaus: Capitalism and Schizophrenia*, trans. Brian Massumi (Minneapolis: University of Minnesota Press, 1987), especially 351–423.

25 Gonzales-Day, *Lynching*, 108.

26 Jacqueline Goldsby, *A Spectacular Secret: Lynching in American Life and Literature* (Chicago: University of Chicago Press, 2006), 281.

27 John Steinbeck, *The Pearl, Novels 1942–1952*, ed. Robert DeMott (New York: Library of America, 2001), 298.

28 Steinbeck, "The Vigilante," 86.

29 Goldsby, *Spectacular Secret*, 231. Goldsby observes that Black men were photographed to display the full extent of their wounding and humiliation.

30 See Walter White, *A Man Called White: The Autobiography of Walter White* (New York: Viking, 1948), 166–67.

31 Kate Flint, *Flash!: Photography, Writing, and Surprising Illumination* (Oxford: Oxford University Press, 2017), 173, 170.

32 Apel, "Lynching Photographs and the Politics of Public Shaming," in Apel and Smith, *Lynching Photographs*, 58. For the young flirting couple in the Marion photograph, writes Apel, "it is as though the myth of the hypersexed black male, now safely controlled, has now become an invisible erotic power haunting their relation" (58).

33 Steinbeck, "The Vigilante," 89.

34 Susan Stewart, *On Longing: Narratives of the Miniature, the Gigantic, the Souvenir, the Collection* (Durham, NC: Duke University Press, 1993), 135, 133, 136. Goldsby also draws from Stewart in her description of lynching souvenirs (*Spectacular Secret*, 275–76).

35 Steinbeck, "The Vigilante," 91, 87. See Stewart, *On Longing*, on experiences being "not for sale" (136).

36 Stewart, *On Longing*, 136.

37 See Goldsby, *Spectacular Secret*, 20–21, 25.

38 Steinbeck, "The Vigilante," 89.

39 John Steinbeck, "Johnny Bear," *The Grapes of Wrath and Other Writings, 1936–1941*, ed. Robert DeMott (New York: Library of America, 1996), 107.

40 Willa Cather, *The World and the Parish: Willa Cather's Articles and Reviews, 1893–1902*, vol. 1 (Lincoln: University of Nebraska Press, 1970), 166.

41 Steinbeck, "Johnny Bear," 95.

42 Verging on the superhuman, he moves with complete lack of effort (Steinbeck, "Johnny Bear," 98).
43 Steinbeck, "Johnny Bear," 95.
44 Steinbeck, "Johnny Bear," 97.
45 Steinbeck, "Johnny Bear," 104.
46 Steinbeck, "Johnny Bear," 109.
47 Steinbeck, "Johnny Bear," 98. Flattered by Johnny's performance of his encounter with Mae, our narrator imitates the barman Carl's clipped sentences. He also becomes unsure of how the details of events come to be known (107).
48 The cook "smoked Cuban cigarettes in a bamboo holder. I didn't like the way his fingers twitched in the morning. His hands were clean – floury like a miller's hands" (Steinbeck, "Johnny Bear," 101).
49 Edgar Allan Poe, "Twice-told Tales," *Graham's Magazine* 20.5 (May 1842), reprinted in John L. Idol Jr. and Buford Jones (eds.), *Nathaniel Hawthorne: The Contemporary Reviews* (Cambridge: Cambridge University Press, 1994), 63–68.
50 Eudora Welty, "Where Is The Voice Coming From?" *The Collected Stories of Eudora Welty* (New York: Harcourt Brace Jovanovich, 1980), 603–7.
51 Eudora Welty, *One Time, One Place: Mississippi in the Depression, A Snapshot Album* (Oxford: University Press of Mississippi, 1996), 4.
52 Julio Cortázar, "Some Aspects of the Short Story," in Charles E. May (ed.), *The New Short Story Theories* (Athens: Ohio University Press, 1994), 245–55. See my discussion of "The Snake" in Chapter 1.
53 Nadine Gordimer, "The Flash of Fireflies," in Charles E. May (ed.), *Short Story Theories* (Athens: Ohio University Press, 1978), 178–81.
54 See Yi-Ping Ong, *The Art of Being: Poetics of the Novel and Existentialist Philosophy* (Cambridge, MA: Harvard University Press, 2018), especially 23–45.
55 Roland Barthes, *Camera Lucida: Reflections on Photography* (New York: Hill & Wang, 2010), 119.
56 Susan Sontag describes photographs as reinforcing a "view of social reality as consisting of small units" in *On Photography* (New York: Picador, 1990), 22.
57 "Photographed images do not seem to be statements about the world so much as pieces of it," writes Sontag in *On Photography*, 4.
58 Sontag, *On Photography*, 74, 10.

4 Becoming Animal: Theories of Mind in *The Red Pony*

1 Edmund Wilson, *The Boys in the Back Room: Notes on California Novelists* (San Francisco, CA: Colt Prss, 1941), 43. The original essay, "The Californians: Storm and Steinbeck," appeared in *New Republic* 103 (December 9, 1940), 784–87.

2 Ralph Thompson, "Books of the Times," *New York Times* (September 21, 1938), in Joseph R. McElrath Jr., Jesse S. Crisler, and Susan Shillinglaw (eds.), *John Steinbeck: The Contemporary Reviews* (Cambridge: Cambridge University Press, 1996), 138.

3 Luc Perry, *The New Ecological Order* (1995), quoted in Bruce Holsinger, "Of Pigs and Parchment: Medieval Studies and the Coming of the Animal," *PMLA* 124.2 (March 2009), 618.

4 Joanna Picciotto, quoted in Holsinger, "Of Pigs and Parchment," 617. Picciotto's phrase was used as the title of a colloquium at Princeton University in June 2003 sponsored by the Center for the Study of Religion.

5 Cary Wolfe, *Animal Rites: American Culture, the Discourses of Species, and Posthumanist Theory* (2003), quoted in Michael Lundblad, "From Animal to Animality Studies," *PMLA* 124.2 (March 2009), 497.

6 Susan McHugh, "Literary Animal Agents," *PMLA* 124.2 (March 2009), 487.

7 Michael Lundblad, *The Birth of a Jungle: Animality in Progressive-Era US Literature and Culture* (Oxford: Oxford University Press, 2013), 6.

8 "Saint Katy the Virgin" was conceived as a verse-parody, based on literary conventions and cultural practices of the Middle Ages that Steinbeck had gleaned from a Stanford history class on European civilization. See Jackson J. Benson, *John Steinbeck, Writer: A Biography* (New York: Penguin, 1990), 253.

9 John Steinbeck, letter to Carlton A. Sheffield (June 30, 1933), in Elaine Steinbeck and Robert Wallsten (eds.), *Steinbeck: A Life in Letters* (New York: Penguin, 1989), 78.

10 Steinbeck, unfinished Letter to George Albee (1933), in Steinbeck and Wallsten (eds.), *A Life in Letters*, 71.

11 Benson, *John Steinbeck*, 14, 62.

12 Benson, *John Steinbeck*, 205.

13 Blakey Vermeule, *Why Do We Care about Literary Characters?* (Baltimore, MD: Johns Hopkins University Press, 2010), 35.

14 Hannah Walser, "Mind-Reading in the Dark: Social Cognition in Nineteenth-Century American Fiction," Ph.D dissertation, Stanford University, June 2016.

15 See Walser, "Mind-Reading in the Dark."

16 John Steinbeck, *The Red Pony, The Grapes of Wrath and Other Writings, 1936–1941*, ed. Robert DeMott (New York: Library of America, 1996), 132.

17 William James, *The Principles of Psychology*, vol. 2 (New York: Dover, 1950), 450.

18 Steinbeck, *Red Pony*, 132.

19 John Dewey, *My Pedagogical Creed* (New York & Chicago, IL: E. L. Kellogg, 1897), 6.

20 Steinbeck, *Red Pony*, 136.
21 Steinbeck, *Red Pony*, 147.
22 Steinbeck, *Red Pony*, 142–43.
23 Steinbeck, *Red Pony*, 143.
24 Silvan Tomkins, *Shame and Its Sisters: A Silvan Tomkins Reader*, eds. Eve Kosofsky Sedgwick and Adam Frank (Durham, NC: Duke University Press, 1995), 136.
25 Steinbeck, letter to George Albee (1933), in Steinbeck and Wallsten (eds.), *A Life in Letters*, 83.
26 Steinbeck, *Red Pony*, 157–58.
27 Karl Steel, "How to Make a Human" (2008), quoted in Holsinger, "Of Pigs and Parchment," 617.
28 Steinbeck, *Red Pony*, 158.
29 Steinbeck, *Red Pony*, 173.
30 Steinbeck, *Red Pony*, 178.
31 Steinbeck, *Red Pony*, 184.
32 Steinbeck, *Red Pony*, 188.
33 Steinbeck, *Red Pony*, 192.
34 Steinbeck, *Red Pony*, 182.
35 Steinbeck, *Red Pony*, 162.
36 Steinbeck, *Red Pony*, 162–64. Bartleby's famous refrain in Melville's "Bartleby, the Scrivener" (1853) is, of course, "I would prefer not to."
37 Steinbeck, *Red Pony*, 169.
38 Steinbeck, *Red Pony*, 170–71.
39 "And now he was different. Out of a thousand centuries they drew the ancient admiration of the footman for the horseman. They knew instinctively that a man on a horse is spiritually as well as physically bigger than a man on foot. They knew that Jody had been miraculously lifted out of equality with them, and had been placed over them" (Steinbeck, *Red Pony*, 139).
40 Donald Houghton quoted in R. S. Hughes, *John Steinbeck: A Study of the Short Fiction* (Boston, MA: Twayne, 1989), 66.
41 Steinbeck, *Red Pony*, 204.
42 For this developing idea of the phalanx in *To a God Unknown*, see John Steinbeck, *Novels and Stories, 1932–1937*, ed. Robert DeMott (New York: Library of America, 1994), 182, 247, 268–69, 318.
43 In the summer of 1923, Steinbeck enrolled in an elementary zoology class at Hopkins Marine Station and was struck by William Emerson Ritter's concept of the "superorganism," in which the whole exercises a measure of determinative influence over its parts. See Benson, *John Steinbeck*, 240–41.
44 Benson, *John Steinbeck*, 268. See also Richard Astro, *John Steinbeck and Edward Ricketts: The Shaping of a Novelist* (Minneapolis: University of Minnesota Press, 1973), 63–65.

45 Gilles Deleuze and Félix Guattari, *Kafka: Toward a Minor Literature*, trans. Dana Polan (Minneapolis: University of Minnesota Press, 1986), 13. For an exploration of Deleuze and Guattari's ideas, see Gerald L. Bruns, "Becoming-Animal (Some Simple Ways)," *New Literary History* 38.4 (Autumn 2007): 703–20.

46 Deleuze and Guattari, *Kafka*, 36, 82, 84.

47 Gilles Deleuze and Félix Guattari, *A Thousand Plateaus: Capitalism and Schizophrenia*, trans. Brian Massumi (Minneapolis: University of Minnesota Press, 1987), 239.

48 See Rosi Braidotti, "Animals, Anomalies, and Inorganic Others," *PMLA* 124.2 (March 2009), 528, and Brian E. Railsback, *Parallel Expeditions: Charles Darwin and the Art of John Steinbeck* (Moscow: University of Idaho Press, 1995).

49 See Deleuze and Guattari, *A Thousand Plateaus*, 238, and Astro, *John Steinbeck and Edward Ricketts*, 65.

50 Deleuze and Guattari, *Kafka*, 37, 84.

51 Steinbeck, *Red Pony*, 204.

52 Steinbeck, *Red Pony*, 203, 200.

53 See Deleuze and Guattari, *A Thousand Plateaus*, 247, and *Kafka*, 15.

54 Deleuze and Guattari, *A Thousand Plateaus*, 247.

55 Frederick Jackson Turner, *The Significance of the Frontier in American History* (New York: Ungar, 1963), 27.

5 What Is It Like to Be a Plant?: "The Chrysanthemums" and "The White Quail"

1 John Steinbeck, letter to Elizabeth Otis (December 7, 1958), in Elaine Steinbeck and Robert Wallsten (eds.), *Steinbeck: A Life in Letters* (New York: Penguin, 1989), 608.

2 John Steinbeck, "Growing Vegetables," *Once There Was a War* (New York: Penguin, 2007), 67.

3 Steinbeck, "Growing Vegetables," 68.

4 John Steinbeck, letter to Carl Wilhelmson (Fall 1930), quoted in Jackson J. Benson, *John Steinbeck, Writer: A Biography* (New York: Penguin, 1990), 220.

5 John Steinbeck, "Johnny Bear," *The Grapes of Wrath and Other Writings, 1936–1941*, ed. Robert DeMott (New York: Library of America, 1996), 93.

6 John Steinbeck, "Always Something to Do in Salinas," *America and Americans, and Selected Nonfiction*, eds. Susan Shillinglaw and Jackson J. Benson (New York: Penguin, 2003), 6.

7 Steinbeck, "Always Something to Do in Salinas," 6–7.

8 "Food power" is Allison Carruth's term. Allison Carruth, *Global Appetites: American Power and the Literature of Food* (Cambridge: Cambridge University Press, 2013), 4.

9 Edmund Wilson, *The Boys in the Back Room: Notes on California Novelists* (San Francisco, CA: Colt Press, 1941), 43.

10 Steinbeck, letter to George Albee (February 25, 1934), in Steinbeck and Wallsten (eds.), *A Life in Letters*, 91.

11 Carol wrote a gardening seed book, now lost; see Susan Shillinglaw, *Carol and John Steinbeck: Portrait of a Marriage* (Reno: University of Nevada Press, 2013), 220–21.

12 John Steinbeck, "The Chrysanthemums," *The Grapes of Wrath and Other Writings, 1936–1941*, ed. Robert DeMott (New York: Library of America, 1996), 6.

13 Steinbeck, "Chrysanthemums," 11.

14 We will return to Ricketts's idea of "breaking through" in Chapter 8.

15 Thomas Nagel, "What Is It Like to Be a Bat?" *The Philosophical Review* 83.4 (October 1974): 435–50.

16 Nagel, "What Is It Like to Be a Bat?" 442.

17 Jeffrey T. Nealon, *Plant Theory: Biopower and Vegetable Life* (Stanford, CA: Stanford University Press, 2015), 11. See also Matthew Hall, *Plants as Persons: A Philosophical Botany* (Albany: State University of New York Press, 2011) and Eduardo Kohn, *How Forests Think: Toward an Anthropology Beyond the Human* (Berkeley: University of California Press, 2013).

18 See Judith A. Richardson, "Nathaniel Hawthorne's Secret Garden," *Nathaniel Hawthorne Review* 45.2 (2019): 171–97.

19 Nealon, *Plant Theory*, 87, 106.

20 Laura Marks, "Vegetable Locomotion" (2012), quoted in Nealon, *Plant Theory*, 87.

21 Steinbeck, "Chrysanthemums," 8.

22 I have in mind here the Thayer and Eldridge edition of Whitman's *Leaves of Grass* (1860–61).

23 Steinbeck, "Chrysanthemums," 11.

24 Elaine Miller, *The Vegetable Soul* (2002), quoted in Nealon, *Plant Theory*, 98.

25 Louis Owens, *Steinbeck's Re-vision of America* (Athens: University of Georgia Press, 1985), 109.

26 Steinbeck, "Chrysanthemums," 13.

27 Steinbeck, "Chrysanthemums," 5.

28 The reader may wish to consult the ideas of Professor Gerald Pollack, among others, at http://prn.fm/can-humans-photosynthesize-by-gerald-pollack-phd/

29 When his sweet peas bloom, Peter sits on his porch to look at the pink and blue in a moment of porous receptivity not unlike Elisa's: "When the afternoon

breeze came up, he inhaled deeply. His blue shirt was open at the throat, as though he wanted to get the perfume down next his skin." Peter's "special knowledge" and his "prophetic" powers stem from a profound connection to the land and its plants. See John Steinbeck, "The Harness," *The Grapes of Wrath and Other Writings, 1936–1941*, ed. Robert DeMott (New York: Library of America, 1996), 72–85.

30 Edward Weston, *The Daybooks of Edward Weston*, vol. 2: *California*, ed. Nancy Newhall (New York: Horizon Press, 1966), 181.

31 Steinbeck, "Chrysanthemums," 14.

32 See Hamedreza Kohzadi, "The Marriage of Hysteria and Feminism in John Steinbeck's 'The Chrysanthemums': Elisa Allen as a Married but Virgin Feminist Homosexual Hysteric," *Interdisciplinary Literary Studies* 20.4 (2018): 429–69. For a more conventional and compelling reading, see Christopher S. Busch, "Longing for the Lost Frontier: Steinbeck's Vision of Cultural Decline in 'The White Quail' and 'The Chrysanthemums,'" *Steinbeck Quarterly* 26.3–4 (1993): 81–90.

33 Steinbeck, letter to George Albee (February 25, 1934), in Steinbeck and Wallsten (eds.), *A Life in Letters*, 91. William V. Miller argues that the tinker plays the role of the artist who has the power to transform his readers. See Miller, "Sexual and Spiritual Ambiguity in 'The Chrysanthemums,'" *Steinbeck Quarterly* 5 (Summer-Fall 1972), 71.

34 Steinbeck, "Chrysanthemums," 16.

35 Steinbeck, "Chrysanthemums," 9.

36 Alexandra Minna Stern, *Eugenic Nation: Faults and Frontiers of Better Breeding in Modern America* (Berkeley: University of California Press, 2005), 124, 128.

37 Luther Burbank, *The Training of the Human Plant* (New York: Century Co., 1907), 14, 30, 82.

38 Paul Popenoe, letter to his parents, quoted in Stern, *Eugenic Nation*, 157.

39 See Stern, *Eugenic Nation*, 156–57.

40 Popenoe, quoted in Jill Lepore, "Fixed," *New Yorker* (March 22, 2010) www.newyorker.com/magazine/2010/03/29/fixed.

41 John Steinbeck, "The White Quail," *The Grapes of Wrath and Other Writings, 1936–1941*, ed. Robert DeMott (New York: Library of America, 1996), 17.

42 Steinbeck, "White Quail," 24.

43 Steinbeck, "White Quail," 17.

44 Steinbeck, "White Quail," 21.

45 Steinbeck, "White Quail," 22.

46 Steinbeck, "White Quail," 25.

47 Arthur L. Simpson Jr. argues that Mary's identification of herself with the quail is an act of self-anesthetization, a "movement out of life and into art." See Simpson, "'The White Quail': A Portrait of an Artist," in Tetsumaro Hayashi

(ed.), *A Study Guide to Steinbeck's "The Long Valley"* (Ann Arbor, MI: Pierian Press, 1976), 11–16.

48 Mary's thought continues: "The marvelous candy from Italy. 'Don't eat it, dear. It's prettier than it's good.' Mary never ate it, but looking at it was an ecstasy like this. / 'What a pretty girl Mary is. She's like a gentian, so quiet.' The hearing was an ecstasy like this. / 'Mary dear, be very brave now. Your father has – passed away.' The first moment of loss was an ecstasy like this." Steinbeck, "White Quail," 25–26.

49 Steinbeck, "White Quail," 19.

50 Steinbeck, "White Quail," 21.

51 Steinbeck, "White Quail," 23.

52 Lepore, "Fixed."

53 Popenoe recommends that "a husband determine whether his bride is 'frigid, normal, or ardent,' as 'some frigid women require surgical treatment'" (Lepore, "Fixed").

54 See Lepore, "Fixed."

55 Paul Popenoe and Roswell Hill Johnson, "Increasing Marriages of Superiors," *Applied Eugenics* (1920), quoted in Lepore, "Fixed."

56 Steinbeck, "White Quail," 24.

57 We might think too of another white animal, the "white elephants" in Ernest Hemingway's "Hills Like White Elephants" (1927), another story of the reproductive angst of a young couple.

58 D. H. Lawrence, *Studies in Classic American Literature* (New York: Penguin, 1977), 169.

59 See C. L. R. James, *Mariners, Renegades, and Castaways: The Story of Herman Melville and the World We Live In* (New York: C. L. R. James, 1953).

60 Steinbeck, "White Quail," 28, 27, 17.

61 Nina Baym, "Melodramas of Beset Manhood: How Theories of American Fiction Exclude Women Authors," *American Quarterly* 33 (1981): 123–39. In a letter from 1948, Steinbeck describes his own garden war against snails and varmints and follows it immediately with negative comments about the intelligence, sexuality, and castrating presence of American women – as if the story's links between gardening and alleged "frigidity" were again surfacing in his mind. Steinbeck, letter to Bo Beskow (November 19, 1948), in Steinbeck and Wallsten (eds.), *A Life in Letters*, 343.

62 Toni Morrison's *Playing in the Dark: Whiteness and the Literary Imagination* (Cambridge, MA: Harvard University Press, 1992) is the pioneering account of this fundamental importance of race.

63 See Carruth, *Global Appetites.*

64 Steinbeck, *The Grapes of Wrath and Other Writings*, 304.

65 Michael Denning, *The Cultural Front: The Laboring of American Culture in the Twentieth Century* (London: Verso, 1997), 264–65. Denning attributes the success of *Grapes* to its blend of racial populism and conservative vitalism. In *Radical Visions and American Dreams: Culture and Social Thought in the Depression Years* (New York: Harper & Row, 1973), Richard H. Pells also describes *Grapes* as unconsciously conservative (219) and unable to locate clearly the causes of the Great Depression (216).

66 Steinbeck, *Grapes of Wrath*, 211.

67 Brian Railsback writes in *Parallel Expeditions: Charles Darwin and the Art of John Steinbeck* (Moscow: University of Idaho Press, 1995): "Steinbeck's extensive use of personification and anthropomorphism underscores his view of Homo sapiens as just another species" (132).

68 Steinbeck, *Grapes of Wrath*, 211.

69 For an excellent account of Rothstein's photography in the context of Roy Stryker's ideas about the photography of the Resettlement Administration, see James Hewitson, "Documenting Disasters: Rothstein's 'Steer Skull' and the Use of Photographic Evidence in Environmental and Political Narratives," *Photographs, Histories, and Meanings*, eds. Marlene Kadar, Jeanne Perreault, and Linda Warley (New York: Palgrave Macmillan, 2009), 43–58.

70 Dorothea Lange and Paul S. Taylor, *An American Exodus: A Record of Human Erosion* (New York: Reynal & Hitchcock, 1939).

71 Mary Austin, *The Land of Little Rain* (Boston and New York: Houghton Mifflin, 1903), 26.

72 Steinbeck, *Grapes of Wrath*, 211.

73 See Hewitson, "Documenting Disasters," 52.

74 Steinbeck, *Grapes of Wrath*, 213–14.

75 It is not insignificant that Woody Guthrie's *Dust Bowl Ballads* (1940), generally considered to be the first "concept album" (featuring a sustained narrative across multiple songs), was directly inspired by *Grapes*. Guthrie strings his ballads into an epic of suffering and emergence into movement, as dust becomes an aesthetic product, a form of blues defined by cyclical repetition and moving on, with narrative emerging from environmental trauma: "Buried head over heels in the black old dust,/I had to pack up and go./An' I just blowed in, an' I'll soon blow out again."

76 Barbara A. Heavilin and Kathleen Hicks describe this environment as "a crime scene as well as a sad dirge bemoaning the maltreatment of the sweet land," where plowing is a vicious rape of a vulnerable woman. Heavilin and Hicks, "Editors Column: John Steinbeck, Pope Francis, and Deep Ecology," *The Steinbeck Review* 12.2 (2015): v–x.

77 Julianna Restivo discusses Steinbeck's intent on restoring male generative power, as it relates both to the land and to the generative power of the

female body in opposition to male production. She writes: "It is not difficult to understand Steinbeck's motivation for such a revision: the male body in the late nineteenth and early twentieth century was under constant threat of being replaced – by the machine and by banks or corporations that cut them off from the land and meaningful production. The female body's inherent connection to the land via the generative power of childbirth offers Steinbeck a solution to such threats in male domination." See Restivo, "Steinbeck's Pregnant Bodies: Childbirth, Land, and Production," *The Steinbeck Review* 12.2 (2015): 117–29.

78 Steinbeck, *Grapes of Wrath*, 581.

6 On Not Being a Modernist: Disability and Performance in *Of Mice and Men*

1 The language of the Supreme Court of the United States *Atkins* case, cited in the American Civil Liberties Union brief amicus curiae on behalf of Bobby James Moore, "Summary of Argument," 6. www.scotusblog.com/wp-content/uploads/2016/08/15-797-ACLU-amicus-pet.pdf

2 For a list of the various parts of the Lennie standard, see the ACLU amicus, 3–4.

3 Cochran's 2004 decision, cited in Julie Barton, "Judging Steinbeck's Lennie," *Life of the Law* (September 3, 2013). www.lifeofthelaw.org/2013/09/judging-steinbeck-lennie/

4 The decision was not based on "someone in the mild end of the spectrum," according to Margaret Nygren, head of the American Association for Intellectual and Developmental Disabilities, which was the original intention of the Supreme Court's decision. See Barton, "Judging Steinbeck's Lennie," para. 16.

5 This is the view of John Blume, a law professor at Cornell University, who points to the fact that Lennie attempts to cover up his crime and is gainfully employed. See Barton, "Judging Steinbeck's Lennie," paras. 20–21.

6 Peter Lisca, *The Wide World of John Steinbeck* (New Brunswick, NJ: Rutgers University Press, 1958), 133. For an excellent collection of critical reactions to *Of Mice and Men*, see Michael J. Meyer (ed.), *The Essential Criticism of John Steinbeck's "Of Mice and Men"* (Lanham, MD: Scarecrow Press, 2009).

7 Edmund Wilson, *The Boys in the Back Room: Notes on California Novelists* (San Francisco, CA: Colt Press, 1941), 52.

8 See Mark McGurl, *The Novel Art: Elevations of American Fiction after Henry James* (Princeton, NJ: Princeton University Press, 2001); Richard Volney Chase, *The American Novel and Its Tradition* (Garden City, NY: Doubleday, 1957); and James Berger, *The Disarticulate: Language, Disability, and the Narratives of Modernity* (New York: New York University Press, 2014).

9 Ato Quayson, *Aesthetic Nervousness: Disability and the Crisis of Representation* (New York: Columbia University Press, 2007).

10 Quayson, *Aesthetic Nervousness*, 55–56, 84.

11 Steinbeck, letter to Wilbur Needham (February 1936), quoted in Jackson J. Benson, *John Steinbeck, Writer: A Biography* (New York: Penguin, 1990), 325–26.

12 Winfried Menninghaus, "On the 'Vital Significance' of Kitsch: Walter Benjamin's Politics of 'Bad Taste,'" in Andrew Benjamin and Charles Rice (eds.), *Walter Benjamin and the Architecture of Modernity* (Melbourne, Australia: re.press, 2009), 41.

13 Quayson, *Aesthetic Nervousness*, 52.

14 Anne Loftis, "A Historical Introduction to *Of Mice and Men,*" in Meyer (ed.), *Essential Criticism*, 123.

15 Steinbeck forewarns us of each development in his flawless plot, according to James Ross Oliver in "Book News and Views," *Peninsula Herald* (Monterey), February 25, 1937, in Joseph R. McElrath Jr., Jesse S. Crisler, and Susan Shillinglaw (eds.), *John Steinbeck: The Contemporary Reviews* (Cambridge: Cambridge University Press, 1996), 74–75.

16 Dorothea Brande Collins, "Reading at Random," *American Review* 9 (April 1937), in McElrath, Crisler, and Shillinglaw (eds.), *Contemporary Reviews*, 90.

17 Lewis M. Terman, *The Measurement of Intelligence* (Boston, MA: Houghton Mifflin, 1916), 92.

18 John Steinbeck, *Of Mice and Men, Novels and Stories, 1932–1937*, ed. Robert DeMott (New York: Library of America, 1994), 814.

19 Anon., "Young Man's Dream," *Time* 28 (March 1, 1937); Anon., "*Of Mice and Men,*" London *Mercury* 36 (October 1937), in McElrath, Crisler, and Shillinglaw (eds.), *Contemporary Reviews*, 85, 93.

20 "Dubbed 'the new modesty in literary criticism' by Jeffrey Williams, this array of overlapping but distinct approaches includes post-critique, surface reading, distant reading, thin description, the sociological turn, and new formalism. The critics associated with these approaches call for alternatives to 'symptomatic reading' – that is, to interpretive modes whose primary aim is to expose the ruses of ideology, decode the encryptions wrought by the unconscious, or otherwise penetrate the surfaces of texts to get at their truer, occulted depths." Paul K. Saint-Amour, "Weak Theory, Weak Modernism," *Modernism/Modernity* 25.3 (September 2018), 439.

21 Steinbeck, *Of Mice and Men*, 855.

22 Carey McWilliams, *Factories in the Field: The Story of Migratory Farm Labor in California* (Boston, MA: Little, Brown and Company, 1939).

23 Steinbeck's writing of *Of Mice and Men* coincided with his acquaintance with personalities in Hollywood and was published a year after Charlie Chaplin's film *Modern Times* was released. Chaplin was a fan of Steinbeck's books and "simply drove up to Steinbeck's house one day – in a large, black chauffeured

limousine – jumped out of the car, extended his hand, and introduced himself. … According to Chaplin's son Charles, Jr., his father 'was fascinated by Steinbeck's books and used to drive around the countryside where his stories were laid, trying to place the characters in the books in their proper locations.'" Benson, *John Steinbeck*, 383–84.

24 Steinbeck, *Of Mice and Men*, 841.

25 Steinbeck, *Of Mice and Men*, 798.

26 Steinbeck, "Notes on the Text," *Novels and Stories, 1932–1937*, 903.

27 Steinbeck, *Of Mice and Men*, 806.

28 Steinbeck, *Of Mice and Men*, 807; emphasis in original.

29 "Lennie was a real person. He's in an insane asylum in California right now," claimed Steinbeck in "Men, Mice, and John Steinbeck," *New York Times* (December 5, 1937), in Thomas Fensch (ed.), *Conversations with John Steinbeck* (Jackson: University of Mississippi Press, 1988), 9.

30 Edmund Wilson, "John Steinbeck," *Classics and Commercials: A Literary Chronicle of the Forties* (New York: Farrar, Straus, and Co., 1950), 35. See also Joseph Henry Jackson, "Steinbeck's Art Finds Powerful Expression in *Of Mice and Men*," *San Francisco Chronicle* (February 28, 1937), in Meyer (ed.), *Essential Criticism*, 11.

31 "Sentimentalism might be defined as the political sense obfuscated or gone rancid. Sentimentalism, unlike the modes of genuine sensibility, never exists except in tandem with failed political consciousness." Ann Douglas, *The Feminization of American Culture* (New York: Farrar, Straus, Giroux, 1998), 254.

32 Candy continues talking to Curley's Wife after she is dead, as if it really makes no difference. Steinbeck, *Of Mice and Men*, 871. For the rapidity of George's reaction to her, see Steinbeck, *Of Mice and Men*, 819–20.

33 Harry Thornton Moore, *The Novels of John Steinbeck: A First Critical Study* (Chicago, IL: Normandy House, 1939), 50–52.

34 Nina Baym, "Melodramas of Beset Manhood: How Theories of American Fiction Exclude Women Authors," *American Quarterly* 33 (1981): 123–39.

35 Fiedler defines the American literary tradition as a drama in which "a white and a colored American male flee from civilization into each other's arms." He asserts that interracial male bonding is "the central myth of our culture … the most deeply underlying image of ourselves." Leslie Fiedler, *Love and Death in the American Novel* (New York: Criterion Books, 1960), 12, 182.

36 Charles Johnson, "Reading the Character of Crooks," in Meyer (ed.), *Essential Criticism*, 249.

37 Johnson, "Reading the Character of Crooks," 236.

38 Johnson, "Reading the Character of Crooks," 247.

39 "Nobody got any right in here but me," says Crooks in Steinbeck, *Of Mice and Men*, 847.

40 Steinbeck, *Of Mice and Men*, 857.

41 Terman, *Measurement of Intelligence*, 4.

42 Steinbeck, *Of Mice and Men*, 821.

43 Susan Sontag, "Notes on 'Camp,'" *Against Interpretation and Other Essays* (New York: Picador, 1966), 284.

44 Sontag, "Notes on 'Camp,'" 284.

45 The Hindu temple dance, which Steinbeck may have had in mind, featured female dancers who were viewed as existing somewhere between prostitutes and nuns. See Amrit Shrinivasan, "The Hindu Temple-Dancer: Prostitute or Nun?" *The Cambridge Journal of Anthropology* 8.1 (1983): 73–99.

46 Sontag, "Notes on 'Camp,'" 279.

47 Josiah Flynt, *Tramping With Tramps: Studies and Sketches of Vagabond Life* (Montclair, NJ: Patterson Smith, 1972), 55–58.

48 Steinbeck, *Of Mice and Men*, 840.

49 The other characters are naturally intrigued (perhaps sexually panicked?) by the trouble George takes over Lennie, the nature of his "interest." When George says, "He's my .... cousin" (813), George's pause speaks volumes as he tries to explain the "funny" (825) nature of their relationship that is outed elsewhere in the closet language of homosexuality. "Oh, so it's that way," comments Curley about George and Lennie traveling around together (815) – *way* signifying queerness in contemporary literature of the period (for example, at the end of Ernest Hemingway's "The Light of the World"). The scene in which Lennie cripples Curley by squeezing his hand might make us think of Herman Melville's "A Squeeze of the Hand" chapter in *Moby-Dick*, perhaps the quintessential description of implicitly queer relationships in the context of global capitalism.

50 Irr's aim in her essay is to juxtapose the novels by Steinbeck and Baird and employ the trope of queerness to think about US-Canadian relations more broadly. Caren Irr, "Queer Borders: Figures from the 1930s For U.S.-Canadian Relations," in Meyer (ed.), *Essential Criticism*, 162, 164.

51 Steinbeck, *Of Mice and Men*, 878.

52 "Like unemployment or transience then, queerness is supposedly ironic, marginal, and non-normative." Irr, "Queer Borders," in Meyer (ed.), *Essential Criticism*, 178.

53 Wilson, *Boys in the Back Room*, 48, 52.

54 John Steinbeck, "The Novel Might Benefit by the Discipline and Terseness of the Drama," *Stage* 15 (January 1938), 50–51, quoted in Lisca, *Wide World of John Steinbeck*, 133.

55 Steinbeck to Wilbur Needham: "Between us I think the novel is painfully dead. I've never liked it. I'm going into training to write for the theatre which seems to be waking up. I have some ideas for a new dramatic form which I'm experimenting with" (quoted in Benson, *John Steinbeck*, 327).

56 Loftis, "A Historical Introduction," in Meyer (ed.), *Essential Criticism*, 123.
57 Steinbeck, "The Novel Might Benefit," quoted in Lisca, *Wide World of John Steinbeck*, 133.
58 David Kurnick, *Empty Houses: Theatrical Failure and the Novel* (Princeton, NJ: Princeton University Press, 2012), 1–4.
59 Kurnick, *Empty Houses*, 9, 25.
60 Ralph Thompson, "Books of the Times," *New York Times* (March 2, 1937), 19, in Meyer (ed.), *Essential Criticism*, 19.
61 Edward Weeks, "The Bookshelf," *Atlantic* 159 (April 1937), 14, 16, in Meyer (ed.), *Essential Criticism*, 27.
62 The quotation continues: "We shall remember it about that long." Mark Van Doren, "Wrong Number," *Nation* 144 (March 6, 1937), 275, in Meyer (ed.), *Essential Criticism*, 23.
63 Steinbeck, *Of Mice and Men*, 797.
64 Steinbeck, *Of Mice and Men*, 809.
65 Loftis, "A Historical Introduction," in Meyer (ed.), *Essential Criticism*, 123.
66 Steinbeck, *Of Mice and Men*, 875.
67 Samuel Beckett, *Waiting for Godot* (New York: Grove), 1.
68 Benson, *John Steinbeck*, 911. We may also detect more than a few Steinbeckian echoes in Harold Pinter's *The Dumb Waiter* (1960).
69 Leo Bersani and Ulysse Dutoit, *Arts of Impoverishment: Beckett, Rothko, Resnais* (Cambridge, MA: Harvard University Press, 1993), 17.
70 Bersani and Dutoit, *Arts of Impoverishment*, 86, 24, 27.
71 Quayson, *Aesthetic Nervousness*, 54–85.
72 Vivian Mercier, "The Uneventful Event," *The Irish Times* (February 18, 1956), 6.
73 See John Timmerman, "John Steinbeck's Fiction: The Aesthetics of the Road Taken," in Meyer (ed.), *Essential Criticism*, 106.
74 Steinbeck, *Of Mice and Men*, 876.
75 Bersani and Dutoit, *Arts of Impoverishment*, 24.
76 Samuel Beckett, *Worstward Ho* (London: J. Calder, 1983), 7.
77 Steinbeck, *Of Mice and Men*, 873–74.
78 See Walter Benjamin, *The Arcades Project*, trans. Howard Eiland and Kevin McLaughlin (Cambridge, MA: The Belknap Press of Harvard University Press, 1999), especially 126, 212, 395–96, 909.
79 Menninghaus, "On the 'Vital Significance' of Kitsch," 41.
80 At the beginning of the novel, rabbits occupy the scene, "little gray, sculptured stones," which flee when George and Lennie first appear. Steinbeck, *Of Mice and Men*, 797.
81 Menninghaus, "On the 'Vital Significance' of Kitsch," 41.
82 Sianne Ngai, *Our Aesthetic Categories: Zany, Cute, Interesting* (Cambridge, MA: Harvard University Press, 2012), 53. Ngai describes how cuteness became

associated with softness in children's toys at the beginning of the twentieth century even as it was related to recognitions of the aggressiveness of children (75). Ngai also describes this ambivalence in cuteness, its switch from the sentimental to the antisentimental (60).

83 Menninghaus, "On the 'Vital Significance' of Kitsch," 41.

84 See Susan Shillinglaw, "Introduction," *Of Mice and Men* (New York: Penguin Books, 1994), xvi.

85 "My idea was to write a play in the form of a novel. It was an experiment. I wanted to call it at first 'a play to be read.' I constructed it in scenes and filled in the character descriptions and painted in the background." Steinbeck, in "Men, Mice and Mr. Steinbeck," in Fensch (ed.), *Conversations with John Steinbeck*, 9.

86 Steinbeck, in "Men, Mice and Mr. Steinbeck," in Fensch (ed.), *Conversations with John Steinbeck*, 9

87 Benson, *John Steinbeck*, 327.

88 John Steinbeck, *Working Days: The Journals of "The Grapes of Wrath," 1938–41*, ed. Robert DeMott (New York: Viking, 1989), 5.

89 Steinbeck continues, "I'll love it once I get down to work," letter to Louis Paul (February 1936), in Elaine Steinbeck and Robert Wallsten (eds.), *Steinbeck: A Life in Letters* (New York: Penguin, 1989), 120.

90 George S. Kaufman, in Steinbeck and Wallsten (eds.), *A Life in Letters*, 136.

91 For example, he includes a single "NOTE" in the play that has close parallels to the things/props presented to us in the novel: "Articles in the boxes on wall are soap, talcum powder, razors, pulp magazines, medicine bottles, combs, and from nails on the sides of the boxes a few neckties." John Steinbeck, *Of Mice and Men: A Play* (New York: Penguin Books, 2014), 35.

92 Steinbeck, *Of Mice and Men: A Play*, 62–65.

93 Steinbeck, letter to Claire Luce (1938), in Steinbeck and Wallsten (eds.), *A Life in Letters*, 154.

94 Daniel Griesbach, "Reduced to Nothing: Race, Lynching, and Erasure in the Theater Revision of Steinbeck's *Of Mice and Men*," in Meyer (ed.), *Essential Criticism*, 272. Griesbach argues that the Broadway version weakens the story's response to racial segregation and anti-Black violence (255).

95 See Gavin Jones, *Failure and the American Writer: A Literary History* (New York: Cambridge University Press, 2014).

7 Emergence and Failure: The Middleness of *The Grapes of Wrath*

1 Michael Szalay, *New Deal Modernism: American Literature and the Invention of the Welfare State* (Durham, NC: Duke University Press, 2010), 162–82.

2 Cyrus Ernesto Zirakzadeh, "Revolutionary Conservative, Conservative Revolutionary? John Steinbeck and *The Grapes of Wrath*," *A Political Companion*

to John Steinbeck, eds. Cyrus Ernesto Zirakzadeh and Simon Stow (Lexington: University Press of Kentucky, 2013), 19–48. For a recent, convincing argument for Steinbeck's close engagement with the Left in the years around *Grapes of Wrath*, see Milton A. Cohen, *The Pull of Politics: Steinbeck, Wright, Hemingway, and the Left in the Late 1930s* (Columbia: University of Missouri Press, 2018).

3 Mark Greif, *The Age of the Crisis of Man: Thought and Fiction in America, 1933–1973* (Princeton, NJ: Princeton University Press, 2015), 3.

4 Greif, *Age of the Crisis of Man*, 12.

5 The essential aridity of the West, wrote Wallace Stegner, necessitates mobility, movement, migration: a "series of brief visitations or a trail to somewhere else." Stegner, *Where the Bluebird Sings to the Lemonade Springs: Living and Writing in the West* (New York: Random House, 1992), 55, 72.

6 John Steinbeck, *The Grapes of Wrath and Other Writings, 1936–1941*, ed. Robert DeMott (New York: Library of America, 1996), 215–23.

7 Michael Denning, *The Cultural Front: The Laboring of American Culture in the Twentieth Century* (London: Verso, 1997), 264.

8 See Paul Humphreys, *Emergence: A Philosophical Account* (Oxford: Oxford University Press, 2016), especially 4–5, 8, 23, 39.

9 Steinbeck, *Grapes of Wrath*, 215–16.

10 See Jane Tompkins, *West of Everything: The Inner Life of Westerns* (New York: Oxford University Press, 1993), 50–60.

11 John Steinbeck, *Working Days: The Journals of "The Grapes of Wrath," 1938–41*, ed. Robert DeMott (New York: Viking, 1989), 25.

12 Steinbeck, letter to Elizabeth Otis, June 1, 1938, in Elaine Steinbeck and Robert Wallsten (eds.), *Steinbeck: A Life in Letters* (New York: Penguin, 1989), 167.

13 Steinbeck, *Grapes of Wrath*, 243.

14 Steinbeck, *Grapes of Wrath*, 226.

15 Steinbeck, *Grapes of Wrath*, 284–85.

16 Steinbeck, *Grapes of Wrath*, 315.

17 See Franz Roh, "Magical Realism: Post-Expressionism," *Magical Realism: Theory, History, Community*, eds. Lois Parkinson Zamora and Wendy B. Faris (Durham, NC: Duke University Press, 1995), 22; and Irene Guenther, "Magic Realism, New Objectivity, and the Arts during the Weimar Republic," in Zamora and Faris (eds.), *Magical Realism*, 36.

18 Bill Brown, *A Sense of Things: The Object Matter of American Literature* (Chicago, IL: University of Chicago Press, 2004), 5, 7–8, 13, 16–17.

19 Steinbeck, *Grapes of Wrath*, 255. Chapter nine is a sustained contemplation of the breakdown between subjectivity and objectivity. Things are "belongings." They embody human longing and history; they confer individuality: "the thousand pictures, that's us." Things are also "possessions." They possess

people, just as they become possessed or haunted by suffering: to buy somebody's junk is to buy a "packet of bitterness to grow in your house and to flower, some day." Things are vessels for humanity: "The pain on that mattress there – that dreadful pain – that's you." Steinbeck, *Grapes of Wrath*, 301–4.

20 Steinbeck, *Grapes of Wrath*, 315.

21 Steinbeck, *Working Days*, 39.

22 "He drank too much when he could get it, ate too much when it was there, talked too much all the time." Steinbeck, *Grapes of Wrath*, 292.

23 See the wonderful description of Ma in *Grapes of Wrath*, 287–88. In *Working Days*, Steinbeck spoke of this need to "build her up" (70).

24 Steinbeck, *Working Days*, 27, 91.

25 *New York Times* review of *The Grapes of Wrath*, in Joseph R. McElrath Jr., Jesse S. Crisler, and Susan Shillinglaw (eds.), *John Steinbeck: The Contemporary Reviews* (Cambridge: Cambridge University Press, 1996), 160.

26 Steinbeck's 1953 letter to a Columbia student, quoted in Susan Shillinglaw, *On Reading The Grapes of Wrath* (New York: Penguin, 2014), 36.

27 In chapter twenty, the slow descriptions of the Joads discovering the lay of the land in the first makeshift migrant camp they enter are broken suddenly by a moment of horrific violence, as an aggressive cop fires suddenly from the ground, taking the knuckles off a woman's hand. This is a sudden turning point in the novel (Casy steps in, kicks the cop in the neck, and is forced to flee the scene), created by a violence *in the representation itself* – an increase in speed, without any protective trigger-warning for the reader. Steinbeck, *Grapes of Wrath*, 491–92.

28 Steinbeck was roused to write the book by his anger that families of migrants were starving in California's interior valleys (see Zirakzadeh, "Revolutionary Conservative," 28). He wrote to Pare Lorentz that the book has a job to do "and I don't care if it isn't good literature. In fact I don't want it to be. It isn't written for literary people" (see Shillinglaw, *On Reading*, 63). In 1958 Steinbeck again writes about anger: "I think any young man or any man who isn't angry at one time or another is a waste of time. No, no. Anger is a symbol of thought and evaluation and reaction; without it what have we got? I'm tired of non-angry people. I think anger is the healthiest thing in the world" (quoted in Shillinglaw, *On Reading*, 65).

29 "By slow violence I mean a violence that occurs gradually and out of sight, a violence of delayed destruction that is dispersed across time and space, an attritional violence that is typically not viewed as violence at all." Rob Nixon, *Slow Violence and the Environmentalism of the Poor* (Cambridge, MA: Harvard University Press, 2011), 2.

30 Steinbeck, *Working Days*, 43.

31 Steinbeck, *Grapes of Wrath*, 369.
32 Zirakzadeh, "Revolutionary Conservative," 41.
33 Steinbeck, *Grapes of Wrath*, 369.
34 Steinbeck, *Grapes of Wrath*, 370.
35 Steinbeck, *Working Days*, 50, 35, 90.
36 Steinbeck, *Working Days*, 6.
37 Steinbeck quoted in Peter Lisca, *The Wide World of John Steinbeck* (New Brunswick, NJ: Rutgers University Press, 1958), 147.
38 Michael Warner, *Publics and Counterpublics* (Brooklyn, NY: Zone Books, 2002), 66–68, 75.
39 Warner, *Publics and Counterpublics*, 72.
40 Steinbeck originally planned to collaborate with Collins, editing and rewriting his reports. See Shillinglaw, *On Reading*, 75.
41 At times the novel seems aware of this life-world of circulation, for example, in chapter twenty-three, which describes the manufacture of pleasure in the form of popular culture – a multimedia world of song, story, movie, newsreels – that lifts individuals to become more than themselves: not merely passive consumers of commercial products but producers and participators in a dynamic, ongoing process. Steinbeck, *Grapes of Wrath*, 556–61.
42 Steinbeck, *Working Days*, 105.
43 Walter Lippmann, *Public Opinion* (New York: Hartcourt, Brace, 1922), 15, 29, 31. Lippmann used the example of a man's love for and knowledge of the automobile as an example of a three-dimensional world (69): the detailed attention throughout *Grapes* to the inside of cars similarly constructs a pseudo-environment.
44 Lippmann, *The Phantom Public* (New York: Macmillan, 1927), 29, 96, 137.
45 "In a curious adaptation, 'the public' often becomes, in administrative fact, 'the disengaged expert', who, although ever so well informed, has never taken a clear-cut and public stand on controversial issues. He is the 'public' member of the board, the commission, the committee. What 'the public' stands for, accordingly, is often a vagueness of policy (called 'open-mindedness'), a lack of involvement in public affairs (known as 'reasonableness'), and a professional disinterest (known as 'tolerance')." C. Wright Mills, "The Structure of Power in American Society," *The British Journal of Sociology* 9.1 (March 1958), 39.
46 Warner, *Publics and Counterpublics*, 91.
47 Steinbeck, *Grapes of Wrath*, 418.
48 Zirakzadeh, "Revolutionary Conservative," 38. The isolation of Weedpatch from the rest of the novel is marked by the speed bump the Joads hit when they enter the camp at the beginning of chapter twenty-two. Other studies of California agriculture, such as Carey McWilliams's *Factories in the Fields* (1939), reached similar conclusions: that the camps were no final solution;

they merely enabled work for low wages even as they provided the agency through which labor organization could be achieved. Carey McWilliams, *Factories in the Field: The Story of Migratory Farm Labor in California* (Boston, MA: Little, Brown and Company, 1939), 303.

49 Lippmann, *Phantom Public*, 43; Lippmann, *Public Opinion,* 249.

50 We can align Steinbeck's vision with that of Lippmann's opponent, John Dewey, who held a nostalgic faith in democracy, reconstructed through an act of will that promotes a revival of community, one dependent on the state for its cultural formation and maintenance. See Bruce Robins (ed.), *The Phantom Public Sphere* (Minneapolis: University of Minnesota Press, 1993), 80–84.

51 Casy has a vision of collective action but cannot explain it to Tom: "it's need that makes all the trouble," he vaguely suggests (*Grapes*, 616). He has murky notions of an oversoul that, when connected to the notion of collective land ownership, has no realized political framework to enact it (655).

52 Steinbeck, *Grapes of Wrath*, 242.

53 See Nixon, *Slow Violence*, 2–3.

54 Steinbeck, *Grapes of Wrath*, 394–95.

55 Lawrence Buell, *The Dream of the Great American Novel* (Cambridge, MA: Harvard University Press, 2014), 407, 410–11.

56 Steinbeck, *Grapes of Wrath*, 656. As Szalay points out, Tom only gains agency when he vanishes (*New Deal Modernism*, 166).

57 Steinbeck, *Grapes of Wrath*, 656.

58 Writing in the *New Yorker* (April 15, 1939), Clifton Fadiman noted that Steinbeck's overreaching, mystical thinking "is based on an emotion that can just as easily be discharged into the channels of reaction. In other words, are not these simple, tormented Okies good Fascist meat, if the proper misleaders are found for them?" Fadiman, "Books," in McElrath, Crisler, and Shillinglaw (eds.), *Contemporary Reviews*, 155.

59 Steinbeck, *Grapes of Wrath*, 458.

60 Steinbeck, *Their Blood Is Strong* (San Francisco, CA: Simon J. Lubin Society, 1938), 28.

61 "With the end of the easy business of exploiting competing racial groups in sight, the farm industrialists shifted the area of exploitation and began to manipulate the flow of labor to their own advantage. The entry of white workers into the fields symbolized the industrial maturity of California agriculture." McWilliams, *Factories in the Field: The Story of Migratory Farm Labor in California*, 199.

62 See, for example, Denning, *The Cultural Front*, 265; Buell, *Dream of the Great American Novel*, 419–20; Sarah Wald, *The Nature of California: Race, Citizenship, and Farming Since the Dust Bowl* (Seattle: University of Washington Press, 2016), 53–65. Comparing *Grapes* unfavorably to Sanora

Babb's *Whose Names Are Unknown* (written in the late 1930s, published in 2004), Wald argues that Steinbeck whitens his migrants to assert their claims to freedom and citizenship in land ownership against those who would deprive them of this Jeffersonian ideal. Writes Wald, "the novel critiques racist prejudice when it is visited upon white migrants, but falls short of criticizing racism against people of color" (59).

63 Zirakzadeh, "Revolutionary Conservative," 41.

64 See Zirakzadeh, "Revolutionary Conservative," 27.

65 A section of this letter to Otis, written during the composition of "L'Affaire Lettuceberg," is quoted in Steinbeck and Wallsten (eds.), *A Life in Letters*, 162. Tom Joad becomes "sensy" in Steinbeck, *Grapes of Wrath*, 477.

66 Warner, *Publics and Counterpublics*, 120.

67 Steinbeck, *Grapes of Wrath*, 692.

68 Michael Ignatieff, *The Needs of Strangers* (New York: Picador, 1984).

69 Szalay, *New Deal Modernism*, 170, 175.

70 One month into writing the book, Steinbeck wrote in his journal: "I went over the whole of the book in my head – fixed on the last scene, huge and symbolic, toward which the whole story moves" (*Working Days*, 36). Jackson J. Benson suggests that the scene may be based on an anecdote Steinbeck heard in the early 1920s. See Benson, *John Steinbeck, Writer: A Biography* (New York: Penguin, 1990), 47–48.

71 Covici quoted in Shillinglaw, *On Reading*, 144–45.

72 Steinbeck, letter to Pascal Covici (January 16, 1939), in Steinbeck and Wallsten (eds.), *A Life in Letters*, 178.

73 Steinbeck, *The Log from the Sea of Cortez, The Grapes of Wrath and Other Writings, 1936–1941*, ed. Robert DeMott (New York: Library of America, 1996), 872.

74 Leslie Fiedler, "Looking Back After 50 Years," *The Devil Gets His Due: The Uncollected Essays of Leslie Fiedler*, ed. Samuel F. S. Pardini (Berkeley, CA: Counterpoint, 2008), 171.

75 Steinbeck, *Their Blood Is Strong*, 22.

76 The novel's famous handbills, driving surplus labor to California, are another example. Despite a government investigation of this alleged practice, not a single handbill ever emerged, something that "defies the laws of bibliography," in the words of the historian Kevin Starr. The burning of the Hooverville and the forced evacuation of the migrants that Steinbeck describes with such emotive power were also convincingly contested at the time. See Starr, *Endangered Dreams: The Great Depression in California* (New York: Oxford University Press, 1996), 261.

77 Steinbeck, letter to Covici (January 16, 1939), in Steinbeck and Wallsten (eds.), *A Life in Letters*, 178–79.

8 Borderlands: Extinction and the New World Outlook in *Sea of Cortez*

1 John Steinbeck, *Working Days: The Journals of "The Grapes of Wrath," 1938–41*, ed. Robert DeMott (New York: Viking, 1989), 125. The final entries in Steinbeck's journal after finishing *Grapes* are particularly bleak as he describes his sense of "coming tragedy" (123): "I am ill – ill in the mind. My head is a grey cloud in which colors drift about and images half-form." This final entry describes his "staggered mind," lostness, and loneliness (127).

2 John Steinbeck, letter to Carlton A. Sheffield (November 13, 1939), in Elaine Steinbeck and Robert Wallsten (eds.), *Steinbeck: A Life in Letters* (New York: Penguin, 1989), 193–94.

3 John Steinbeck, letter to Wilbur Needham (September 29, 1940), in Jackson J. Benson, *John Steinbeck, Writer: A Biography* (New York: Penguin, 1990), 468.

4 See Edward F. Ricketts and Jack Calvin, *Between Pacific Tides: An Account of the Habits and Habitats of Some Five Hundred of the Common, Conspicuous Seashore Invertebrates of the Pacific Coast between Sitka, Alaska and Northern Mexico* (Stanford, CA: Stanford University Press, 1948).

5 Gloria Anzaldúa, *Borderlands/La Frontera: The New Mestiza* (San Francisco, CA: Aunt Lute Books, 2007), 108.

6 Steinbeck, letter to Wilbur Needham (early 1935), in Steinbeck and Wallsten (eds.), *A Life in Letters*, 106.

7 Steinbeck, letter to Mavis McIntosh (April 1935), in Steinbeck and Wallsten (eds.), *A Life in Letters*, 108.

8 Steinbeck, letter to Elizabeth Otis (October 2, 1932), The John Steinbeck Collection, 1902–1979, Stanford University Libraries, Department of Special Collections, Box 2, Folder 6 ("John Steinbeck to Elizabeth Otis, 1931–1936").

9 See Benson, *John Steinbeck*, 321–22.

10 Philip D. Ortego, "Fables of Identity: Stereotype and Caricature of Chicanos in Steinbeck's *Tortilla Flat*," *The Journal of Ethnic Studies* 1.1 (Spring 1973), 42; "forgotten people" is Ortego's quotation from George Sanchez, *Forgotten People: A Study of New Mexicans* (Albuquerque, NM: Calvin Horn, 1967), which we return to later.

11 Steinbeck, letter to A. Grove Day (November 1929), in Steinbeck and Wallsten (eds.), *A Life in Letters*, 15.

12 See John Steinbeck, *Cup of Gold: A Life of Sir Henry Morgan, Buccaneer, with Occasional Reference to History* (New York: Penguin, 2008), 58.

13 Susan Shillinglaw, *A Journey into Steinbeck's California* (Berkeley, CA: Roaring Forties Press, 2011), 61.

14 In 1931, Waldo Frank published *America Hispana: A Portrait and Prospect*, a study of Latin American culture and history, which also begins with the Panama Canal and a dream of an organically unified Americas, its peoples

and the various gifts of North and South merging into a New Wholeness. See Waldo Frank, *America Hispana: A Portrait and a Prospect* (New York: C. Scribner's Sons, 1931), 3–22.

15 Ella Winter, "Sketching the Author of *Tortilla Flat*," San Francisco *Chronicle* (June 2, 1935), in Joseph R. McElrath Jr., Jesse S. Crisler, and Susan Shillinglaw (eds.), *John Steinbeck: The Contemporary Reviews* (Cambridge: Cambridge University Press, 1996), 39–40.

16 William Rose Benét, "Affectionate Bravos," *Saturday Review* 12 (June 1, 1935), in McElrath, Crisler, and Shillinglaw (eds.), *Contemporary Reviews*, 35. "When this book was written, it did not occur to me that the paisanos were curious or quaint, dispossessed or underdoggish," he wrote in the preface to the 1937 Modern Library edition of the work: "They are people whom I know and like, people who merge successfully with their habitat." See notes to John Steinbeck, *Novels and Stories, 1932–1937*, ed. Robert DeMott (New York: Library of America, 1994), 907.

17 Paul S. Taylor, *An American-Mexican Frontier: Nueces County, Texas* (Chapel Hill: University of North Carolina Press, 1934), 245, 269.

18 Paul S. Taylor, *Mexican Labor in the United States*, vols. 1–3 (Berkeley: University of California Press, 1928–34).

19 Taylor, *American-Mexican Frontier*, 255–57, 275.

20 Sanchez, *Forgotten People*, 82.

21 Sanchez, *Forgotten People*, 10.

22 McWilliams sought to discount what he called "the fantasy heritage," concentrated in myths of Spanish *Californios* – myths designed to maintain the subordination of Mexican immigrants. See Carey McWilliams, *North from Mexico: The Spanish-Speaking People of the United States*, new edition updated by Matt S. Meier (New York: Greenwood, 1990), 46, originally part of J. B. Lippincott's multiethnic series, "Peoples of America," ed. Louis Adamic.

23 McWilliams, *North from Mexico*, 66.

24 Anzaldúa, *Borderlands*, 99.

25 Anzaldúa, *Borderlands*, 101, 23. This is the first verse of the poem that opens *Borderlands*.

26 Steinbeck and Ricketts are quoting their favorite conchologist Philip P. Carpenter, who published *The Mollusks of Western North America* (Washington, DC: Smithsonian Institution, 1872). John Steinbeck and Edward F. Ricketts, "Annotated Phyletic Catalogue," *Sea of Cortez: A Leisurely Journal of Travel and Research, with a Scientific Appendix Comprising Materials for a Source Book on the Marine Animals of the Panamic Faunal Province* (New York: Viking, 1941), 483. To remain consistent with the choice of the Library of America edition of Steinbeck's writings throughout this book, subsequent quotations from the log section of *Sea of Cortez* are from

The Log from the Sea of Cortez, The Grapes of Wrath and Other Writings, 1936–1941, ed. Robert DeMott (New York: Library of America, 1996); references to the second section of *Sea of Cortez* are listed "Annotated Phyletic Catalogue" and are from the 1941 Viking edition of *Sea of Cortez.*

27 Steinbeck and Ricketts (S&R), "Annotated Phyletic Catalogue," 294.

28 S&R, "Annotated Phyletic Catalogue," 303.

29 The passage on the etymology of California emphasizes its hemispheric reach, beyond national distinctions, and its basis in relational experience of place rather than geopolitical lines. Steinbeck, *The Log*, 791–93.

30 For a recent article, see Richard Grant, "John Steinbeck's Epic Ocean Voyage Rewrote the Rules of Ecology," *Smithsonian Magazine* (September 2019). www.smithsonianmag.com/arts-culture/ship-sent-john-steinbeck-epic-ocean-voyage-may-ride-again–180972847/. See also Michael J. Lannoo, *Leopold's Shack and Ricketts's Lab: The Emergence of Environmentalism* (Berkeley: University of California Press, 2010).

31 See John A. Britton, *Revolution and Ideology: Images of the Mexican Revolution in the United States* (Lexington: University Press of Kentucky, 1995), 11, 15.

32 Steinbeck, *The Log*, 950. Compare with Edward F. Ricketts, "Verbatim Transcription of Notes of Gulf of California Trip, March-April 1940," *Breaking Through: Essays, Journals, and Travelogues of Edward F. Ricketts*, ed. Katherine A. Rodger (Berkeley: University of California Press, 2006), 176.

33 Stuart Chase, in collaboration with Marian Tyler, *Mexico: A Study of Two Americas* (New York: Macmillan, 1931).

34 Frank, *America Hispana,* 233. See also Roy S. Simmonds, *John Steinbeck: The War Years, 1939–1945* (Lewisburg, PA: Bucknell University Press, 1996), 111.

35 Steinbeck, *The Log*, 751, 970.

36 See Steinbeck, *The Log*, 815–16.

37 Steinbeck, *The Log*, 859.

38 See Simmonds, *The War Years*, 65

39 Ricketts quoted in Steinbeck, *Working Days*, 104–5. Steinbeck and Ricketts collaborated earlier on a Handbook of San Francisco Bay Invertebrates, which was never completed.

40 Ricketts studied at the University of Chicago under W. C. Allee, who taught Ricketts that "individual animals have instinctive drives toward communal life, toward aggregation." See Richard Astro, *Edward F. Ricketts* (Boise, ID: Boise State University Press, 1976), 8.

41 Steinbeck, "About Ed Ricketts," *The Log*, 738: "His scientific interest was essentially ecological and holistic" (738).

42 See Katherine A. Rodger, "Introduction" to Ricketts, *Breaking Through*, 8.

43 Ricketts, *Breaking Through*, 21, mentioned in Steinbeck, *The Log*, 780.

44 Ricketts, *Breaking Through*, 22.

45 Anzaldúa, *Borderlands*, 61, 72, 101.
46 Steinbeck, *The Log*, 875.
47 Ricketts commented to Joseph Campbell on Steinbeck's careful building of *Sea of Cortez*: "The increasing hints towards purity of thinking, then building up toward the center of the book, on Easter Sunday, with the non-tel essay. The little waves at the start and the little waves at the finish, and the working out of the microcosm-macrocosm thing towards the end." See Simmonds, *The War Years*, 77.
48 Steinbeck, *The Log*, 862.
49 Steinbeck, *The Log*, 874.
50 Steinbeck, *The Log*, 872–73. One of S&R's main examples is from the Great Depression: we cannot blame members of society for their unemployment but can only seek to describe the total picture in which a certain number of people are inevitably unemployed (*The Log*, 859–60).
51 Anzaldúa, *Borderlands*, 103. See Anzaldúa's note, which draws on ideas of Ilya Prigogine: substances interact unpredictably to produce new and more complex structures (120). This is very similar to S&R's desire for a mutation in consciousness. Anzaldúa strives in her writing to move past the dualistic individual self toward a "cosmic" consciousness, the "total self" beyond traditional racial designations. "At the confluence of two or more genetic streams, with chromosomes constantly 'crossing over,' this mixture of races, rather than resulting in an inferior being, provides hybrid progeny, a mutable, more malleable species with a rich gene pool." Anzaldúa, *Borderlands*, 105, 99.
52 Steinbeck, *The Log*, 860. The only reference is in the "Annotated Phyletic Catalogue," to "the-fish-that-bit-Carol" (576).
53 Arguments are divided into (A) (B) (C) with numeric subsections, and are frustratingly circular: "they're tall because they're tall" (*The Log*, 863). See also Steinbeck, *The Log*, 867.
54 See Steinbeck, *The Log*, 859. The idea of a "cosmic" identity, for example, emerges from a text of the Mexican Revolution, José Vasconcelos's *The Cosmic Race* (1925), referred to directly by Anzaldúa in *Borderlands*, 99.
55 Jeffers quoted in Rodger, "Introduction" to Ricketts, *Breaking Through*, 6.
56 Jeffers quoted in Ricketts, "The Philosophy of 'Breaking Through,'" *Breaking Through*, 94.
57 Robinson Jeffers, "The Beauty of Things," *Poetry* 77.4 (January 1951), 190.
58 See Steinbeck, *The Log*, 918, 896, which echoes Frank's *America Hispana*.
59 Steinbeck quoted in Susan Shillinglaw, *Carol and John Steinbeck: Portrait of a Marriage* (Reno: University of Nevada Press, 2013), 218.
60 See Ursula K. Heise on E. O. Wilson and debates over species-thinking, in *Imagining Extinction: The Cultural Meaning of Endangered Species* (Chicago, IL: The University of Chicago Press, 2016), 224–25.

61 Steinbeck, letter to Pascal Covici (July 4, 1941), in Steinbeck and Wallsten (eds.), *Life in Letters*, 232.

62 Steinbeck, *Working Days*, 101. Steinbeck described the great poetry that lay in scientific writing as a "life saver" and wrote: "The song of the microscope. There is something. Glass tubing – x-ray. These are poems worth writing. These are things that could make for rebirth." Steinbeck, *Working Days*, 107, 101.

63 In her Ph.D dissertation (Stanford University, Department of English), "To Describe America, 1835–1967," Rachel Bolten begins with John James Audubon's and George Catlin's efforts, respectively, to represent the birds of America and its Native American peoples in face of fears of their extinction.

64 See Steinbeck, *The Log*, 870–71.

65 Steinbeck, *The Log*, 863. This exact same point is made twice, as if to de-emphasize narrative progression.

66 S&R, "Annotated Phyletic Catalogue," 286.

67 S&R, "Annotated Phyletic Catalogue," 288. They see this descriptive act as opposing the particular challenge of "nondescript" animals (338, 369).

68 S&R, "Annotated Phyletic Catalogue," 480.

69 See Donna Jeanne Haraway, *When Species Meet* (Minneapolis: University of Minnesota Press, 2008), 17.

70 S&R, "Annotated Phyletic Catalogue," 305.

71 S&R, "Annotated Phyletic Catalogue," 291. See Steinbeck, *The Log*, 799, 800, 890, and 923–24 for this ideal of long, careful collecting, and absorbed observation of minutiae.

72 S&R, "Annotated Phyletic Catalogue," 292.

73 See Clifford Geertz, *Interpretation of Cultures: Selected Essays* (New York: Basic Books, 1973), 3; S&R, "Annotated Phyletic Catalogue," 304, 496–97.

74 To differentiate their own approach, S&R quote an early colonialist description of discovery of the Gulf of California from Richard Hakluyt's *The Voyages of the English Nation to America* (1598–1600). See "Annotated Phyletic Catalogue," 581.

75 S&R, "Annotated Phyletic Catalogue," 481.

76 Steinbeck, *The Log*, 875; Susan Stewart, *On Longing: Narratives of the Miniature, the Gigantic, the Souvenir, the Collection* (Baltimore, MD: Johns Hopkins University Press, 1984), 158.

77 S&R outline these difficulties in "Annotated Phyletic Catalogue," 496, and they recognize the second generation of specialists capable of discovering minute differentials "at which times the names bestowed by the original describers will be revived as valid species" (538).

78 S&R, "Annotated Phyletic Catalogue," 350.

79 See Geertz, *Interpretation of Cultures*, 20.

80 S&R, "A Note on Preparing Specimens," in *Sea of Cortez* (New York: Viking, 1941), 275–77. In "To Describe America," Bolten discusses how Audubon's descriptive art was dependent on the killing of his subjects.
81 "The descriptive method lacks humanity," wrote Georg Lukács in his 1936 essay "Narrate or Describe?": "Its transformation of men into still lives is only the artistic manifestation of its inhumanity." Georg Lukács, *Writer and Critic, and Other Essays*, ed. and trans. Arthur Kahn (London: Merlin Press, 1970), 140, 146.
82 See Benson, *John Steinbeck*, 429.
83 "Why do men, sitting at the microscope, examine the calcareous plates of a sea-cucumber, and, finding a new arrangement and number, feel an exaltation and give the new species a name, and write about it possessively?" The process of collecting, observing, and describing defines an aspect of the human species, its "curiosity." Steinbeck, *The Log*, 751.
84 Steinbeck, *The Log*, 809. See also the moments when they correct guidebook descriptions of the region (836–38), and the lengthy descriptions of the *botete* (851–54).
85 Steinbeck, *The Log*, 763–64.
86 Steinbeck, *The Log*, 752.
87 Steinbeck, *The Log*, 797–98; see 812–13 for more lists.
88 Stewart, *On Longing*, 151; Steinbeck, *The Log*, 798, 842.
89 See Stewart, *On Longing*, 159, 166.
90 See Steinbeck, *The Log*, 801–2.
91 Steinbeck, *The Log*, 920. Compare with *The Log*, 793–94, on the importance of finding the right name.
92 Steinbeck, *The Log*, 862.
93 Steinbeck, *The Log*, 868.
94 Steinbeck, *The Log*, 929, 819–20. Man must first admit "to himself his cosmic identity," "one factor in a surge of striving" (886).
95 Steinbeck, *The Log*, 928.
96 Dimock describes deep time as "at once projective and recessional, with input going both ways, and binding continents and millennia into many loops of relations, a densely interactive fabric." Wai Chee Dimock, *Through Other Continents: American Literature Across Deep Time* (Princeton, NJ: Princeton University Press 2006), 3–4. Dimock discusses Spivak and the idea of planetarity as the elusive horizon of collective responsibility (6). S&R also describe a seeing in deep time, beyond the "warping lens" of our present time sense. Steinbeck, *The Log*, 967.
97 Steinbeck, *The Log*, 753.
98 Steinbeck, *The Log*, 956, 928.

99 Ironically, there is something about the way individuals act together, ultimately working as a species, that brings the destruction of our natural resources. See Steinbeck, *The Log*, 956.
100 See Steinbeck, *The Log*, 786–87, 925–26, 911.
101 See Simmonds, *The War Years*, 34.
102 Steinbeck, *The Log*, 762, 778, 776.
103 "It is one diagnostic trait of *Homo sapiens* that groups of individuals are periodically infected with a feverish nervousness which causes the individual to turn on and destroy, not only his own kind, but the works of his own kind. It is not known whether this be caused by a virus, some airborne spore, or whether it be a species reaction to some meteorological stimulus as yet undetermined." Steinbeck, *The Log*, 764.
104 Steinbeck, *The Log*, 820–22. S&R suggest that the industrial revolution may itself be a mutation of the species (*The Log*, 821).
105 Steinbeck, *The Log*, 767.
106 Steinbeck, *The Log*, 822–23.
107 Man in "his thinking or reverie status admires the progression toward extinction." Steinbeck, *The Log*, 829.
108 Steinbeck, *The Log*, 820, 841, 829.
109 Steinbeck, *The Log*, 811.
110 Frank, *America Hispana*, 234, 236, 239, 253.
111 Steinbeck, *The Log*, 820; this point is repeated on 831.
112 John Elof Boodin, *A Realistic Universe: An Introduction to Metaphysics* (New York: The MacMillan Company, 1916), xvi.
113 Roy Scranton, *Learning to Die in the Anthropocene: Reflections on the End of a Civilization* (San Francisco, CA: City Lights Books, 2015), 24.
114 Scranton, *Learning to Die*, 24, 92. Like Steinbeck, Scranton uses the idea of insect and animal groupings to understand the behavior of the human animal and he describes destructive violence as a species trait (25).
115 See Steinbeck, *The Log*, 921, 926.
116 Heise, *Imagining Extinction*, 5.
117 Scranton, *Learning to Die*, 108.
118 Heise, *Imagining Extinction*, 225.
119 Lukács, "Narrate or Describe?" 110–19.
120 Steinbeck, *The Log*, 803–4.
121 See Steinbeck, *The Log*, 923.
122 See Steinbeck, *The Log*, 972.
123 Heise discusses power differentials that endow some humans with authority to categorize others as belonging to the human species or not. Heise, *Imagining Extinction*, 198.

124 Ricketts, "Verbatim Transcription," *Breaking Through*, 177; Steinbeck, *The Log*, 951.

125 Benson, *John Steinbeck*, 439.

126 S&R give the example of anemones in an aquarium. Steinbeck, *The Log*, 908.

127 Steinbeck, *The Log*, 952. His "teleologies are just as full of nonsense as ours" (*The Log*, 923).

128 See Steinbeck, *The Log*, 952.

129 "Where and when species meet, that heritage must be untied and better knots of companion species attempted within and across differences. Loosening the grip of analogies that issue in the collapse of all of man's others into one another, companion species must instead learn to live intersectionally." Haraway, *When Species Meet*, 18.

130 See Steinbeck, *The Log*, 939, 800–1.

131 Steinbeck, *The Log*, 751.

9 Mexican Revolutions: *The Forgotten Village*, *The Pearl*, and the Global South

1 John Steinbeck, *The Log from the Sea of Cortez, The Grapes of Wrath and Other Writings, 1936–1941*, ed. Robert DeMott (New York: Library of America, 1996), 810.

2 William Faulkner, *Lion in the Garden: Interviews with William Faulkner, 1926–1962*, eds. James B. Meriwether and Michael Millgate (New York: Random House, 1968), 255.

3 See Tanya T. Fayen, *In Search of the Latin American Faulkner* (Lanham, MD: University Press of America, 1995).

4 Gabriel García Márquez and Mario Vargas Llosa, *La Novela en América Latina: Diálogo* (1968), quoted in Antonio C. Márquez, "Faulkner in Latin America," *The Faulkner Journal* 11.1–2 (Fall 1995–Spring 1996), 83, 93.

5 For this view, see Susan Willis's pioneering essay on Faulkner in global context, "Aesthetics of the Rural Slum: Contradictions and Dependency in 'The Bear,'" *Social Text* 2 (Summer 1979), 103. See also Ramón Saldívar and Sylvan Goldberg, "The Faulknerian Anthropocene: Scales of Time and History in *The Wild Palms* and *Go Down, Moses*," *The New Cambridge Companion to William Faulkner*, ed. John T. Matthews (New York: Cambridge University Press, 2015), 185–203; and Hosam Aboul-Ela, *Other South: Faulkner, Coloniality, and the Mariátegui Tradition* (Pittsburgh, PA: University of Pittsburgh Press, 2007).

6 See Fayen, *In Search of the Latin American Faulkner*, xi. For an excellent account of Faulkner's reception in Latin America, see Deborah Cohn, "'He Was One of Us': The Reception of William Faulkner and the U.S. South by Latin American Authors," *Comparative Literature Studies* 34.2 (1997): 149–69.

7 For an interesting recent argument, see Wanda Raiford, "Fantasy and Haiti's Erasure in William Faulkner's *Absalom, Absalom!*" *South: A Scholarly Journal* 49.1 (Fall 2016): 101–21.

8 See Ramón Saldívar, "Looking for a Master Plan: Faulkner, Paredes, and the Colonial and Postcolonial Subject," *The Cambridge Companion to William Faulkner*, ed. Philip M. Weinstein (Cambridge: Cambridge University Press, 1995), 118. It could be argued that Faulkner's idea of Mexican ancestry adds little to inflect the understanding of mixed-race identity found elsewhere in his work.

9 The most valiant attempt to establish an enabling relationship of Greater Mexico to Faulkner's work is José Limón, "South by Southwest: William Faulkner and Greater Mexico," *Faulkner's Geographies*, eds. Jay Watson and Ann. J. Abadie (Jackson: University Press of Mississippi, 2015). Limón himself admits that his claims for Faulkner's knowledge are "inferential and conditional" (85).

10 Jackson J. Benson, *John Steinbeck, Writer: A Biography* (New York: Penguin, 1990), 280.

11 Steinbeck's screenplay for *Viva Zapata!* and his historical and archival work on the revolutionary leader can be found in John Steinbeck, *Zapata*, ed. Robert Morsberger (New York: Penguin, 1993).

12 For a precursor to my argument about Steinbeck, see Jerry W. Wilson, "Steinbeck, Fuentes, and The Mexican Revolution," *Southwest Review* 67.4 (Autumn 1982): 430–40. See also Adela Eugenia Pineda Franco, *The Mexican Revolution on the World Stage: Intellectuals and Film in the Twentieth Century* (Albany: State University of New York Press, 2019).

13 See Marijane Osborn, "Participatory Parables: Cinema, Social Action, and Steinbeck's Mexican Dilemma," *A Political Companion to John Steinbeck*, eds. Cyrus Ernesto Zirakzadeh and Simon Stow (Lexington: University of Kentucky Press, 2013), 268.

14 See Steinbeck's letter to Carlton A. Sheffield (November 3, 1939), in Elaine Steinbeck and Robert Wallsten (eds.), *Steinbeck: A Life in Letters* (New York: Penguin, 1989), 193.

15 Steinbeck and Wallsten (eds.), *A Life in Letters*, 162.

16 Steinbeck, letter to Pascal Covici (August–September 1949), quoted in Benson, *John Steinbeck*, 649. See Osborn, "Participatory Parables," 241.

17 See Herbert Kline, "On John Steinbeck," *Steinbeck Quarterly* 4.3 (1971), 84. A letter from Steinbeck to Kline suggests a story of the democratic process "from hacienda to ejido," interrupted by forces of ignorance, disease, and "finally the revolt of the reactionary." John Steinbeck, letter to Herbert Kline (April 22, 1940), in "Papers Relating to the Production of Steinbeck's *The Forgotten Village*, 1941," Stanford University Libraries, Department of Special Collections, M1350, Box 1.

18 Steinbeck had been talking to people everywhere, mostly poor fisherman, only to find "100% of the people of this region for Almazán," he wrote in an undated letter to Herbert Kline, from Loreto, Baja California, in "Papers Relating to the Production of Steinbeck's *The Forgotten Village*, 1941," Stanford University Libraries, Department of Special Collections, Box 1, M1350. In the same letter he noted the general opinion that the land cooperatives had been a failure, and the broad support for Almazán even among those he considered better educated: "And when it is suggested that he will tie up with American capital, there is hearty agreement. Indeed, he has promised to do so. And most Mexicans we have talked to want him to do just that. They want Fords and canned fruit and store clothes, want them intensively, want them much more than ideas." Noting that the peasant class has always had tremendous power in Mexico, Steinbeck worried that he had misunderstood the people's desire to be lifted out of poverty.

19 Kline, "On John Steinbeck," 82, 84.

20 Osborn, "Participatory Parables," 227–46.

21 See Waldo Frank, *America Hispana: A Portrait and a Prospect* (New York: C. Scribner's Sons, 1931), 239, on the Mexican Revolution being "not yet over."

22 John Steinbeck, *The Forgotten Village: With 136 Photographs from the Film of the Same Name*, eds. Rosa Harvan Kline and Alexander Hackensmid (New York: Viking, 1941), 5. Steinbeck described the culture he encountered as a complex mix of an indigenous Aztec and a Spanish-Catholic "social-religious frame" combined with "the thrusting toward social betterment which has been Mexico's drive for the past fifty years" (6).

23 Public sanitation, electrical power, and scientific agriculture would improve life, Redfield thought; cars and movies were much more risky, for they brought with them factory-made products and alien values. See John A. Britton, *Revolution and Ideology: Images of the Mexican Revolution in the United States* (Lexington: University Press of Kentucky, 1995), 109.

24 Steinbeck, *Forgotten Village*, 6.

25 Frank Tannenbaum, *Peace by Revolution* (1933), quoted in Britton, *Revolution and Ideology*, 123. For Dewey's similar view, see Britton, *Revolution and Ideology*, 88.

26 Kline, "On John Steinbeck," 85.

27 According to Kline, Trini and the women's unselfconscious performance of an Aztec childbirth ritual yielded "the most gripping and effective scene of our film." Kline also describes the various tricks and suggestions made by the filmmakers to help the peasants relive bits of life without self-consciousness. Kline, "On John Steinbeck," 85–86.

28 Steinbeck, *Forgotten Village*, 55, 85.

29 The film is available at the Internet Archive, see https://archive.org/details/forgotten_village

30 Steinbeck, *The Forgotten Village*, 141–42.

31 John Steinbeck, "Holograph Manuscript of the Screenplay for *The Forgotten Village*," in "Papers Relating to the Production of Steinbeck's *The Forgotten Village*, 1941," Stanford University Libraries, Department of Special Collections, M1350, Box 1.

32 Steinbeck, "Holograph Manuscript of *The Forgotten Village*," 5–6.

33 Steinbeck, *The Forgotten Village*, 6.

34 Klein, "On John Steinbeck," 86.

35 Steinbeck, "Holograph Manuscript of *The Forgotten Village*," 22.

36 Steinbeck, "Holograph Manuscript of *The Forgotten Village*," 23.

37 Steinbeck, letter to Herbert Kline (Wednesday), in "Papers Relating to the Production of Steinbeck's *The Forgotten Village*."

38 See Steinbeck, "Holograph Manuscript of *The Forgotten Village*," 24.

39 Edward F. Ricketts, "Thesis and Materials for a Script on Mexico Which Shall Be Motivated Oppositely to John's 'Forgotten Village,'" *Breaking Through: Essays, Journals, and Travelogues of Edward F. Ricketts*, ed. Katherine A. Rodger (Berkeley: University of California Press, 2006). The script was based on Ricketts's experiences with Kline and crew during the planning and making of the film. According to Ricketts, the "Region of Outward Possessions" was defined by what we can broadly call "progress" whose forces were primarily those of narrative: "The emphasis is on change, acquisition, progress. Symbols are: high-tension lines, modern highways, modern schools" (206). The opposite, inner forces emphasize instead static relationships, between human beings, and between humans and the land primarily (203). The values of this "other side" are closely related to Ricketts's ideal of non-teleological thinking and are captured in vignettes that describe the deep being of transcendent joy – say, a junky merry-go-round that Ricketts encounters in Guadalajara, bringing joy to impoverished infants in an ongoing, circular, existential moment, one that would be destroyed by the observer's participation (208–9).

40 Ricketts, "Thesis and Materials for a Script on Mexico," 212.

41 José David Saldívar, *Trans-Americanity: Subaltern Modernities, Global Coloniality, and the Cultures of Greater Mexico* (Durham, NC: Duke University Press, 2012), xvii.

42 Steinbeck describes these war-related symptoms, and his subsequent, partial breakdown in Mexico, in a letter to Carlton A. Sheffield (April 12, 1944), in Steinbeck and Wallsten (eds.), *Life in Letters*, 268.

43 See Roy Simmonds, *John Steinbeck: The War Years, 1939–1945* (Lewisburg, PA: Bucknell University Press, 1996), 220.

44 See Fernando Fabio Sánchez, "From the Silver Screen to the Countryside: Confronting the United States and Hollywood in 'El Indio' Fernández's

The Pearl," *Mexico Reading the United States*, eds. Linda Egan and Mary K. Long (Nashville, TN: Vanderbilt University Press, 2009), 85.

45 Steinbeck, letter to Joseph Henry Jackson (January 1945), quoted in Benson, *John Steinbeck*, 565.

46 Steinbeck, letter to Bo Beskow (May 22, 1948), in Steinbeck and Wallsten (eds.), *Life in Letters*, 313.

47 Steinbeck, *The Log*, 833.

48 Steinbeck, *The Log*, 834–35.

49 The *curandera* is present in the movie versions, but not in the novel of *The Pearl*, though the narrator explicitly comments that the traditional remedy of Juana, Kino's wife, was probably better than that of the doctor. See Steinbeck, "The Pearl of the World" (1945), unpublished screenplay, the Martha Heasley Cox Center for Steinbeck Studies, San Jose State University; and Steinbeck, *The Pearl*, *Novels 1942–1952*, ed. Robert DeMott (New York: Library of America, 2001), 245.

50 See Ana M. López, "A Cinema for the Continent," *The Mexican Cinema Project*, eds. Chon A. Noriega and Steven Ricci (Los Angeles: University of California–Los Angeles Film and Television Archive, 1994), 9. See also Desirée J. Garcia, "'The Soul of a People': Mexican Spectatorship and the Transnational *Comedia Ranchera*," *Journal of American Ethnic History* 30.1 (Fall 2010), 73.

51 Ricketts, "Thesis and Materials for a Script on Mexico," 212.

52 See Alfred Neumeyer, "Orozco's Mission," *College Art Journal* 10.2 (Winter 1951), 130. See also José Clemente Orozco, *An Autobiography* (Austin: University of Texas Press, 1962), 82, 87.

53 Orozco, *Autobiography*, 50, 65, 76–77; Neumeyer, "Orozco's Mission," 127.

54 See Mark K. Coffey, "Toward an Industrial Golden Age: Orozco's *Epic of American Civilization*," *Orozco at Dartmouth: The Epic of American Civilization* (Dartmouth, NH: Hood Museum of Art, 2017), 14. See also Orozco, *Autobiography*, 149 on the idea of "Dynamic Symmetry."

55 Ramirez-Berg cited in Sánchez, "From the Silver Screen to the Countryside," 85.

56 Steinbeck, letter to Elizabeth Otis (May 3, 1945), in Steinbeck and Wallsten (eds.), *A Life in Letters*, 281

57 See Susan Shillinglaw, *On Reading The Grapes of Wrath* (New York: Penguin, 2014), 43.

58 For an article that counters my argument on music in *The Pearl*, see Carroll Britch and Cliff Lewis, "Shadow of the Indian in the Fiction of John Steinbeck," *MELUS* 11.2 (Summer 1984), 42.

59 Steinbeck, *The Pearl*, 256.

60 Steinbeck, *The Pearl*, 294.

61 Another good example: "The family song was alive now and driving him down on the dark enemy. The harsh cicada seemed to take up its melody, and the twittering tree frogs called little phrases of it." Steinbeck, *The Pearl*, 300.
62 Steinbeck, *The Pearl*, 272.
63 Steinbeck, *The Pearl*, 252.
64 In their influential paper "The Extended Mind" (1998), Andy Clark and David Chalmers write about "active externalism" in which "the human organism is linked with an external entity in a two-way interaction, creating a *coupled system* that can be seen as a cognitive system in its own right. All the components in the system play an active causal role, and they jointly govern behavior in the same sort of way that cognition usually does." www.nyu.edu/gsas/dept/philo/courses/concepts/clark.html . For responses to this idea, see Richard Menary (ed.), *The Extended Mind* (Cambridge, MA: MIT Press, 2010).
65 Steinbeck, *The Pearl*, 266.
66 Steinbeck, *The Pearl*, 234, 240–41. See Simmonds, *The War Years*, 258.
67 Steinbeck, *The Pearl*, 250, 275.
68 Steinbeck, *The Pearl*, 254–55, 265, 263.
69 Steinbeck, *The Pearl*, 277.
70 Steinbeck, letter to Anne Laurie Williams (January 12, 1945), quoted in Simmonds, *The War Years*, 252.
71 See Margaret Cohen, "Underwater Optics as Symbolic Form," *French Politics, Culture & Society* 32.3 (Winter 2014): 1–23. We rarely dive below the surface in *Sea of Cortez.*
72 Steinbeck, *The Pearl*, 253.
73 See Cohen, "Underwater Optics," 7.
74 Steinbeck, *The Pearl*, 244.
75 See Kyoko Ariki, "From 'Flight' to *The Pearl*: A Thematic Study," *The Steinbeck Review* 3.1 (Spring 2006), 89.
76 The place where Kino retrieves the pearl bears qualities of Pulmo Reef in *Sea of Cortez* (its concealment, its little erosion caves, etc.) that are made evident in the film. See Steinbeck, *The Log*, 808–14.
77 Steinbeck, *The Pearl*, 298.
78 Steinbeck, *The Pearl*, 301.
79 Steinbeck, *The Pearl*, 231.
80 Steinbeck, *The Pearl*, 231; emphasis added.
81 Steinbeck, *The Pearl*, 272.
82 "This rural hero has been shut in a dungeon of logic, sandwiched between a past of savage misery and a present of barbaric wealth." Roger Bartra, *La jaula de la melancolía: identidad y metamorfosis del mexicano* (1996), quoted in Sánchez, "From the Silver Screen to the Countryside," 88.

83 See Simmonds, *The War Years*, 260.

84 Steinbeck, *The Pearl*, 254–55. In the 1945 film script of *The Pearl of the World* a group of young men long for guns, the one thing that can realize the potential of their revolutionary thoughts (63).

85 Steinbeck, *The Pearl*, 241.

86 Steinbeck, *The Pearl*, 303.

87 Steinbeck, *The Pearl*, 257–58.

88 Steinbeck, letter to Jack Wagner (May 2, 1946), in Steinbeck and Wallsten (eds.), *A Life in Letters*, 290.

89 Dolores Tierney, *Emilio Fernández: Pictures in the Margins* (Manchester, UK: University of Manchester Press, 2007), 99–101.

90 See Simmonds, *The War Years*, 290.

91 Steinbeck quoted in Morsberger's introduction to Steinbeck, *Zapata*, 21.

92 See Osborne, "Participatory Parables," 240.

93 Steinbeck, *The Pearl*, 302.

94 Steinbeck, *The Pearl*, 302.

95 "It is in the very nature of a beginning to carry with itself a measure of complete arbitrariness. Not only is it not bound into a reliable chain of cause and effect, a chain in which each effect immediately turns into the cause for future developments, the beginning has, as it were, nothing whatsoever to hold on to; it is as though it came out of nowhere in either time or space. For a moment, the moment of beginning, it is as though the beginner had abolished the sequence of temporality itself, or as though the actors were thrown out of the temporal order and its continuity." Hannah Arendt, *On Revolution* (New York: Viking, 1963), 207.

Epilogue: The Aftertaste of *Cannery Row*

1 John Steinbeck, letter to Carlton A. Sheffield (September 1944), quoted in Jackson J. Benson, *John Steinbeck, Writer: A Biography* (New York: Penguin, 1990), 554; Steinbeck, letter to Joseph Henry Jackson (August 1944), quoted in Roy Simmonds, *John Steinbeck: The War Years, 1939–1945* (Lewisburg, PA: Bucknell University Press, 1996), 227.

2 Steinbeck, letter to Pascal Covici (January 15, 1945), quoted in Benson, *John Steinbeck*, 562.

3 Orville Prescott, "Books of the Times," *John Steinbeck: The Contemporary Reviews*, eds. Joseph R. McElrath Jr., Jesse S. Crisler, and Susan Shillinglaw (Cambridge: Cambridge University Press, 1996), 276–77; Cowley review, "Steinbeck delivers a mixture of farce and Freud" (1945), quoted in Simmonds, *The War Years*, 237.

4 John Steinbeck, "My Short Novels," *America and Americans, and Selected Nonfiction*, eds. Susan Shillinglaw and Jackson J. Benson (New York: Penguin, 2003), 160.

5 Steinbeck, letter to Ritchie and Tal Lovejoy (July 1944), quoted in Benson, *John Steinbeck*, 553.
6 Roy Scranton, *Learning to Die in the Anthropocene: Reflections on the End of a Civilization* (San Francisco, CA: City Lights Books, 2015), 24, 92.
7 John Steinbeck, *Cannery Row, Novels 1942–1952*, ed. Robert DeMott (New York: Library of America, 2001), 119. The chapter "The Time the Wolves Ate the Vice Principle" was removed from the published version of the manuscript on the grounds of its gruesome violence.
8 Colleen Lye, *America's Asia: Racial Form and American Literature, 1893–1945* (Princeton, NJ: Princeton University Press, 2005), 224.
9 Lye, *America's Asia*, 190.
10 Lye, *America's Asia*, 250, 253.
11 See the confrontation between young Andy and the Old Chinaman in Steinbeck, *Cannery Row*, 114.
12 Steinbeck, *Cannery Row*, 108.
13 See Heidi Kim, *Invisible Subjects: Asian America in Postwar Literature* (New York: Oxford University Press, 2016), 51.
14 Steinbeck, *Cannery Row*, 106.
15 Steinbeck, *Cannery Row*, 108.
16 See Stephen Schryer, *Maximum Feasible Participation: American Literature and the War on Poverty* (Stanford, CA: Stanford University Press, 2018), 32–33.
17 Steinbeck, *Cannery Row*, 193.
18 Spengler quoted in Schryer, *Maximum Feasible Participation*, 32.
19 For Mikhail Bakhtin's idea of the carnivalesque, see *Rabelais and His World*, trans. Hélène Iswolsky (Bloomington: Indiana University Press, 1984).
20 Matthew Garrett, *Episodic Poetics: Politics and Literary Form After the Constitution* (New York: Oxford University Press, 2014), 5. Garrett's introduction offers an excellent discussion of episodic form.
21 Steinbeck, *Cannery Row*, 209–10.
22 Steinbeck, *Cannery Row*, 117, 165.
23 See Wolfgang Paalen, "Totem Art," *DYN* 4–5 (December 1943).
24 See Ad Reinhardt, *How to Look: Art Comics* (New York: David Zwirner Books, 2013).
25 See Christina Klein, *Cold War Orientalism: Asia in the Middlebrow Imagination, 1945–1961* (Berkeley: University of California Press, 2003), 64.
26 Steinbeck, *Cannery Row*, 113.
27 Ross Posnock, *Renunciation: Acts of Abandonment by Writers, Philosophers, and Artists* (Cambridge, MA: Harvard University Press, 2016), 377.

Index

Titles of works by John Steinbeck are in bold.